A.305 8942

D0336832

The revision of Englishness

Published in our
centenary year
～ 2004 ～
MANCHESTER
UNIVERSITY
PRESS

The revision of Englishness

Edited by David Rogers and
John McLeod

Manchester University Press
Manchester and New York

distributed exclusively in the USA by Palgrave

Published by Manchester University Press
Oxford Road, Manchester M13 9NR, UK
and Room 400, 175 Fifth Avenue, New York, NY 10010, USA
www.manchesteruniversitypress.co.uk

Distributed exclusively in the USA by
Palgrave, 175 Fifth Avenue, New York,
NY 10010, USA

Distributed exclusively in Canada by
UBC Press, University of British Columbia, 2029 West Mall,
Vancouver, BC, Canada V6T 1Z2

British Library Cataloguing-in-Publication Data
A catalogue record for this book is available from the British Library

Library of Congress Cataloging-in-Publication Data applied for

ISBN 0 7190 6972 6 *hardback*
EAN   978 0 7190 6972 7

First published 2004

13 12 11 10 09 08 07 06 05 04   10 9 8 7 6 5 4 3 2 1

Typeset by
D R Bungay Associates, Burghfield, Berks

Printed in Great Britain
by Bell & Bain Ltd, Glasgow

for our families

Contents

Notes on contributors   *page* viii

Acknowledgements   xi

Introduction: measuring Englishness *John McLeod*   1

Part I Changing Englishness in the post-war years

1 Modernity, Jewishness and 'being English' *Vic Seidler*   15

2 Queen's English *Alan Sinfield*   30

3 The miasma of Englishness at home and abroad in the 1950s
   Elizabeth Maslen   40

Part II Revising the myth

4 An activity not an attribute: mobilising Englishness *James Wood*   55

5 The English and the European: the poetry of Geoffrey Hill
   David Gervais   65

6 A case of red herrings: Englishness in the poetry of Philip Larkin
   and Ted Hughes *Antony Rowland*   81

7 The love that dares not speak its name: Englishness and suburbia
   Vesna Goldsworthy   95

8 'Dying of England': melancholic Englishness in Adam Thorpe's *Still*
   Ingrid Gunby   107

Part III New Englands

9 *Bhaji on the Beach*: South Asian femininity at 'home' on the 'English'
   seaside *Bilkis Malek*   121

10 *The Black Album*: Hanif Kureishi's revisions of 'Englishness'
    Bart Moore-Gilbert   138

11 Beyond revisions: Rushdie, newness and the end of authenticity
    Martin Corner   154

Postcript: Englishness in transition: Swift, Faulkner and an outsider's
staunch belief *David Rogers*   169

Index   185

Notes on contributors

Martin Corner is Principal Lecturer in English Literature at Kingston University. He has published widely on the work of Matthew Arnold, Virginia Woolf, John Updike and Saul Bellow.

David Gervais is an Honorary Fellow of the University of Reading and an editor of the *Cambridge Quarterly*. He is the author of *Literary Englands: versions of Englishness in modern writing* (Cambridge University Press, 1993) and of numerous articles on French and English literature.

Vesna Goldsworthy is the author of *Inventing Ruritania: The imperialism of the imagination* (Yale University Press, 1998), which has been translated into Bulgarian, Greek, Romanian and Serbian. She has also written chapters in books published by MIT Press, Routledge, Macmillan, Cambridge University Press and Wieser Verlag; and articles in journals published in Britain, France, the USA and a number of Eastern European countries. She teaches English literature at Kingston University where she founded the Centre for Suburban Studies in 2003.

Ingrid Gunby has a PhD from the University of Leeds, and teaches English at the University of Otago, Dunedin, New Zealand. She has published on Adam Thorpe's novel *Ulverton* and on the work of George Orwell and Elizabeth Bowen, and is working on a study of violence in post-war British writing.

John McLeod is Lecturer in English at the University of Leeds, where he teaches postcolonial literatures. He is the author of *Beginning Postcolonialism* (Manchester University Press, 2000) and *Postcolonial London: rewriting the metropolis* (Routledge, 2004), and has edited two special issues of *Kunapipi: journal of postcolonial writing* (21:2 (1999) and 25:1 (2003)). His forthcoming publications include (as editor) *The Routledge Companion to Postcolonial Studies*.

Bilkis Malek lives in London. Her previous essays include 'Not Such Tolerant Times' in *Young Britain*, ed. Jonathan Rutherford (Lawrence & Wishart, 1998), and 'A Game of Two Halves: "English" identity fifty years after Windrush', *Soundings*, 10. She currently works as a freelance researcher and consultant in the fields of race and diversity.

Elizabeth Maslen is a member of staff at the School of Advanced Study, Institute of English Studies, University of London. Her publications include *Doris Lessing*

(Northcote House, 1994) and *Political and Social Issues in British Women's Fiction, 1928-1968* (Palgrave, 2001).

Bart Moore-Gilbert is Professor of Postcolonial Studies at Goldsmiths College, University of London. His publications include *Postcolonial Theory: contexts, practices, politics* (Verso, 1997), *Postcolonial Criticism: a reader* (Longman, 1998) and *Hanif Kureishi* (Manchester University Press, 2001).

David Rogers was born in Magnolia, Arkansas and moved to England from New Jersey in 1986. He publishes on English and American literature and is currently Head of the School of Humanities at Kingston University, London. He is married to an English academic and has two very English children. His last essay on William Faulkner appeared in *Renaissance and Modern Studies* (2001).

Antony Rowland is Senior Lecturer at the University of Salford. His first critical book was *Tony Harrison and the Holocaust* (Liverpool University Press, 2001). He has also co-edited two collections of essays – *Signs of Masculinity* (Rodopi, 1998) and *'Choosing Tough Words': the poetry of Carol Ann Duffy* (Manchester University Press, 2003) – and two special editions of journals: '"Hating Tradition Properly": the legacy of the Frankfurt School', *New Formations*, 1999; and 'Performing Postmodern Poetries', *Critical Survey*, 2002. He was recently on Arts and Humanities Research Board-funded research leave finishing a book on post-Holocaust poetry for Edinburgh University Press. He is also a published poet, and was included in the *New Poetries III* anthology (Carcanet, 2002).

Vic Seidler is Professor of Social Theory in the Department of Sociology, Goldsmiths College, University of London. He has written widely in the areas of ethics, philosophy, social theory and gender. His recent work includes *Unreasonable Men: masculinity and social theory* (Routledge, 1994), *Recovering the Self: morality and social theory* (Routledge, 1995), *Man Enough: embodying masculinities* (Sage, 1999), and *Shadows of the Shoah: Jewish identity and belonging* (Berg, 2000).

Alan Sinfield is Professor of English at the University of Sussex, England, where he teaches on the Sexual Dissidence and Cultural Change programme. His books include *Literature, Politics and Culture in Postwar Britain* (Blackwell, 1989), *Faultlines: cultural materialism and the politics of dissident reading* (Clarendon, 1992), *The Wilde Century: effeminacy, Oscar Wilde and the queer moment* (Cassell, 1994), *Cultural Politics – Queer Reading* (Routledge, 1994), *Gay and After: gender, culture and consumption* (Serpent's Tail, 1998) and *Out on Stage: lesbian and gay theatre in the twentieth century* (Yale University Press, 1999). He lives in Brighton.

James Wood is an editor for the *New Republic* magazine. He is the author of *The Broken Estate: essays on literature and belief* (Pimlico, 1999), a novel, *The Book against God* (Jonathan Cape, 2003), and *The Irresponsible Self* (Jonathan Cape, 2004). He is a frequent contributor to the *London Review of Books*, the *New Yorker* and the *Guardian*.

Acknowledgements

We would like to thank the contributors to this volume for their support and patience, and their prompt responses to our editorial enquiries. It has been a pleasure to work with each of them. This book's achievements are a product of their energy and expertise (its weaknesses are, of course, entirely our responsibility). We owe much to Matthew Frost at Manchester University Press, not least for believing in this project and helping it grow from a proposal into a typescript and eventually into production. Philippa Grand at MUP was also extremely helpful during the production of this book.

Introduction: measuring Englishness

John McLeod

[Milan] Kundera: ... You see, if you're English, you never question the immortality of your nation because you are English. Your Englishness will never be put in doubt. You may question England's politics, but not its existence.
[Ian] McEwan: Well, once we were very big. Now we are rather small.
Kundera: Not all that small, though.
McEwan: We ask ourselves who we are, and what our position in the world is. We have an image of ourselves that was formed in another time.[1]

England has changed. (CARYL PHILLIPS)[2]

In 'Interference', a short story taken from his collection *Cross Channel* (1995), Julian Barnes depicts an old and reclusive English composer, Leonard Verity. Long exiled from England, Verity spends his twilight years in a provincial French village, Saint-Maure, with his French wife, Adeline, whom he first met in Berlin. He reads Nietzsche and Edgar Wallace, and listens to Beethoven, Grieg and Chopin. The story concerns the radio broadcast of Verity's latest and final masterpiece, 'The Four English Seasons', a 'kinetic observation of the memory of those seasons filtered through the known reality of other, non-English seasons'.[3] Adeline dismisses the piece as an exercise in nostalgia, but Verity's engagement with the memory of England is purposeful. As far as he is concerned, England is the enemy of the artist:

In England, the soul lived on its knees, shuffling toward a non-existent God like some butcher boy. Religion had poisoned art. 'Gerontius' was nauseating. Palestrina was mathematics. Plainsong was ditchwater. You had to leave England to find the upper slopes, to let the soul roar. That comfortable island dragged you down into softness and pettiness, into Jesus and marriage.[4]

England is sick; a new English aesthetic, exposed to the influences of other times and places, must save it.

Verity's composition has been recorded by the BBC, yet in a comic twist the recording is held up by customs officials at Calais and Leonard is forced to try to

---

1 Ian McEwan, 'An Interview with Milan Kundera' (1984) in *The Novel Today: contemporary writers on modern fiction*, new ed, ed. Malcolm Bradbury (London: Fontana, 1990), pp. 205–21 (p. 210).
2 Caryl Phillips, *A Distant Shore* (London: Secker & Warburg, 2003), p. 3.
3 Julian Barnes, 'Interference' in *Cross Channel* (1995; London: Picador, 1996), pp. 3-20 (p. 6).
4 Barnes, 'Interference', pp. 12–13.

listen to its radio broadcast from England. In order to receive clear radio signals, his wife has been compelled in the past to ask the villagers of Saint-Maure (with whom Leonard has a frosty relationship) to desist from using electrical equipment during certain hours of the day as it interferes with the clarity of the radio signal. Leonard wishes to surprise his wife with the broadcast and asks her to beg the village's silence for the scheduled time of its transmission, pretending that he wishes to listen to something else. Adeline fails to alert the village. When she hears the introduction to the barely audible broadcast and realises it is her ailing husband's final work, she runs from their house distraught. On returning she knows that Leonard is dead. Three weeks later, the vinyl recordings of 'The Four English Seasons' arrive in a parcel marked 'fragile'. Adeline breaks them into pieces.

As an English author whose writing has frequently looked to France for intellectual, aesthetic and creative inspiration, Barnes explores in his story a number of pertinent issues with which this book is also concerned. Verity's disillusionment with England is born out of a sense of its constriction, its social and intellectual narrowness when compared with the imaginative daring and adventurousness he comes to associate with Continental Europe. His desire to refract the English seasons through the known reality of non-English seasons is an attempt to confront English insularity, to open up England to the sensibilities which exist across the Channel and contest the sense of contemporary England's isolation, in more ways than one, from the rest of Europe. It is a deliberately revisionary act: in choosing England's seasons as the inspiration for his work, Verity reaches for a familiar register of romantic English pastoral almost as an act of aesthetic resuscitation, in order to bring a new vitality to a familiar way of eulogising England. His garrulousness and dissatisfaction with England is itself a kind of homage (in which Adeline rightly detects more than a hint of nostalgia): '[Verity] was not an exile, since that implied a country to which he could, or would, return. Nor was he an immigrant, since that implied a desire to be accepted, to submit yourself to the land of adoption … No, he was an artist.'[5] As the story suggests, there is a fine line between critical revision and intransigent recuperation. Verity's turning to art as a way of solving what he considers to be the problems of contemporary England is a potential mode of escapism. He is not interested in the social conditions of England and the challenges they might pose for conventional representations of Englishness which may require urgent revision. Rather, the appropriation of the pleasures of Continental European art as a way of resolving England's sterility smacks of superficiality and a contempt for difference and change. The story's irony, both comical and oddly poignant, rests upon the fact that Verity cannot fully escape from the world into art, from a disappointing England into a recuperative Englishness paradoxically cosmopolitan – the unwelcome radio interference which the French villagers generate marks both the irruption of the social into art and the impossibility of recuperating an aesthetic of Englishness which will rescue

---

5 Barnes, 'Interference', p. 8.

a sterile country. Art cannot remain untouched by social and material realities, by other voices which interfere with its transmission.

The chapters in this book are also concerned, in their different ways, with modes of interference that have impacted severally upon the social conditions of England and the creative and imaginative representation of Englishness. Since the end of the Second World War, both the material circumstances of England and the ways it has been envisaged and projected have undergone sustained revision for a number of reasons. England has changed; it is the function of this volume to reflect upon these changes. In terms of social conditions, England's relations to the rest of the British Isles and the world overseas have altered profoundly. The end of the British Empire inaugurated a new phase of immigration in the post-war decades (of 'New Commonwealth' workers, European refugees and other peoples) that significantly altered an already heterogeneous people, creating a new multi-cultural English population as well as triggering myths of an embattled national identity which turned increasingly to race and heterosexuality as the prime markers of legitimacy and belonging. The ascendancy of the USA and USSR after the war, coupled with the increasing influence of American culture in popular music, film, television, the visual arts and literature, has seen a shift in the perception of England both at home and abroad as at the centre of international power and global culture. The vexed relations with Continental Europe have also been affected by, firstly, membership of the EEC (Common Market) in 1973 and, more recently, the debate over joining a single European currency – issues which have been seen as challenging national sovereignty.

Domestically, the shifting status of England within Britain in recent years in the light of the Good Friday Agreement in Northern Ireland (1998), Devolution in Scotland (1998) and the establishment of the Cynulliad Cenedlaethol Cymru/National Assembly for Wales (1999) has questioned the marginalisation of other British nations as a Celtic 'fringe' and further affected the consistency of Britain's political and economic relationship with Europe as new transnational economic and political relationships are formed by British countries outside of England. Indeed, the common slippage between Englishness and Britishness seems increasingly unsafe at the turn of a new century. Iain Chambers has remarked that there are two versions of 'Britishness'. The first is 'Anglo-centric, frequently conservative, backward-looking, and increasingly located in a frozen and largely stereotyped idea of the national, that is English, culture. The other is ex-centric, open-ended and multi-ethnic.'[6] In Chambers' formulation, Englishness has conventionally been definitive of a common culture while remaining aloof from historical or demographic divergencies and differences, as well as the influence of the other British nations. For Angela Carter, writing in the 1980s about the construction of the Union Jack from the flags of England,

---

6 Iain Chambers, *Border Dialogues: journeys in postmodernity* (London and New York: Routledge, 1990), p. 27.

Scotland and Wales, these relationships could be described with the following equation: 'Great Britain = Greater England. The greedy flag [of St. George] swallowed up its constituent parts and became a sign, not of a nation but of a state of mind.'[7] England ruled Britannia, indeed *was* Britannia, both economically and as the source of an artistic Anglocentric tradition which reflected very little of the social lives and cultural heterogeneity of the English.

Yet old hierarchies are slipping. Arguably the most popular British fictions of the 1990s were written from and about other British countries – one thinks of the success of Iain Banks and Irvine Welsh. Additionally, Englishness is increasingly approached through a second-generation diaspora sensibility (in the fiction and films of Hanif Kureishi and Meera Syal) or from a proudly and self-consciously 'regionalised' position also deemed to be at some distance from official Englishness (as in the poetry of Tony Harrison or, in a different mode, Simon Armitage). Increasingly, an Englishness beyond the reach of 'ex-centrics' cannot be guaranteed, and its definitive role in constructions of Britishness is, at the turn of a new century, precarious. New cultural initiatives have complicated the extent to which notions of English and British culture can any longer be meaningfully synchronised.

As well as the domestic recalibration of England in conjunction with the other British nations, England has also had to contend with a number of social transformations, global in reach yet also impacting upon domestic notions of Englishness. These include the 'sexual revolution' often identified with the 1960s, and the beginning of an end to the social stigmatisation of gay, lesbian and bisexual people (as well as continuing prejudice at the levels of both street and state). A coterminous development concerns the continuing impact of feminist politics on English social, cultural and economic institutions, challenging received notions of masculine and feminine English identities.

These and other social and cultural shifts might be narrated in terms of decline. In Ian McEwan's comment to Milan Kundera – 'once we were very big. Now we are rather small' – the political, economic and cultural fortunes of England are inflected with a dying fall. Such a way of envisioning England has recurred in recent decades and is characteristic of one way of plotting England's recent past. In August 1983, the novelist Beryl Bainbridge, accompanied by a BBC television film crew, retraced the approximate route J. B. Priestley had recorded fifty years earlier in *English Journey* (1934). The revisionary route of her travels invited comparisons between Priestley's depressed England of 1933 and the Thatcherite England of the early 1980s. During the recession of the 1930s Priestley could still boast of the new graving dock at Southampton, the biggest in the world at the time. In his comments on the great liners which docked at Southampton – the *Berengaria*, the *Empress of Britain* – Priestley remarked that if 'another Gibbon

---

7 Angela Carter, 'So There'll Always be an England' in *Shaking a Leg: collected journalism and writings*, ed. Jenny Uglow (London: Vintage, 1997), pp. 185–9 (p. 186).

describes our decline and fall, what play he will make with these names!'[8] But Bainbridge's journey up the River Itchen on a trawler, from Hamble to Southampton's docks, takes her past the rusting, empty supertanker *Burmah Endeavour*, 'built during the Suez crisis to take oil the long way round and stranded in the Solent because she's no longer needed and there's nothing else she's fit for. Her salvation would be another crisis, another war.'[9] England is no longer an admirable endeavour epitomised by its economic and naval power but now lies moribund like the wrecked supertanker, barely afloat and gradually disintegrating. In Manchester Bainbridge is dazzled by the Town Hall in Albert Square, its 'silver plate and busts, its marble columns and mosaic floors … What a world it represented – cotton and shipping and commerce, the like of which we shall never see again.'[10] Similar sentiments are voiced as she sits in the centre of Bristol, on the banks of a wharf awaiting development:

On the opposite bank of the river stood a massive warehouse, windows smashed in their oval frames, the roof sprouting hollyhocks. It was sinking into the mud. Nothing shoddy about nineteenth-century architecture. Whether the purpose of the building was to store stacks of sugar or works of art, the exterior, with its balustrades, porticoes and columns of granite, was a monument to wealth and the permanence of imperialistic trade. I expect the warehouse will be gutted and made into a supermarket or flats for executives, and no one but a filing clerk in some dusty department of the Town Hall will remember what it used to be.[11]

The architecture might not be shoddy, but the 'purpose' of the building certainly was. It is unclear whether Bainbridge is unable or unwilling to realise that the nineteenth-century trade in goods such as sugar, dependent upon Caribbean slavery and colonial economics, created the wealth with which Bristol's bourgeoisie could afford to commission or purchase the works of art that hung on their walls. In recognising that the 'permanence of imperialistic trade' is in ruins she both mocks imperial self-aggrandisement and rehearses a historical narrative of decline. The image of this 'monument' sinking unceremoniously into the mud uneasily buttresses a certain nostalgic admiration not only for the buildings which empire created, but also the days when such economic and imperial greatness kept the warehouses fully stocked. Between her mapping of decline and the mocking of the empire's terminal fortunes there lies a revealing awkwardness. Her conflicted attitude – one that shares Leonard Verity's contradictory loathing and nostalgia for England – is clinched in the image of the empty warehouse sinking sadly in the Bristol mud which figures an Englishness represented by the contradictory coupling of ruined endurance and inevitable disappearance. Dereliction permits indulgence – of a seemingly empty, decaying warehouse whose external

8 J. B. Priestley, *English Journey* (1934; London: Mandarin, 1994), p. 14.
9 Beryl Bainbridge, *English Journey: or the road to Milton Keynes* (London: Duckworth/BBC, 1984), p. 15.
10 Bainbridge, *English Journey*, p. 81.
11 Bainbridge, *English Journey*, p. 41

splendours can be made to seem more important than the sordid business of its past or the vacancy of its present.

The aesthetic appeal of the warehouse, the beauties of which have outlived the circumstances which produced it, obscures a variety of other histories and voices central to the fortunes of both England and Englishness. If the social and economic fortunes of England have been made at the expense of others through the English pursuit of supremacy and authority both internationally and within the British Isles, in a similar vein ways of representing and imagining England's history, current condition and future have also been based upon a series of significant elisions. The problematic and disharmonious relationship between the transhistorical aesthetics of Englishness and the socially evolving and diverse constituencies of the English has been heightened in recent decades. As both Barnes' and Bainbridge's examples show, in recent years the articulation of Englishness has often proceeded through a revisionary register as writers have looked again at England self-consciously through the lenses of received traditions or inherited texts. But whereas Bainbridge's revisioning of Englishness seems caught inside an imperious optic that regards the end of power and status as lamentable, several other figures during the same period have attempted to re-envisage Englishness through creative acts of revision in order to admit English experiences, values and representations which actively challenge prevailing attitudes. These figures, frequently critical of both traditions of English representation and popular representations of England, are often motivated by their own ambiguous relationship with Englishness – as well as a profound sense that, as Caryl Phillips writes, England has changed. For these figures, the revision of Englishness becomes a subversive, empowering and perhaps even democratising act.

Ian Baucom has written of the important role of the *lieux de memoire* of Englishness: 'objects of pilgrimage and veneration, the jealously guarded ruins of cultural ensembles possessed by a need to stop time or, better yet, to launch a voyage of return to the past … They are places where an identity-preserving, identity-enchanting, and identity-transforming aura lingers, or is made to appear.'[12] As he explains, certain locations have become identified with the mystical sense of Englishness, and returning to them promises access to this 'aura' (which explains why, perhaps, Bainbridge spends so long on her English journey at England's rusting docks or the derelict warehouses). Importantly, Baucom's argument leads to a consideration of the possibilities of *transformation* that may be created when one is exposed to the potent influence of such *lieux de memoire*. In seeking to revise Englishness for the purposes of contestation and change, it seems necessary to go over old ground.

Consider, for example, Angela Carter's narrative of her visit to the historic English town of Bath, as described in her essay 'Bath, Heritage City' (1976), seven

---

12 Ian Baucom, *Out of Place: Englishness, Empire and the locations of identity* (Princeton: Princeton University Press, 1999), p. 18.

years prior to Bainbridge's sojourn down the road in Bristol. 'Bath is dotted with blue plaques', she records. 'Wordsworth was here, Southey was here, Jane Austen was here, almost everybody came for a weekend but Malthus was actually buried here.'[13] Yet Carter's vision of Bath is of a different hue, peopled by New Age occultists, West Indian grocers and alcoholics, and she uncovers another history here, of English madness and fear: 'the Anglo-Saxons wouldn't live here, they thought it was haunted. Too cack-handed and primitive themselves to build in stone, they thought that only giants or devils could have done so and left the Roman ruins well alone.'[14] Her visit to Bath attempts to discover its wonders – Great Pulteney Street, The Circus, the Royal Crescent, Lansdown Crescent perched above remarkable sloping fields – in terms different to officious representations of its Englishness, in order to engage with it in new ways. There is much for Carter to treasure in Bath, but its rewards are not akin to the nostalgic sentiments of Englishness which, in her vision, seem as unsubstantial as 'taste', as flat and lifeless as the repetitive blue plaques which speckle the city's walls. Here the allegedly auratic English countryside (Leonard Verity's obsession, of course) becomes transformed in a different vision:

that sense of pervasive pastoral, the feeling for countryside typified in wild gardens, it isn't really anything to do with the countryside at all but a liking for parks, for landscaped mead-ows, for contained nature, for garden cities ... the water-colour aesthetic as of English art, whose favourite seasons are the moist ones, early spring, early autumn, and all of whose landscapes are gently haunted. Bath, a city so English that it feels like being abroad, has been so distorted by what Pevsner called the Englishness of English art that the city itself has become almost an icon of sensibility.[15]

Those watercolours effect a falsification, a dissolution of the social, a draining away of other stories which uncannily haunt the calm tranquillity of such scenes and jostle for position with the 'official' English heritage ghosts of the nose-pinch-ing middle classes. Carter's vision of Bath is a critical revisioning, an approach to place through familiar lenses. It resembles Bainbridge's meanderings in the succeeding decade in terms of its mode, but its substance instead attempts to show the narrowness of such vistas as well as the two-dimensionality of the aesthetic 'aura' of received Englishness.

In Carter's writing, the perceived vacuity of an officious Englishness affords the opportunity, not for sentiments of loss, decline and nostalgia, but for celebra-tion, optimism, a looking forward to a brighter, better place liberated from those imperious and exclusive constructions which informed the architecture of the town halls and warehouses so admired by Bainbridge, and helped set the *social* limits of English identity. In a brilliant essay entitled 'So There'll Always be an

---

13 Angela Carter, 'Bath, Heritage City' in *Shaking a Leg*, pp. 161–5 (p. 161).
14 Carter, 'Bath, Heritage City', p. 163.
15 Carter, 'Bath, Heritage City', p. 165.

England' (1982), Carter recalls celebrating Empire Day at school in South London in the years immediately after the war. This theatrical confection featured a procession of flags and emblems, always with a blonde, blue-eyed young schoolgirl playing the part of the Rose Queen, before whose feet rose petals were liberally scattered. The occasion revealed to Carter how such representations of Englishness, while necessarily referring to older received images, cannot avoid the dangers of absurdity, anachronism and trivialisation: 'at the core of the ritual, the essential nub of Empire Day was of all things a cut-down version of an operetta, Merrie England for juveniles … [featuring] a purpose-built maypole which was far removed from the phallic splendour of the ethnic originals'.[16] Juxtaposing two of the roles for the children in the pageant – one child wearing a uniform and carrying the nation's flag, another dressed as a rose skipping merrily around a maypole – Carter decodes the mixed message of Englishness as she perceived it:

There is a rigid authoritarianism that presumes a passive submission; and then there is the marshmallow sentimentality with which the English have chosen to smother their bloody, bellicose and unexemplary history in order to make it digestible … Think of the costume of the Yeoman of the Guard which the leader of the English National Party dons to enliven by-elections. Intended, presumably, to invoke England's glorious past, it is reminiscent only of Gilbert and Sullivan (operetta, again). The reality of it is as if, in 400 years' time, some patriot, touting for votes on a nostalgia ticket, chose to don the garb of our present-day SAS.[17]

In revealing the process of selection in representations of Englishness, here exemplified by the Yeoman of the Guard happily liberated from the bloody chambers of history, Carter registers some of the rubric of post-war Englishness, its very dependency upon acts of revision which invoke and anaesthetise a bloodthirsty history in constructing the more palatable confection of 'tradition'. Yet, if Englishness is conceived ultimately as a theatrical mode, dependent upon the inevitable acts of revisitation to maintain its presence, then the future is surely bright. 'There is a chance', she moots, that the England of succeeding generations 'will resemble a kind of permanent Notting Hill carnival … a place that does not now have, nor ever has had, the consciousness that it has been singled out for a special fate'.[18] This vista is in contrast to Carter's experience of 1980s England, one in which most women, the working class and the communities created and changed by new arrivants are *not* included in the performance of Englishness, nor registered in its pathetic images of the 'foreign stereotypes of the comic, toff, milord or district commissioner' which mask a brutal and violent reality of poverty, discrimination and racism, and about which (I'm sure her tone must be ironic here) even 'lots of perfectly ordinary, ethnically English people … think all

---

16 Angela Carter, 'So There'll Always be an England', p. 186.
17 Carter, 'So There'll Always be an England', p. 187.
18 Carter, 'So There'll Always be an England', p. 187.

this is *terrible*.[19] But the future can be changed by revising the dominant tropes of Englishness, enabling its aesthetics to be transformed by the different constituencies of 'the English' who are allowed access at last to its production. Carter herself envisions replacing 'uniform Englishness' with something more heteroglot and untidy, embracing Englishness in terms of historical flux rather than in terms of the stasis and petrification of English 'heritage'. As she demonstrates, Englishness requires revising to make it more responsive to the different kinds of socially negotiated English identities which post-war England has cradled; an Englishness best conveyed for her by the image and spirit of the Notting Hill Carnival.[20]

In referring to particular scenes and received representations, conjuring again vistas located in another time, revisions provoke the familiarity of a tradition while inevitably participating in it. They possess the potential to confront the pedagogical protocols of received wisdom with the performative interference of the present. Acts of revision may function to unsettle received representations and the values which have become attached to them. Revisions can chart and effect historical change; they take the measure of the present by confronting the extent to which it no longer conforms to familiar patterns. For some they open a strategy for dissent and subversion; for others (such as diasporic peoples or those descended from immigrants) they are a way of claiming critically as their legitimate property a tradition of national cultural authority. But if revisions can involve the questioning of received representations for the purposes of dissent and change, they do not constitute a demolition of tradition. Revision is not the same as ruin; it is not concerned with fully dismantling, dispatching or discarding Englishness by unravelling the political subtexts which underwrite its representations. Indeed, the biggest challenge of this volume is perhaps its attempt to read exactly *how* and *why* Englishness is being refurbished and reconstructed by some of its fiercest critics, rather than dismantled and discarded once and for all. How ironic is Angela Carter's titular sentiment, 'so there'll always be an England'? Is the revision of Englishness always underwritten or compromised by nostalgic impulses in the last instance?

The vocabulary of legitimacy, authenticity and belonging is frequently complicated by the poets, novelists and film-makers that form the focus of this volume's essays. For such figures, it is often difficult – for reasons of race, ethnicity, sexuality, class, gender and so on – to engage with Englishness; each acts as its own disruptive and potentially terminal act of interference. These difficulties are also often felt by the contributors to this volume themselves, who in their different ways have also been faced with the challenge of negotiating with England

---

19 Carter, 'So There'll Always be an England', pp. 188, 189.
20 I have often wondered whether it was the creative energy, cross-cultural fusions and daring possibilities of the Notting Hill Carnival, held every August Bank Holiday in London, that animated Carter's fiction in the 1980s – most notably in *Nights at the Circus* (1984) – rather than the more idealised and historically remote sense of the 'carnivalesque' as described by Mikhael Bakhtin in *Rabelais and his World* (trans. Hélène Iswolsky (Cambridge, Mass.: MIT Press, 1968)).

and Englishness from an ambivalent position. My own circumstances may prove instructive here. I was born in England in 1969 and have lived in the country throughout my life. Yet I have never met the people who created me (an Irish woman and a Scottish man). I was adopted as a baby by my parents, Scottish migrants to Canada who had arrived in England only a few years prior to my birth, and was raised in Manchester as a Catholic. Scotland has always been a major presence in my life – when taking frequent trips to Glasgow as a child my mother would always refer to it as 'going home'. At school I spoke with a Mancunian accent and seemed like any other local kid; at home my accent involuntarily changed into a Scottish lilt (a habit which both my sister and I have kept to this day – I find it hideously embarrassing to speak 'in English' to my parents). My family's Catholicism added to my sense of ambivalence with England. Although I lived there, England did not exhaust my childhood world and it became peculiar to think of myself as either English or Mancunian – my birth in London complicated the latter. My emotional attachment was to Scotland and, later, Ireland; I thought of England simply as where I lived. At my local comprehensive school I supported the Scotland football team during the (now defunct) Home International tournament, partly out of loyalty to my family, although in truth I found it increasingly hard to choose between England and Scotland as I got older. Today I still find it difficult when asked to explain where I am 'from': I have left Manchester, have never lived in London, Scotland or Ireland, but know that 'England' does not do justice to my story even while recognising that I cannot disaffiliate from it or think neutrally about it. Too much of my past interferes with my ability to reach unproblematically for England and Englishness as secure markers of home, an identity or an attitude. Perhaps this is why I have become impatient with Englishness, and have come to regard it as restrictive, exclusionary and officious, representing a partial and narrow band of English experience yet arrogating to itself the claim of generality.

Those who have undergone fierce, perhaps violent, acts of discrimination in England due to the continuing presence of intolerance and prejudice may regard the story of my circumstances as unexceptional, if not one of good fortune and privilege. I would not for a moment want to propose my narrative as remarkable. Indeed, my point is entirely the opposite. That is to say, I wonder if my position is perhaps quite typical: most people living in England today may regard themselves also as sharing an ambivalent relationship with Englishness. It is in a similar spirit of self-conscious criticism that in commissioning essays for this volume, contributors were invited if they wished to reflect self-consciously upon their relationship with Englishness as a part of their critical endeavours, to allow their own positioning vis-à-vis Englishness actively to interfere with their scholarly readings of texts and hence open up the academic essay to other modes of writing. In the chapters which follow, several contributors reflect upon their engagement with English culture, either overtly or surreptitiously, as influenced by their childhood, education, sexuality and other significant dynamics. And in keeping with the spirit of revision – of looking back and looking again – I have eschewed in this introduction the convention of looking forward to the essays to come; in his post-script David Rogers engages retrospectively with several of the points raised in this collection while offering his own thoughts about the revision of Englishness in recent decades from the point of view of an American in England.

At the turn of a new century, where is Englishness? This collection offers a number of responses to the question, always partial, never conclusive. For some, its revisioning is to be welcomed not least because the newly emerging vistas are more sensitive to the demography and politics of contemporary England, as well as reflective of the transnationality of both the English and Englishness: the hybridity created from the continual crossings of people across England, the rest of the British Isles, Europe, the 'old' and 'new' Commonwealth, and North America. For others, revisionary responses have ranged from the antiquated and isolationist jingoism and the anti-European politics of the United Kingdom Independence Party, to the wistfulness of writers such as A. N. Wilson or the film-makers Merchant Ivory Productions. This collection constitutes its own 'interference' with Englishness, transmitted from many positions and for different reasons. As the essays which follow demonstrate in a variety of conflicting and fascinating ways, those often secreted by an imperious Englishness have effected a range of revisions of representations which are cross-hatched with radical and reactionary impulses – an interference created out of the dissonant moods of recuperation and refutation, survival and loss, retrieval and renewal. We shall see evidence of a number of conflicting attitudes towards Englishness in this collection, in the creative works which are the focus of the essays and in the attitudes of the contributors themselves. For each, revision remains a meaningful and significant means by which Englishness can be approached, for good or ill.

Part I   Changing Englishness in the post-war years

1 Modernity, Jewishness and 'being English'

Vic Seidler

In memory of Leo Seidler

English identities and the Jews

James Shapiro recently published *Shakespeare and the Jews*, a book not so much about Shakespeare as about the culture of which he was a part.[1] A professor of English and comparative literature at Columbia, Shapiro argues that scholars have overlooked the role that Jews played in helping the English define themselves. Events in the sixteenth and seventeenth centuries worked to complicate stable notions of English identity. The Reformation had pitted Catholics against Protestants and the quest for empire was reshaping nations. In an interview for *The Chronicle of Higher Education* (2 February 1996) Shapiro says that: 'At a time when many writers were trying to reinvent what it meant to be English, the English increasingly defined themselves by whom they were not. Very often that was the Jews. I would argue that the English were obsessed with the Jews.'

Like many post-Holocaust Jewish scholars, James Shapiro had kept his Jewish identity separate from his professional work. Though he was raised in a traditionally observant family and continued his religious education until he finished high school, his undergraduate education at Columbia in the 1970s and his graduate work at the University of Chicago brought him into an intellectual world that gave little acknowledgement to his Jewishness. Within the terms of an Enlightenment vision of modernity his Jewishness became a matter of private concern and individual belief. It was disconnected from the public discourses of the university where it had no space. Shapiro chose to specialise in the English Renaissance, a culture deeply infused with Christianity.

Not only is his Jewishness silenced but its suppression organises a field of intellectual work. As Shapiro recalls,

When I got to graduate school, I was told that there were no Jews, or only a handful, in Shakespeare's England – and so no issues to discuss about the Jews. I was always conscious of what was being suppressed – the discussion of Jews that I was seeing in the texts. Finally, I realised that I'm both a professor of English and a Jew, and I wanted to know how my people had shaped the culture I was studying.[2]

---

1 James Shapiro, *Shakespeare and the Jews* (New York: Columbia University Press, 1996).
2 Shapiro explores the ways it is very easy to forget one's Jewishness, to regard it as something that can be easily disavowed as a religious belief one no longer holds to, so that it is too easy to lose a sense of how one is positioned in relation to Shakespeare's texts. That there were so few Jews in

This is already an unsettling notion for scholars who have learnt to conceive of their Jewishness as a matter of individual religious belief alone. Within the tighter terms of a post-war English culture that teaches Jews that they need to assimilate into a dominant culture, they have less space than the other ethnic identities of post-war United States.

Shakespeare and the Jews explores how the English in Shakespeare's time focused upon the Jews as a way of exploring troubling questions about themselves. The English explored issues of nationhood through considering whether the Jews, without a homeland, could be a nation. The issue of whether the English could be considered a race was often thought about in terms of whether a religious group like the Jews had a radical identity. English writers in the sixteenth and seventeenth centuries repeatedly contrasted the Jews to the English. Theirs was often a gendered discussion relating to masculinities, though Shapiro does not seem to frame it in these terms. Jewish men were said to be effeminate – even to menstruate – while English men were 'manly'; the Jews smelled bad while the English were clean.

The writings Shapiro examines seem to return again and again to a deep anxiety about who was and who was not a Jew. This apprehension in fact seemed to mask a widespread concern about the stability of English identity. The question he sees obsessing the English was whether the English could lose their own identity and become Jews or take on attributes of Jews. This question seemed to be part of the fascination – and revulsion – for a figure like John Traske who was imprisoned in the seventeenth century for founding a sect of Christians who followed some Jewish doctrines. It echoes anxieties that have their source in the long-standing Western denial of the Jewishness of Jesus. This repression was often linked to the demonising of Jews as the 'other' within the West, where the wandering Jew became a figure of punishment.

In his exploration of *The Merchant of Venice* Shapiro is concerned to show how the portrayal of Jews would have resonated with contemporary audiences. He goes back to early editions of sources from which Shakespeare could have drawn for the story that likens a Jew's demanding a pound of flesh to male circumcision. He argues that the story would have provoked widespread fears that non-Jews could become Jews. Such questions recur in the play's many allusions to religious conversion. This recurrence reflects widespread uncertainties in relation to the stability of English identities. In different periods of upheaval and uncertainty issues in relation to Jewish identities have been framed in ways that allow for reflections upon the re-visioning of England.

Being Jewish/being 'English'

Growing up in England in a refugee family which had escaped from Continental Europe just before the war was to grow up in the shadow of the Holocaust. In some

Shakespeare's England says very little about the ways that Englishness can still be re-visioned in relation to a Jewish 'other'.

sense it was to grow up without representation, to be 'invisible'. I was born in England in 1945. I shared with many others the name of 'Victor', for the Second World War had been a 'victory' that was to be remembered and celebrated in the streets. After years of a long and difficult war, there was to be a time of peace and reconstruction. England was to be reborn out of the ashes of the Blitz and this was a time to look forward, not to dwell on the past. Not only had England been victorious, but it was to bring into being a period of social justice when the fruits of the peace were assumed to be shared by all.

I was named after this victory and as I was named so I was also marked. I carried a public name which carried meaning beyond the personal boundaries of family. But I was also to carry this mark as a sign of protection for it was a promise of what I was to become – 'English', like everyone else – if I was not already. I was born in Hendon, North London. In those days, since I was born in England, I was entitled to 'be English', even though my parents were 'foreign' because they had been born in Poland and in Austria. It was not easy for them to become English, and over fifty years later it can still be difficult for them to feel that they are accepted or that they 'belong'. They were largely to remain 'Continental' in their own terms. They did not 'speak right' in a culture where accent was so important. But they felt gratitude for a country that had provided them with refuge and did not really want to be reminded about the many who were refused refuge when they had nowhere to go.

The Jewish community that was established was not always welcoming to these 'Continentals' who had their own practices and traditions. They were expected to 'fit in' and to accommodate to 'English ways'. The Jews who had come over from Russia and Poland towards the end of the nineteenth century were already on the way to assimilating into a dominant culture. They were to 'be English' even if they happened to have different religious beliefs. This forced assimilation was a matter of individual belief and was not thought to affect their status as equal citizens. Our parents could not feel so confident in the hopes and aspirations of a liberal culture, for they had experienced the revoking of their rights in Germany and Austria which supposedly cherished the ideals of an Enlightenment modernity. But it was in these 'civilised' communities that their rights as free and equal citizens were revoked, even though their families had the medals to prove the sacrifices they had made in the First World War.

Often there was a silent and unspoken feeling of rejection. They did not speak easily about the communities which they had come from and felt so integrated with. They carried the pain of rejection. At some level this burden was transformed in the aspiration they had for their children who were to be 'protected' from the truth of these pains. They were to have their own revenge through splitting from their pasts and in feeling that they could give to their children the precious gift of 'becoming English'. But this gift was also important at another level, for to be English was to be 'safe'.

It was this safety that my parents were ready to make sacrifices for and it was part of their deep and unquestioned gratitude to England that they did their best to pass on this sense of safety to their children. They would not have a bad word spoken about England. I remember how difficult it was for them when I went to join a Ban the Bomb march on its way back from Aldermaston. My stepfather Leo had learnt from his experience at the hands of the Nazis in Germany that Jews should not be involved in politics. As a Jew you had to learn to keep your head down. You were to learn to be invisible. As far as he was concerned you had to learn to behave properly, 'to be seen and not heard'. This was a message I was never consciously happy with, but it left its mark. It made me careful and at some level held me back. I learnt not to take too many risks.

Our parents looked forward to their children 'becoming English'. They felt this new identity as one of the gifts they could offer us. It was part of working for a future and refusing to look back to the past. It was also a way of coping with not being overwhelmed by the sufferings of the recent past. There was a determination to make a living in England so that they could provide for their children what they did not have themselves. The children were to come first for they were the future. They allowed their parents to focus on the future so that the parents did not have to deal with the past. It was also that we were to be different from all those Jews, all those uncles, aunts, grandparents, brothers and sisters who had died in the camps.

This was to be a new beginning, and England in the 1950s was to be a land of hope and opportunity in which the past could be left behind. We as children were not to be like them, though often we carried the names of the dead, as this was the ancient Jewish custom. We were to know that we were 'English', though somehow we were also supposed to be proud of being Jewish. We were to carry the hopes of our parents for a better life. We were often not allowed to be sad or unhappy or depressed because such emotions threatened to remind them of feelings they did not want to touch. Rather it was our duty to be constantly happy and, if we felt different, we soon learnt to keep these feelings to ourselves.

Names matter, but often we carry quite ambivalent feelings about our names and who we might be named after. It can be part of an uncertain family inheritance, especially if, as happened in so many Jewish families, you were named after a family member who had died in the Holocaust. This legacy creates its own link and responsibility, but it can produce its own rifts if, as in my case, you have a 'public' name that turns you outwards towards the world whilst you also carry an inner name. I was called 'Victor' for the world. This was a form of self-protection and in the 1950s it was still called your 'Christian' name. But I also carried the name 'Jacob' which was an inner name. It was my Jewish name or my Hebrew name. But it was not necessarily a name that I felt more easy with. It remained hidden and was spoken only within the rituals of the synagogue. It remained a private name and at some level I felt uneasy, even ashamed, in relation to it.

I did not feel easy about being called 'Victor', however, since with the destruction of European Jewry, there was little to celebrate. As far as the Jewish people were concerned, it had not been a victory but a devastating defeat. So it was a name that I carried but which I felt it difficult to identify with. I soon shortened it to 'Vic' as if I wanted to make myself less visible. As children growing up in the 1950s we did not really knowingly embody this sense of defeat for we were often left with very ambivalent feelings towards our own sense of Jewishness. It was so much easier to think that we could be English like everyone else. Even if our families were to be protected from the cruelties of the past, we were to represent hope and the future and we were to live without the stains and injuries of the past. This ambivalence was to protect us as children, but it was also to make things easier for our parents who found it difficult to speak about what had happened to them. To speak was to make it real and to expose yourself to a pain you often did not want to be reminded of.

The histories of the war and of pre-war life in Continental Europe were not to be talked about. These histories were often not to be shared, for the sense of rejection they threatened to bring to the surface could not be tolerated. At some level it was as if these histories had not really happened. There was an anxiety growing up in immigrant communities in the 1950s that the children 'be normal' and so be 'like everyone else'. If we wondered why we did not have uncles and aunts to visit, we were not told that this was because they had been killed in the Warsaw Ghetto or in Treblinka or Buchenwald. These names were not really mentioned in the family or only in passing. It was just said as a matter of fact that we had little extended families. And so as to reassure us friends of our mothers were renamed as 'auntie' so that again we would not feel deprived. It was important for our parents that we thought of ourselves as having happy childhoods and for us to think that we were not really different from other children.

This pretence of normality was even sustained when my father died in 1950 when I was just five. He had just found out what had happened to his brother during the war. I felt that he had died from a broken heart, but that was a story that I created for myself. It felt true at some level. These were difficult times, especially for my mother who had been left with heavy debts. She had to work to support four young children on her own. I felt then that being 'without a father' put us in a different situation from other children, especially at school. We learnt not to talk about it, but we still owed it to our mother to 'feel happy', or at least not to allow the inner depression we carried to show. At some level this obligation helped me realise that there was something different about the childhood we had and the circumstances our refugee families had to come to terms with. But I can still find it difficult to acknowledge fully what a particular experience we had as children growing up in the shadows of the Shoa.

Modernity and Jewishness

The idea that as Jews growing up in England we were 'like everyone else' was part of the dream of an Enlightenment vision of modernity. We were to grow up into a liberal moral culture which believed that our primary identities were as free and equal rational selves. We were to learn, as Sartre explores it in *Anti-Semite and Jew*,

to treat Jewishness as if it were contingent and accidental.[3] It did not in any mean-
ingful sense define 'who' we were, which meant that if you did not happen to share
these particular religious beliefs you could dispense with 'being Jewish' altogether.
This is the path towards a universal vision of the rational moral agent which an
Enlightenment vision prepared for those Jews who were keen to assimilate. What
is more, they could welcome the Enlightenment as the realisation of the universal
aspiration of a prophetic Judaism.

In terms of Kant's moral theory, history and culture were deemed to be forms
of unfreedom and determination. As we had to learn to rise above inclinations
which reflect an animal nature, so we also have to rise above history and culture.
We had to learn to think for ourselves as free and autonomous moral agents. So it
was that Jewishness became a matter of individual private belief. It had nothing to
do with public and civic identities. Within the public realm we were to be 'like
everyone else' and we were guaranteed equal legal and political rights. These
dreams of modernity still held sway in England in the 1950s. At some level it was as
if the Holocaust had not happened.

A dominant English culture had not begun to come to terms with the way the
Holocaust challenges fundamental terms of modernity. The existence of legal and
political rights had not proved a guarantee of the humanity of Jews in Nazi
Germany. Rights had not been able to secure the human dignity of Jews once
these rights could be taken away by the state. This was the crisis that Levinas was
responding too, recognising it as part of a crisis of Western conceptions of
modernity.[4] It had to do with the place of ethics and the poverty of the ethical traditions that treat ethics subjectively, as a matter of individual opinion alone.
Having lived through this time himself, Levinas recognised the importance of
prioritising ethical responsibilities for others. This recognition was a gift that
a Jewish tradition could offer the West and was part of the conflict between
Athens and Jerusalem. It was open for us to acknowledge the priority of ethics
over epistemology.

But there was also a recognition in Levinas of the ways an Enlightenment
vision of modernity, whilst offering a liberal vision of freedom and equality, also
worked to weaken Jews' relationships with their own traditions and histories. For
presenting, in Kant's terms, Jewishness as a form of unfreedom and determination

---

3 Jean-Paul Sartre, *Anti-Semite and Jew* (New York: Schocken Books, 1968). Sartre shows how an
   Enlightenment vision of modernity that is organised around a supposedly universal vision of the
   rational self is able to offer the emancipation of the Jews on condition that they are ready to
   disavow their Jewishness as a particularistic identity. Sartre reveals the intolerance that underpins
   liberal notions of tolerance.
4 Levinas' crucial essay 'Reflections on the Philosophy of Hitlerism' (1934)traces the 'source' of
   National Socialism's 'bloody barbarism' to a possibility of an 'elemental evil in which we can be led
   by logic and against which western philosophy had not insured itself'. A thoughtful discussion
   which helps to place this essay historically is given by Howard Caygill in *Levinas and the Political*
   (London: Routledge, 2002).

tended to deface a person's relationship with their own Jewishness. As we were growing up in post-war England, security lay in 'becoming English' and it seemed as if this could be done only through a process of defacing your own Jewishness. Within modernity it became a matter of private concern alone. In learning to be normal and like everyone else which were central values within an assimilationist culture, we learnt unconsciously that we were not to be visible as Jews. At some level we were not comfortable in thinking of ourselves as Jews at all. With Sartre it was easy to feel that it was the anti-Semite who was to do the naming.

Going to a North London grammar school in the 1950s, even one with a relatively high proportion of Jewish students who held their own assemblies, it was easy to feel that Jewishness was something to be tolerated. You learnt to feel grateful for the tolerance of English society, but this was a tolerance that was often to be paid for in terms of visibility. At some level the very lack of public recognition and expression made you feel that there was something almost shameful in being Jewish. In school you could feel torn between being Jewish and being English as if there was something automatically suspect about having diverse loyalties. The question was in the air of whom you would support in the unlikely circumstance of a war between England and Israel. It was as if you were called upon to declare yourself and to make a choice.

An earlier generation had known this conflict in a different form. Within the terms of an Enlightenment vision of modernity there should be a straightforward response, that you are 'English' and that you happened to have a different religious practice. This was the clear conviction of German Jews in Weimar Germany. But this vision was shattered with the rise of Nazism as Jews were gradually marginalised and excluded from civil society. As far as they had been concerned, religious differences were significant only within the private sphere where different religious beliefs were recognised. But English Jews who felt for their co-religionists in Germany were themselves questioned because they were told that these people who were suffering were Germans or Poles while they were 'English'. So English Jews felt that they had to hide their feelings for what was going on. They were made to feel that it was wrong for them to feel so angry and hurt.

Modernity established a firm distinction between public and private spheres. Within the public sphere of citizenship, we existed as free and equal rational selves. It was only in the private sphere of family that difference was acknowledged, and then only as individual differences of belief. As Jews we were supposed to be 'invisible' in public where we learnt that we were to be 'like everyone else', whilst in the private sphere of the family we were encouraged to feel proud of our Jewish backgrounds. This creates an ambivalence that is familiar to different generations of refugee children. The ease with which you learnt to switch, often assuming different identities within these different spheres, makes switching almost automatic. But you also learn to police these boundaries and you can feel uneasy when school friends come home. I can still feel some of the tension. I can also appreciate the efforts my mother went to to provide an abundance of food, as if to compensate for any grounds of unease.

Double consciousness/double identities

Growing up within the refugee community in north-west London, we often had a limited sense of our parents as 'refugees'. This was partly because they were in many cases the lucky ones who had had the money and the connections to leave. We were living in a relatively prosperous middle-class community. In London in the 1950s to be different was to 'be abnormal' and this was a fear. Often it was important for us, as children, to remind ourselves that we were born in England so we must be 'English'. The logic seemed incontrovertible and so reassuring. At some level we did not want to feel ourselves as different and we invoked the will not to 'be different'.

As children we learnt about the war and were told about the Nazis, but often this lesson was in generalised terms; sometimes as a warning against thinking we might marry anyone who was not Jewish. As Anne Karpf has said recently, 'other children were told stories about monsters, goblins and wicked witches; we learnt about the Nazis'.[5] We learnt but often we were not told directly. It was threat that was there in the background of everyday life to be mentioned at times, but not really to be explained. Often we learnt about what had happened to the Jews during the war through the same newsreel images of dead bodies as anyone else. Often the images were overwhelming and very little was said about them. It was left to us to imagine that they could be our uncles and aunts. It was too terrifying – and the realisation only came much later in adult years – to recognise that they could also be our cousins. We did not want to let these images in, because they threatened the sense we needed of living a 'normal' and 'happy' childhood.

Often we learnt to watch in silence, feeling uneasy for our parents, in some way instinctively wanting to protect them. We learnt not to expect the adults to say much. It was as if we had already absorbed their pain unconsciously as the second generation. At some level we knew that, whatever they had suffered, they had suffered more than enough. It was our task somehow to redeem their lives, to make things better for them. This awareness could be part of an unconscious drive to do well and succeed at school. We did not want to let them down or disappoint them. But at some level we also learnt not to expect very much from them. For many of them found it difficult to give emotionally, after the rejections they had experienced in their own lives. They had been separated from their parents at a young age and often had not received the love they needed. Somehow it was our task as children to make it good for them. We knew the wounds could not be healed, but at least we could learn to expect very little for ourselves. Often we learnt to be responsible before it was time. Many children in the second generation learnt to look after their own parents, automatically forsaking their own needs. This altruism could seem the least they could do.

---

5 Anne Karpf, *The War After* (London: Minerva, 1997). This is a history that I have also explored in Victor Jeleniewski Seidler, *Shadows of the Shoah: Jewish identity and belonging* (Oxford: Berg, 2000).

As children we learnt not to ask about the war and what had happened to the wider family. We learnt that our parents 'had suffered enough'. We learnt to hide and conceal our own unhappiness and depression from them, for we did not want to add to their pain. Rather we learnt to collude in the idea that we had every-thing we could want. I even learnt to believe this when my father died, somehow colluding in the notion that as children 'we were too young to know' so that we did not need to mourn ourselves. We had to exercise grief in the privacy of our own dreams. But children often learn to blame themselves and it was easy for me to promise in my dreams that 'I would be good' if only my dad would come back.

The questions that at some level haunted our childhoods, though they were rarely articulated, were 'How did our parents survive when so many people perished'? 'What entitled them to live when so many died'? These questions were too difficult and painful to voice, so often they were unconsciously passed on to the second generation. But they were not questions that we could ask anyone; rather they were left hanging. Sometimes they were questions whose presence we were not consciously aware of. But they could be part of the unspoken pressure to achieve in whatever arena, to prove that we are entitled to live. Not only did we have to prove our own entitlement but somehow we had to redeem and make good the broken lives of our parents. This act of redemption was not something that was consciously demanded. It could be expressed in a look of disappoint-ment. That was more than enough.

Anglo-Jewry in the 1950s was in many ways a frozen, traumatised community that had not really begun to come to terms with the Shoah. The child refugees, such as Kitty Hart, describe in her *Return to Auschwitz* how quickly they learnt on arrival in England not to talk, even to their closest family, about their camp experi-ence.[6] She was told by her uncle that people would just not want to know and not embarrass them. She kept her silence until the 1970s and her own family were grown-up before she started to share some of her experience. Post-war England wanted to turn its back on the sufferings of the war and did not want to be reminded of what had happened to European Jewry. Life was to get back to normal and people were looking towards a new future. They did not want to be reminded of the past, or else only in the heroic terms of the movies.

The refugees who lived in England throughout the war learnt to fit in as best they could. They were to learn to talk English as best they could. There was a sense in which 'they came from nowhere and did not really have a past'. They had been uprooted, as Simone Weil describes it, in both space and time.[7] Their energies were to be given over to making a living as best they could. So it was hardly surprising if we felt strangely suspended and unrooted as children, doing our best to root ourselves in often not very hospitable English manners and customs. It was easy to

6 Kitty Hart, *Return to Auschwitz* (London: Sidgwick & Jackson, 1981). Hart shares the silences that were imposed upon her when she came to England as a young survivor of Auschwitz. People did not want to hear what she had to say and she learnt to maintain her silence for years.

7 Simone Weil, *The Need for Roots* (London: Routledge & Kegan Paul, 1972).

feel that whatever you did you were 'not right' – your nose was too big or you talked too emotionally with your hands. You learnt to contain yourself, for often it fell to you as children to mediate between your parents and the host community. At some level, despite everything that you did, you felt yourself an outsider. This is why it was so exciting when Colin Wilson published *The Outsider* in the late 1950s. It helped to name a significant feeling and it gave some acceptability to it. Years before postmodernism it created a limited space for difference and named a tradition of double consciousness. The assimilationist English culture was still very much intact, but there were some spaces opening up. It could help to make you a little more self-accepting, a little easier and less judgemental on yourself.

Embodying difference

It was in the 1960s that the cracks in modernity began to show. With the influx of an Afro-Caribbean population and the racism which the community met in terms of jobs and housing, there were others who were not going to be able to live out their dreams of the 'mother country'. The high expectations were soon dashed and the realities of life in an England which was so resistant to the notion of a multicultural community were hard. It took time to recognise that it was not simply an issue of individual prejudice but that there was institutionalised racism that had to be confronted. It was a matter of undoing the link not only between being English and being Christian that the Jewish community had to confront but also between being English and being white. Historically there had also been the issue of whether Jews were 'white' and in earlier times they were not allowed to be, even if they wanted to. Whiteness was tied up with the conditions of modernity.

An Enlightenment vision of modernity insisted that the 'other' could be made like the 'same'. Underlying the differences was the shared reality of existing as rational selves. As rational selves we were supposedly guaranteed equal legal and political rights within the public realm. But this Cartesian vision was already gendered and racialised. It was a dominant white, Christian, heterosexual masculinity that alone could take its reason for granted. Modernity had in a crucial sense encoded a secularised Christian tradition in its antagonism to the body and sexuality as 'the sins of the flesh'. A dominant rationalist tradition, as Nietzsche recognised, showed how the body and sexuality as part of an 'animal nature' had been superseded. Reason was set in categorical distinction to nature, and women, Jews and people of colour were deemed to be 'closer to nature'. They were deemed to be less rational and so could not take their 'humanity' for granted.

As Christianity had supposedly superseded Judaism, as Daniel Boyarin has it, the disembodied spirit had superseded 'carnal Israel', so within modernity the mind was to control the body.[8] The identification of Judaism with the body,

---

8 Daniel Boyarin, *Carnal Israel: reading sex in Talmudic Judaism* (Berkeley: University of California Press, 1993).

sexuality and 'carnality' was central to the anti-Semitic discourses of the West. It helped to produce its own forms of Jewish self-hatred, which Sander Gillman has explored.[9]

The language of minorities often fails to recognise the ease with which 'others' come to see themselves through the eyes of the dominant culture. As Simone Weil grasps it, this failure is part of the workings of power.[10] It is also something that Fanon grapples with in *Black Skin, White Masks* (1952) when he looks into the mirror and has to come to terms with his negative feelings about his own body.[11] His body stands as a reminder of the 'uncivilised' and he has been brought up within a colonial culture to despise it. He shares his inner struggle to shift his atti-tude and feelings about his body and so about himself. Here is an inner link between the internalised oppression of racism and the Jewish self-hatred that Gillman explores in *Jewish Self-Hatred*.[12] Often these struggles take place away from the gaze of the public sphere. In public people learn to hide these inner strug-gles and present themselves in more acceptable ways.

With feminism learning from the movements for black consciousness in the United States about the importance of re-evaluating experience, not only intellec-tually but also emotionally, different ways of theorising the relationship between the personal and the political come into focus. Women refused to see themselves and evaluate their experience through the eyes of a dominant heterosexual masculinity. Postmodernism posited a greater appreciation of a politics of differ-ence and a developing unease about talking of 'women' as a generalised category. If discourse theory can help us identify subaltern voices which have been suppressed and marginalised within dominant theoretical discourses, often, however, it remains within a rationalist framework.

Its attention to the multiplicity of voices within texts can also help to show, as in Bryan Cheyette's work, 'the Jew' as a floating signifier within a variety of dif-ferent literary texts.[13] We can be made aware of the variety of meanings attached to the notion of 'the Jew', so helping us question what is taken to be a 'naive' assumption in relation to a too homogenised vision of 'the Jew'. It is only through the display of meanings within a particular literary text that we can say what meaning is being given to 'the Jew'. But this literary practice, alive as it is to the multiplicities of deferred meanings, involves its own forms of denial. As with

---

9 Sander Gillman, *Jewish Self-Hatred: anti-semitism and the hidden language of the Jews* (Baltimore: Johns Hopkins University Press, 1989).

10 For an exploration of the workings of power in Simone Weil's writings see chapter 8 in Lawrence Blum and Victor J. Seidler, *A Truer Liberty: Simone Weil and Marxism* (New York: Routledge, 1991).

11 Frantz Fanon, *Black Skin, White Masks*, trans. Charles Lam Markmann (1952; London: Pluto Books, 1984).

12 Gillman, *Jewish Self-Hatred*. I also allude to this link in relation to men and masculinities in Victor J. Seidler, *Man Enough: embodying masculinities* (London: Sage, 1999).

13 Bryan Cheyette and Laura Marcus (eds), *Modernity, Culture and the Jew* (Oxford: Polity, 1998). The collection explores the figure of 'the Jew' in diverse literary texts within modernity.

Lyotard's discussion of 'the Jew' this practice finds it difficult to give adequate recognition to realities of anti-Semitism and to the diverse religious and spiritual traditions of the Jews as people. It unwittingly serves to silence this discussion, as it too often gets caught in a circle of representations. It is just this circle that Levinas helps to break in his recognition of ethical obligations to the 'other'.[14]

Modernity is still to be named as a secularised Christian project in its rationalist disdain for the body, sexualities and emotional life. If recent postmodern work has sought to give belated recognition to the body and emotional life as sources of knowledge, it has too often focused upon the play of meanings within text. This focus makes it difficult to recognise how racism and anti-Semitism are entwined within the terms of modernity. In more recent years young Jews have learnt from young black men and women. The notion that 'black is beautiful' involved a re-evaluation of what has so easily been devalued and despised. As young Afro-Caribbean men and women have also had to come to terms with slavery, without being limited by it, so young Jewish men and women have demanded the space to come to terms with the Shoah, without limiting Jewish identities to this experience. These explorations are shared in art and literature as they are in the cinema. The Jewish film festival has been significant in sharing these representations.

We may be able to celebrate the new hybrid identities that are being created, but we must not minimise the pain that is experienced as young people feel torn between different cultural inheritances. The high rate of young Asian women who have committed suicide should make us more aware of the emotional and material difficulties that people have to endure, before they can feel at ease with themselves in these new settings. A re-visioning of England which allows recognition of a multicultural society will offer more space for the exploration of diverse identities and the creation of new hybrid identities. But often we identity with freedom before we have really understood the complex attachments to culture and tradition. If these are not to be automatically defined in negative terms, we need to refigure Enlightenment notions of modernity.

Too often modernity has insisted upon the effacing of cultural and ethnic difference. If I have an obligation to recognise another face to face, as Levinas has it, this obligation has to be a recognition which validates and affirms their difference. When I face another person do I face them as Victor? What difference does it make if I face them as Jacob? For years the letter has been my hidden Jewish name, though it was also a name I carried with some pride. But it could also be a name which was shamed and it takes time to feel pride for what has been culturally shamed. This is an issue that people of colour, gays and lesbians have long struggled with.

---

14 For an appreciation of the way that Lyotard considers Jewish identities after Auschwitz see Jean-François Lyotard, *Heidegger and 'the Jews'* (Minneapolis: University of Minnesota Press, 1990). See also the interesting discussions collected in Robert Fine and Charles Turner (eds), *Social Theory after the Holocaust* (Liverpool: University of Liverpool Press, 2000).

As they have learnt from their own bitter experience, the issue is not exclusively a matter of what representations are available in the broader culture, important as this is, but also how we want to voice our own his/herstories. For a second generation that has grown up in the shadows of the Shoah, it has been a matter of whether you can find a voice at all in the face of the pain of that suffering. It has also been a question, which Rosensweig and Levinas have struggled with, of whether you can speak out of the vitality of a living Jewish tradition within contemporary cultures. This has to be part of a re-visioning of England as much as it has to be part of a reframing of what has been so easily talked about as 'Christian' Europe.

Postscript

Why does it still feel so difficult to talk more personally about these questions of Jewish identities in an academic context? Is it because at some level I still feel that there is something shameful and that I fear being rejected if I share some of these feelings? Is this fear of rejection in the particular form that it takes linked to masculinity, since Jewish feminists seem more easily to blend the personal with the theoretical? Are there particular issues that come into play when it comes to speaking about Jewish masculinities? Is it as if with modernity you can only prove that you are a 'man enough' if you are ready to be silent about your Jewishness? For there is almost a contradiction in terms that bring 'Jewish' and 'man' together, for there is a culturally entrenched notion within modernity that Jewish men are 'really' feminine. This is a fear talked about in relation to Weininger. It means that they are somehow 'pretending' to be other than what they are.

This act of pretence links in complex ways to the issue of being exposed or 'found out', a sense that at some level, as Jewish, you are somehow already guilty and that if people somehow discover that you are Jewish they would show you the door. So you learn automatically to conceal your Jewish identity, unless you feel it is safe to reveal it. This feeling is linked to a fear of being found out even though you may not have the slightest understanding what it refers to. It connects to the familiar feelings, reproduced within the terms of modernity, that if people get to know that you are Jewish they will reject you, so you had better keep this particular piece of information to yourself. This reaction becomes so automatic a part of a process of self-policing that you are barely aware you are doing it. The fear, so present for the second generation, is that you won't be 'safe' and that it is best to keep yourself hidden and concealed.

When I turned up on Sunday morning to give my paper to the conference for which this chapter was originally written, I was very politely told that I had been taken off the programme. The organisers had been trying to reach me for the last two weeks and had not been able to contact me, so assumed that I no longer wanted to do the paper. This explanation made me feel very uneasy: part of me felt that I should just leave there and then; part of me also knew that I had wanted to contact the organisers but had not felt the need, because I was on the last draft of the programme that had been sent out. But at some unconscious level I was struck that it probably also had to do with my unease at talking about some of these issues directly and personally within an academic environment. I know that the suggestion for the paper had been warmly welcomed by the organisers, but this support did not stop me feeling uneasy.

It was as if these issues should not be talked about in public, that it was too risky and too dangerous. At some level I was ambivalent about doing it at all since this was also the first time I was speaking in such a setting on such themes. But once I had begun I felt a lot easier. I felt as if some kind of load had lifted and I felt a little fuller in myself. The discussion it provoked was interesting and fruitful and helped to focus some important questions. But it also made me feel a little odd for it somehow confirmed in public that I had a 'different' past and that I was forced to deal with issues in my growing up that seemed quite strange to many people. It was as if a re-visioning of England and what it could mean to be English was going on in the room.

At the same time as I was talking about a Jewish childhood in which I wanted to be normal and like everyone else – and this is partly how I experienced myself internally – it was also difficult to live in public with the strangeness of the history that I was sharing. It was as if I had to meet myself in a different way in public, possibly for the first time. But in many ways it also helped me explain different things I have felt in the past. From now on I think it is going to be a little easier and I will feel a little more at ease with myself and with my Jewishness. It is part of a process of coming out as Jewish. I do not think it will be easy but it will be easier.

As we went for lunch a young Irishman pulled me aside to say how much he had learnt from the session. He told me that just the week before his mother had come down to Dublin to spend an evening with him. They had shared a bottle of wine. This had almost never happened before and he sensed that she had something to tell him. She wanted to tell him about his middle names – he had two and one was acknowledged as Huguenot and talked about in the family, and the other was Jewish. He heard for the first time that his maternal grandmother had been Jewish. This discovery had been unsettling to the sense of identity which he carried. He had always carried the second middle name but never really knew what it meant – 'it was just a name'.

But it was proving very helpful for him to know about the cultural derivation of this naming for it made a number of things clearer to him. He had always felt very much at ease with Jewish friends and often wondered why this should be so. He had found himself with close Jewish friends at different times in his life. It is easy to think of this discovery as a coincidence but it raises questions, questions we have difficulty thinking about within a rationalist culture about hidden/buried identities and what it is we can be said to 'carry' from our ancestors. These are questions that African traditions have little difficulty with, but, even with the openings of postcolonial literatures, we often refuse to validate traditional forms of knowledge. It could be said, in Walter Benjamin's terms, that some 'space' had been filled out in his aura with this new information that his mother had passed on to him.[15] She had felt the urgency to make a special visit. She had recognised that this was significant information which she had withheld and which, you could say, he had a right to know. It was significant if he was to revise his identity.

Knowing a little more of where he had come from, he also knew a little more about who he is. Within a homogenised vision of England, these knowledges have been long suppressed. People did not often want to recover the complexities of their English identities. In this way they controlled their anxieties about Englishness, so often played out in relation to the Jews. This is not simply a matter of available knowledge, for you have to be ready to hear what is being said. He could have rejected the gifts his mother had brought with her. This is part of a process that cannot be forced, nor is it a matter of will. Often it is a matter of taking the next step when you are ready for it.

Someone else came up who was also from an Irish background, though this had been barely acknowledged when he was growing up. His mother had done her best to present herself as 'English', but now he felt it was important for him to explore his Irish inheritance. This was part of a felt knowledge about himself, though he could not really explain it. He just knew in some way that it was something that he needed to do for himself. It was not simply a matter of reframing experience in terms of a different discourse. Rather it opened up difficult issues about the relationship of language to experience.

Such responses often follow the breaking of a silence and they are heartening when they are made. But often these realisations remain at odds with the dominant ways we theorise identities within contemporary theoretical frameworks. These traditions also have to be shifted if we are to bring light to bear upon complex identities which have for so long been denied and shamed. This shift to complex, previously denied identities is a crucial part of the re-visioning of England. It has often been in the darkness of the cinema or in the privacy of reading literature that some of these connections have been made. It has been through extending the realm of imagination that we have also been able to voice aspects of our his/herstories that have for so long been repressed in the name of an England that has long passed.

---

15 For an exploration of Walter Benjamin's early writings see the essays collected in *One-Way Street, and Other Writings*, trans. Edmund Jephcott and Kingsley Shorter (London: New Left Books, 1979).

2 Queen's English

Alan Sinfield

In summer 1961 I had just left school. I thought of myself in metropolitan terms, as a Londoner; Derek, my best friend, lived near Stratford-upon-Avon and when I visited him we went to see Shakespeare plays there. Both of us were going to study English at university. These reinforcements of Englishness followed upon a sequence of compatible experiences. As a youngster, like millions of others, my first sight of television had been at the house of a friend during the coronation of Queen Elizabeth in 1953. I collected postage stamps of the British Empire, and took photos of Westminster Abbey and the Tower of London with my Brownie 127 camera. Englishness was secured, even more, by 'the War' (there was only one that counted). Despite the formation of NATO and the sudden discovery that the real enemy was the Soviet Union after all, comics, paperbacks and films dwelt upon the war with Nazi Germany far more than on the empire. Though they didn't talk about it much, my mother, aunties and grandparents had been bombed and my uncles had fought. Even more particularly, my father had been reported missing, presumed dead, in the RAF in 1944; my brother Mark was born posthumously. So we were a one-parent family, but no one accused us of fecklessness. No one gave us much support either.

The powers that be sent my mother a sheet of foolscap with the royal coat of arms in colour taking up most of the top half. She had it framed and hung it over the fireplace in her bedroom, so when I managed to get into her bed – in my father's place! – I could read it:

> This scroll commemorates
> Flight Sergeant E. J. Sinfield
> Royal Air Force
> held in honour as one who
> served King and Country in
> the world war of 1939–1945
> and gave his life to save
> mankind from tyranny. May
> his sacrifice help to bring
> the peace and freedom for
> which he died.

It was signed (though not individually) by the King. At the age of eleven I was sent to a kind of orphanage school in Wolverhampton – you had to have one parent deceased – and Armistice Day was a big thing for most of us: 'At the going down of the sun, and in the morning, We will remember them.' England wasn't just where we happened to have been born; we had contributed crucially to its liberty, and once a year everyone recognised this.

By the time I got to summer 1961 all that had been thoroughly reoriented. Like most of the other students I was about to meet at University College London, I was committed, emotionally and intellectually, to the Campaign for Nuclear Disarmament (CND). Now an empire seemed a disgraceful thing and a royal family a waste of money. Armistice Day was a con.

The War was probably all right nonetheless because it was against Hitler. The First World War was another matter; from Wilfred Owen's poems to Joan Littlewood's *Oh! What a Lovely War* (1963), it displayed the selfish and destructive perfidy of the ruling class and the immorality and inefficiency of capitalism. Shakespeare too was probably all right, because the history plays could be rewritten as *The Wars of the Roses* (Stratford, 1963), showing how great magnates dismantled England without regard for the ordinary citizen.

In fact, as has often been remarked, CND was by no means free of English nationalism. It aspired, by withdrawing Britain from NATO, to liberate the country from United States domination. And it imagined that England, in the organised Labour movement and the radical intelligentsia, had access to an authoritative moral tradition that would make a unilateral renunciation of nuclear weapons a compelling example to the rest of the world. Both these factors involved an uninspected assumption that England was a world power capable of acting by itself and likely to be marked by others. 'Tell the leaders of the nations, Let the whole wide world take heed', we sang.

As well as protest songs, English and American folk songs were a significant part of this oppositional subculture. However, these were not perceived as aspects of olde Englande or of US cultural domination. They were envisaged as belonging to an alternative system, transmitted almost without the capitalist cultural apparatus, and invoking love, work and suffering as experienced by the common people. I don't recall anyone saying this idea of the people was patronising, and men, at least, didn't notice the sexism that pervaded many of the songs.

Two further complicating factors in this picture of Englishness should be race, and the intersection between England and Britain. We sang songs from the African American tradition and the Civil Rights movement, but this didn't involve direct contact with any black people. At school in Wolverhampton we should have had a stronger sense of race than many people – Caribbean men appeared on the streets from the mid-1950s. However, I don't remember speaking to any of them, connecting them to American jazz, blues and gospel music, or appreciating that their presence was going to make much of a difference. In 1961 after spending six weeks working in a café in Cornwall and getting a suntan, I got a job in a pub and was asked by a customer where I came from. 'Palmers Green', I replied, but confusion and belligerence ensued, until I realised that I had been heard as saying 'Pakistan'. I realised that I was experiencing racial prejudice, but was mainly at a loss. Not until a few months later would a fellow student (from Birmingham) take me for my first curry.

I can't focus properly how I believed England related to the United Kingdom and the British Isles; from this inability, I deduce that my ideas of Scotland, Wales and Ireland were vague at best. Although I had been moved by the landscape in Wales, my notion of Britain was just England with extra, hilly bits. Perhaps it was 'Britain' for power and glory, and 'England' for core authenticity, sincerity and simplicity. When the Civil Rights movement erupted in Derry in 1968 I had had no idea that Catholics were unable to vote or get jobs or houses in Northern Ireland, and that they were systematically excluded from the apparatus of government. I had known more about oppressed peoples in South Africa and the United States.

I inhabited an Englishness, then, that was not simple, but its dissonances seemed fairly well under control. In fact, in the aspects thus far mentioned, my attitudes were largely those of my generation and class fraction – a youthful left–liberal intelligentsia, struggling up from the lower middle classes through the newly, and unevenly, meritocratic education system.[1]

The problem, in the midst of it all, was that I was in love with Derek, and wanted to have sex with him in some only partly comprehended way. That was illegal and scarcely heard of in England, though not altogether un-English. I could see that Derek knew about my infatuation and that it made him uneasy, so I tried to hold off for fear of driving him away altogether. As it was, I made him impatient and eventually bored with continual jealous sulks and obscure grievances. When I read Tennyson's *In Memoriam* (1850) in my third year at college, when Derek was finally abandoning me, I recognised the pattern of unequal passion all too clearly. I shielded myself from it, while immersing myself in it, by devoting my research degree to a structural analysis of the language of the poem; I didn't write about sexual relations in *In Memoriam* until a second book, published in 1986.

None of my confusion seemed consonant with the Englishness of Queen Elizabeth and her multiplying family, British Empire stamps and snapshots of Westminster Abbey; or with horror at the Holocaust and the Gestapo and amazement at the stiff upper lips of young men in ridiculously fragile Hurricanes and Spitfires. No one observed that hints of queerness were to be found lurking around empire-builders and generals such as Rhodes, Gordon, Baden-Powell, Kitchener, Churchill, Montgomery and Mountbatten. No one mentioned that gays had been held in Nazi death camps.

The culture of radical politics promised a considerably better accommodation with queerness. My comrades and I were pleased to claim for University College and CND a tradition of dissent, one that had spoken up for individual liberties and dared unorthodox lifestyles. However, we didn't know that Jeremy Bentham (whose preserved body was on view in the cloisters at college) had declared laws and prejudice against homosexuals irrational, or that Bertrand Russell had

1 See Alan Sinfield, *Literature, Politics and Culture in Postwar Britain*, 3rd edn (London: Continuum, 2004), chs 11, 12.

cultivated a freethinking, if heterosexual, love-life. We thought of the Suffragettes as a noble episode in our tradition, but most men, at least, supposed that feminist demands had been largely satisfied; indeed, remarking that self-assertive women might be lesbians would have been regarded as a way of putting them down. We were not aware that anyone prominent in CND was gay – Pat Arrowsmith, for instance.

To be sure, people in the peace movement were generally in favour of the decriminalisation of male homosexual practices, as the Wolfenden Commission had recommended in 1957. A survey of 1966 found the progressive view to be held by between 75 per cent and 94 per cent (depending on social class) of CND supporters.[2] However, that was a rational principle. Centrally, CND cultivated a clean-living, juice-drinking image (commercially produced yoghurt was a novelty, I think) which scarcely encouraged sexual indulgence. There was a minor scandal when a newspaper reporter persuaded a boy and girl to get into the same sleeping bag for a photo: what an unfair slur on decent people! Our idea of a photo-opportunity always included parents with a push chair – we made much of the danger to children of fall-out from nuclear testing. 'Will you see your cities crumble, Will you let your children die?' we sang.

The big factor that ought to have afforded some kind of purchase on English queerness was 'doing English'. We had studied some of Shakespeare's sonnets for the verse form and the lofty sentiments, but their intriguingly obscure story appeared to purport a forbidden love: 'Let me confess that we two must be twain, / Although our undivided loves are one' (sonnet 36). Further, the frustration and resentment was me and Derek – 'Being your slave, what should I do but tend / Upon the hours and times of your desire?' (sonnet 57). The critical establishment tried to evade such topics: the sonnets were technical exercises, designed to flatter a patron. It was better to believe that the bard had been insincere, than desecrate such an icon of Englishness with the spectre of queerness. Some scholars still take that line.

Nowadays, our idea of literary activity in early- to mid-twentieth-century England is dominated by images of willowy young gentlemen and over-intense ladies. In film adaptations, biographies and television documentaries, we see them camping around in country houses, London salons and Oxbridge colleges, falling in love with each other, taking advantage of the lower classes, exploiting exotic places and exotic people.

I did pick up bits of all that. Probably I intuited the yearnings of prohibited love among the sufferings of war in the poems of Wilfred Owen and Siegfried Sassoon, though without any encouragement from literary institutions (in 1998, still, the film *Regeneration* shies away from queerness). Virginia Woolf's *Orlando* (1928) was set for A-level examinations and had evident possibilities, but it all got dissipated in whimsy. *Howards End* (1910) was set as well and I read *A Passage to*

---

2 Frank Parkin, *Middle Class Radicalism* (Manchester: Manchester University Press, 1968), p. 43.

India (1924), but I didn't know E. M. Forster was queer; after all, neither did Lionel Trilling when he wrote admiringly of Forster's liberalism in 1944. It was rumoured that W. H. Auden and Christopher Isherwood were gay, but I couldn't see it in the available writings. James Baldwin's *Giovanni's Room* (1956) didn't get into paperback until 1963.

D. H. Lawrence was the top guru on sex, of course. But the chapter on lesbianism in *The Rainbow* (1915) is titled 'Shame', and Birkin's attempt to love a man as well as a woman in *Women in Love* (1917) doesn't work out ('It's an obstinacy, a theory, a perversity', Ursula says on the last page of the novel). Non-English titles were more helpful. Thomas Mann's *Death in Venice* came out in Penguin in 1955, but was a gloomy affair; likewise André Gide's *The Immoralist* (1960). The vulnerability of young people to predatory queers in these books was a doubly worrying theme, since I cast myself in both roles, producing both repugnance for a situation in which I might be regarded as disgusting, and fear of a situation which I might not control. I could neither approach anyone, nor allow myself to be approached. J. D. Salinger's *The Catcher in the Rye* (Penguin, 1958) was discouraging here, as was 'An Encounter', one of the stories in James Joyce's *Dubliners* (1914). The presumption of Derek's reluctance gave me an alibi for not trying.

Other books were so avant-gardiste that you could hardly make out what was supposed to be happening. I pored endlessly over T. S. Eliot but no one mentioned the theory that *The Waste Land* (1922) might be understood as an elegy on the death of a young man – 'mort aux Dardanelles' (as the epigraph to 'Prufrock' has it). I puzzled over whether one or both of the characters in Edward Albee's *The Zoo Story* (1960) were gay, and who was doing what to whom in William Burroughs' *The Naked Lunch* (1959). When paperback translations of Jean Genet's novels began to appear in the mid-1960s I pondered whether some of the 'she's' are 'he's' (it turns out all of them are). Anyway, this is all after the event. As these books appeared, no one was drawing attention to them as a body of writing that might illuminate the queer condition; or positioning them in a spectrum of queer experience; or discussing their moral and psychological implications.

The central irony is that while the intimations of queerness in these and other literary writings were quite inadequate for a boy trying to find out how to set about it, they were sufficient to instil a monstrous anxiety that poetry and the like was for girls and sissies. Thus I felt exposed to an imputation of queer effeminacy while not actually getting anywhere with my sex life.

For, as I have argued elsewhere, the embarrassment of literary culture, in England at least, is that it is gendered.[3] 'Manliness' is celebrated as the backbone of industry, business, the military and empire; and art and literature find themselves, in counterpart, in a 'feminine' stance. When Hermann Goering reaches for his gun, we literary folk reach for our culture. *Howards End* is about culture and gender - the empire-building Wilcoxes versus the artistic Schlegels. Consider

---

3   See Alan Sinfield, *Cultural Politics – Queer Reading,* 2nd edn (London: Routledge, 2004).

Matthew Arnold's phraseology: he sets humanist sweetness and light against the philistines and the barbarians. The latter two may be vulgar, but they do sound like real men.

Literary culture accepts – in the main very gingerly – a touch of the feminine. Its 'human' protest against the inhumanity of capitalism and the modern world (often perceived as the inhumanity of 'man') depends on a strategic deployment of effeminacy: of culture against brutality, the spirit against the system, style against purpose, personal emotion against coercion. Hence the commonplace that the great writer is androgynous. There musn't be too much of the 'wrong' sex, though. The trick is to appropriate sufficient of the radical aura of androgyny, without more than is necessary of the disabling stigma.

Yet there is no evading it: literature is a sissy affair. The consequent anxiety has preoccupied literary criticism, for instance in the work of F. R. Leavis, whose approach became dominant during the 1950s. His project was to make literature fit for a man to study: healthy, mature, tough, robust – these are the epithets of Leavisite approval. Chris Baldick remarks the stress on 'maturity' and how the Leavises elevated the 'fecund' Lawrence against the 'surprising radical adolescence' of Auden.[4] Shelley too is the wrong kind of poet: he is given to 'tender, caressing, voluptuous effects', and 'the conventional bathos of album poeticizing, not excluding banalities about … the sad lot of woman'. Compare the manly stance of Wordsworth: he evinces 'emotional discipline, critical exploration of his experience, pondered valuation and maturing reflection'.[5] Even so, the distinction is not very safe. 'I wandered lonely as a cloud / That floats on high o'er vales and hills' – William Wordsworth. It's not all *that* manly.

Notwithstanding these anxieties, literature was *English* – notionally continuous with saving mankind from tyranny. It was something we were good at (whereas the Germans did music and the Italians did painting). Forster, Lawrence and others had addressed 'the condition of England'. And being an arts student was a good deal more special than it is now. It was all right, in 1961, for Derek and me to lean languidly in the Dirty Duck at Stratford (the pub where the actors were supposed to go – another dodgy group), drinking lager and lime in our cavalry twills and suede shoes. We were at the prestige cultural centre of England. Despite all the obscurity, obliquity and discouragement, I am sure English Literature helped many boys to negotiate a serviceable basis for a purposeful gayness.

For me and others, though, there was a further problem: class. Queer literary Englishness was upper middle class (this was part of Leavis's objection also). Only John Keats, among the canonical nineteenth-century poets, really had to work for his living (we weren't encouraged to take John Clare seriously). While it is true that working people had read literary writers in their own ways, the institutions that

---

4 Chris Baldick, *The Social Mission of English Criticism 1848-1932* (Oxford: Oxford University Press, 1983), p. 217.
5 F. R. Leavis, *Revaluation* (London: Chatto, 1936), pp. 222, 221, 212.

had taken it upon themselves to establish the canon and the proper concerns of criticism were bourgeois (gentleman scholars, universities and public schools, upmarket newspapers and magazines, coterie journals). Virginia Woolf was only trying to join the mainstream when she demanded, for the twentieth-century woman writer, not just a room of her own but a significant private income.

The milieux of queer literary English writing were correspondingly elevated. Even Lawrence's characters, though some of them were technically lower middle class, managed to move in posh circles. They gave dinners and attended garden parties, drank wine and ate exotic foods (figs, for instance), travelled abroad. (We bought wine at Christmas time, and I encountered spaghetti bolognaise for the first time at college – they served it with chips in the refectory; hardly anyone I knew had been abroad, other than in the armed forces.) Some of Lawrence's moneyed characters were presented for disapproval – they were out of touch with their feelings, indeed deathly in some cryptic way. But those were the ones most likely to be queer! Moreover, despite the unorthodox lifestyles and opinions of many characters in these fictions, they were generally mired in a middle-class ethos of good manners, discretion, respectability and keeping up appearances.

It was less Englishness, then, than class which prevented literature from affording a workable concept of gayness. One of the signals on that scroll from the King was my father's rank: flight sergeant. He couldn't have been in *The Colditz Story*, then – the book or the movie – because Colditz was a prison for officers. In *The Cruel Sea* he would have been receiving orders in the engine room, not giving them on the bridge. He wouldn't have had a speaking part in *The Dam Busters*, though we bought the record of the march. The school in Wolverhampton did develop aspirations, but we had almost no relations with public schools and, indeed, were in awe of the local grammar school. All the pupils were poor. By the time I was twenty I hadn't been in a private car more than a few dozen times; I was aware that my British Empire stamps held little value because I could afford only the lower denominations in each series.

Paul Bailey records this problem in his personal memoir, *An Immaculate Mistake* (1990). He couldn't reveal to his family and neighbours that he was

what they called a 'pansy'. They would not have believed me, anyway. I came from working stock, and my ancestors had toiled long and hard to make a humble living. It was common knowledge that pansies were the sons of the idle rich, who had nothing better to do than be waited on, hand and foot. Pansies had weak blood – blood as weak as water – in their veins. You wouldn't find a pansy in our part of London.[6]

In Arnold Wesker's play *Chips with Everything* (1962), which I admired a lot, the Pilot Officer places a hand on the knee of an airman, apparently typifying the exploitative habits of the officer class.[7]

---

6 Paul Bailey, *An Immaculate Mistake* (London: Bloomsbury, 1990), p. 92.
7 Wesker later changed the stage direction here to suggest that a friendly gesture was misread.

There were other writings. *Aubade* by Kenneth Martin (1957) was about an ordinary sort of boy finding out about sexuality, but I didn't know about it until Gay Men's Press reprinted it in 1989. I did see *A Taste of Honey* by Shelagh Delaney when it reached the semi-professional Intimate Theatre in Palmers Green, probably in 1960. Geof is lower class and gay. He has stereotypical mannerisms, but is in quest of emotional reality and is hardly discreet. He knows about drawing, but because he is an art student, not an aesthete – art students were related to the CND ethos and were to spearhead the inventive 1960s subcultures. Even so, Geof is not reported as meeting any sexual partners, and the penalty for relative openness is getting called 'pansified little freak', 'bloody little pansy' and 'that little fruitcake parcel'. Not very heartening.

The class implications of homosexuality were again reinforced, again in 1961, by Basil Dearden's film *Victim*. The character offered for audience identification is a barrister; he is married and trying to stay clear of homosexual liaisons. The lower-class objects of his reluctant attention are a shifty lot and only he is given psychological depth and social implication. I went to see *Victim* with Derek, and we had an earnest discussion in the course of which we distinguished inverts and perverts and decided that one of them might be regarded sympathetically and the other not. I don't remember which was which, or where we got such ideas from.

Angus Wilson's novel *Hemlock and After* (1952) is in the same vein. The protagonist, a famous, gay and married writer, is upper-middle-class in his lifestyle and his access to social, artistic and state power; his sexual partners are treated with sympathy and respect, but they are relatively lightly sketched.

When I had been at college a couple of months, Angus Wilson came to lecture on 'Evil in the English Novel' and I arranged to interview him for the student newspaper. Of course, I didn't ask him about homosexuality. He was courteous, kind and generous, but I took the opportunity, nonetheless, to remark to the tutor who was introducing the lectures that I had found Wilson's handshake limp. Taking an interest in a writer associated with gayness required, to my mind, a gesture of disaffiliation. 'Perhaps he's lonely', the tutor responded. Only years later did I realise that my little piece of self-rejection had been particularly ill-judged because the tutor was himself gay. This simply hadn't occurred to me as a possibility: that there might have been two – no, three – gay men in a room at the same time was beyond my imagining!

So that is why I was wasting my emotional energy being unrequited with Derek. Englishness and English afforded me some opportunities, but they also held me trapped. In the mid-1960s I was to repeat the Derek pattern of relating with Peter, before the Gay Liberation Front arrived from the United States in 1970, with quite different credentials. There was a new way to be gay: up-front, organised, egalitarian, defiant. Within a decade, this approach was to produce the effective resolution of the uneasy stand-off between English Literature and dissident sexuality: Lesbian and Gay Studies, or, more ambitiously perhaps, Queer Studies. Efforts in these fields have produced substantial insights into familiar, canonical texts, while uncovering innumerable new and potent resources in gay life and letters. They have provoked sophisticated reassessments of psychoanalysis, essentialism, post-structuralism and cultural studies. They have sponsored new histories of sexualities, and afforded a base for hitherto unconsidered minorities – transsexuals, transgender people, gay people of colour. Above all, for instance in the University of Sussex MA programme, Sexual Dissidence and Cultural Change, student work of quite extraordinary calibre and intensity has been inspired.

Of course, this gay work in universities has not been uncontentious. The press got news of the Sussex programme when it started in February 1991, in the middle of the tabloid assault on people with AIDS and a couple of years after the infamous Section 28 became law, prohibiting municipalities from spending money on projects that 'promote homosexuality'. Questions were raised by parliamentarians. 'MPs Slam "Degree in Gays"' was the headline in the *Daily Mirror* (25 February 1991): 'Students at a university are being offered a degree course in gay and lesbian studies. But the one year course at Sussex University in Brighton is under attack by Tory MPs. Terry Dicks said it was a waste of taxpayers' subsidy. "The place should be shut down and disinfected", he said.' Nonetheless, the traditional liberal ethos of the university and the imaginative support of particular colleagues have protected our work. Also, the insistence that market forces be respected makes it hard to stop us – so long as we attract good students and publish notable research.

So how secure are such gains? In an opinion piece in the *Times Higher Education Supplement*, Gary Day (of De Montfort University) quarrels with 'literary critics or theorists or whatever they're called these days', who do not value the study of literary history. Day adds, without any apparent linkage: 'And then there's the question of sexuality. Professors can take this very seriously. A friend of mine didn't get a job because he was "weak on queer theory". He should have told them he was strong on the practice. The job? PGCE coordinator for English.'[8] I offered to write a rebuttal in the features section of the paper, but was told a letter would be more appropriate. Aware that brevity is required in such a context, I wrote simply this:

Why the gratuitous jibe against professors who take sexuality seriously, in Gary Day's opinion piece on literature and the past? Lesbians and gay men have been vigorously unearthing our literature and our past. Is this good only when heterosexuals do it?

Suppose, as Day claims, someone didn't get a job as a PGCE coordinator because he was weak on 'queer theory'. If that includes issues of AIDS prevention and bullying of gay school students, it would be an appropriate knowledge. But Day allows the murky inference that gays should be kept away from young people.

Day suggests that queer 'practice' might have influenced the job. He doesn't have to like gays, but he has no cause to impugn our professional integrity.

---

8 Gary Day, 'It's surprising that, with all that it's got going for it, the past comes in for such a battering', *Times Higher Education Supplement* (25 Apr. 2003), p. 13. (PGCE is a qualification for teaching in schools.)

They didn't print my letter. In 2003 gays may have had partnership rights and the repeal of section 28, but in a purportedly serious newspaper Lesbian and Gay Studies can be speared with the imputation that offering your body may get you a job, without even a right of reply.

3 The miasma of Englishness at home and abroad in the 1950s

Elizabeth Maslen

A common dictionary definition of the term 'miasma' is 'an infectious or noxious emanation' and, while this may seem an over-dramatic metaphor for attitudes to and perceptions of Englishness in the 1950s, what is conveyed is central to my argument.[1] For, as has often been argued, the term 'Englishness' has all too often been undefined in discussion, as if what it signified not only could be taken for granted, but should be self-evident. Yet, for the steady flow of incomers in the 1950s and after, not to mention those who arrived long before, this very insubstantial vagueness was soon seen to be exclusive, despite its apparent lack of precision. Indeed, it was all too apparent that the undefined nature of conventional Englishness had been and continued to be a central source of its power and influence. In consequence, the term as used by certain commentators becomes increasingly noxious in the years after the Second World War. All too often, Englishness (frequently, as we know, used interchangeably with Britishness, as if there could be no argument as to their being synonyms) takes for granted that we are an island nation of pure blood. Such an assumption is arrogant enough in ignoring the Celtic peripheries and long-term minorities, and becomes ever more outrageous when it still persists in seeking to exclude the various racial and cultural differences that it now, according to law, embraces. As Raphael Samuel reminds us, 'Minorities have not normally had an easy time of it in Britain'.[2] Citing prejudices against such groups as Catholics, Jews, Gypsies and gays, down the centuries, he goes on to argue:

Politically Britain may be a pluralist society, as it has been, notionally, through three centuries of representative government. Behaviourally, though, it is fearful of departures from the norm … In public discourse 'British characteristics' (as the Prime Minister [Thatcher] calls them) are still spoken of as though they were generic, the 'British' as though they were a single people, 'the British way of life' as though it were organic – a natural harmony which only the malevolent would disturb, a shared condition which newcomers must adapt to.[3]

1 See, for instance, H. W. and F. G. Fowler (eds), *The Concise Oxford Dictionary of Current English*, Rev. 5th edn (Oxford: Oxford University Press, 1964).
2 Raphael Samuel, 'Introduction: The Little Platoons' in *Patriotism: the making and unmaking of British national identity, vol. 2: Minorities and Outsiders*, ed. Raphael Samuel (London and New York: Routledge, 1989), p. ix.
3 Samuel, 'Introduction: The Little Platoons', p. xxii.

Yet what constitutes Englishness (or 'Britishness' according to such as Thatcher), despite being taken for granted, has arguably changed over the centuries, for, as Samuel suggests: 'Ideas of national character have typically been formed by processes of exclusion, where what is British is defined in its relations of opposition to enemies both without and within.'[4] For the post-war era, as Simon Gikandi argues, Englishness could be seen as an imperial concept which had been carried forward, using its experience of alterity to construct itself. Indeed, it could be argued as Gikandi does – and here he agrees with Edward Said's thesis in *Culture and Imperialism* (1993) – that 'colonised peoples and imperial spaces were crucial ingredients in the generation and consolidation of a European identity and its master narratives'.[5]

People inhabiting the British Isles in the 1950s were faced not only with the steadily accelerating loss of empire but with the arrival of increasing numbers of incomers from what had been, they may have felt, reassuringly distant parts of that empire. Many could not come to terms with the alterity within, and either ignored or rejected it. Indeed Enoch Powell in the 1960s would simply provide an already flourishing English nationalism with what Gikandi calls 'its working hypothesis', and which he summarises: 'Empire gave England power and prestige but left its national character untouched; even at the height of its empire, England remained an island untouched by the landscapes and subjects it dominated; now with postimperial migration, the blacks have come to contaminate the realm.'[6] This attitude, whether openly acknowledged or not, was all too prevalent in the 1950s, and has by no means been an anachronism right up to the present time; the hostility to refugees has been fuelled by it. And I would go further, with Samuel: the English, whether at home or abroad, all too often, now as then, cling to a myth of racial purity and imperial superiority, both in relation to their former colonies and indeed to anyone and anywhere perceived as 'foreign', or even more narrowly as 'other'.

The tabloid press affords many current examples of this tendency, often drawing on Second World War slogans to make a dramatic point; slogans which, in their propagandist constructions of what 'England' meant, racially and morally, had already helped to shape the post-war thinking of half a century ago. And they merely mirror perceptions that have been current ever since. Queenie Leavis, for instance, giving a paper on 'The Englishness of the English Novel' in 1980, a few months before her death, illustrates this.[7] As might be expected, there are sharply perceptive comments in this paper. But equally there are remarkable blind-spots and flashes of prejudice – characteristic of Leavis herself certainly, but also

---

4 Samuel, 'Introduction: The Little Platoons', p. xviii.
5 Simon Gikandi, *Maps of Englishness: writing identity in the culture of colonialism* (New York: Columbia University Press, 1996), p. 5.
6 Gikandi, *Maps of Englishness*, p. 86.
7 Q. D. Leavis, 'The Englishness of the English Novel', *English Studies*, 62 (1981), pp. 128–45.

arguably endemic in those of her generation who were rooted in certain habits of mind, where a sort of cultural arrogance spilled over and infected ideas of race, nation and class. Leavis shares with her husband, F. R. Leavis, certainties which bedeviled a way of thinking that was all too common in the years after the Second World War, even among those, like Queenie Leavis, with strong socialist sympathies. For instance, in her paper, Leavis acknowledges how 'a succession of gifted, creative writers, born in different times and places and stations ... saw prose fiction as a suitable medium for expressing their *human* concerns'.[8] But then it becomes clear that such human concerns are indistinguishable from what is *national*: 'the novel', Leavis says, 'is the art most influenced by national life in all its minute particulars'; and later the same merging occurs when the 'major' novelist is defined as

a writer peculiarly sensitive to national tensions and conflicts and one who, by the accidents of his personal history, is specially qualified to feel and register the characteristic and deeper movements of the life of his time, has a true sense of values, and has the wisdom and insights which make him a warning voice for his generation.[9]

'A true sense of values' is a phrase that has to be worrying, whatever it means, since the basis for the claim of 'truth' is never defined. What is more, it soon becomes clear, as the paper develops, that anything remotely foreign, any influence perceived, however arbitrarily, as coming from outside this undefined Englishness must be pernicious. Anything written abroad must either owe its greatness to the Englishness of the English novel (as in Russia) or demonstrably fall short of English achievement (as in America). And again, the lack of definition of the central concept, Englishness, can lead to some unfortunate conclusions. For instance, 'Chaucer is already recognizably an Englishman' despite his (studiously unacknowledged) debts to Europe and ultimately North Africa.[10] Furthermore, the novelists writing in the 1950s, the most recent writers that Leavis chooses to castigate for their betrayal of their English tradition and heritage (writers like Amis, Powell, Graham Greene, Manning) are significantly home-made. Writers like Doris Lessing, V. S. Naipaul and Sam Selvon are conspicuous by their absence, an absence, one suspects, influenced by their tendency to problematise concepts of Englishness.

Queenie Leavis is, of course, celebrated for her quirky dogmatism, and it would be comforting to see her, as we say, as one on her own, or at least as representing only a certain group within her generation. But she does not. *Literary Englands* by David Gervais was published in 1993, and is described in an abstract as meditating 'on the contemporary meanings of "Englishness"'.[11] Inevitably, such a work cannot be all-inclusive, as Gervais readily acknowledges in his Afterword. But it is striking that this

---

8   Leavis, 'The Englishness of the English Novel', p. 128 (emphasis added).
9   Leavis, 'The Englishness of the English Novel', p. 128.
10 Leavis, 'The Englishness of the English Novel', p. 141.
11 David Gervais, *Literary Englands: versions of 'Englishness' in modern writing* (Cambridge: Cambridge University Press, 1993).

Afterword, in acknowledging what it regretfully excludes for want of space ('cosmopolitans' looking to Europe, for instance), does not even acknowledge in its exclusions those members of English society who do not hail from so-called 'white' traditions. There is no mention, for instance, of Hanif Kureishi who famously, in 1990, has his protagonist open *The Buddha of Suburbia* by asserting: 'I am an Englishman born and bred, almost. I am often considered to be a funny kind of Englishman, a new breed as it were, having emerged from two old histories. But I don't care – Englishman I am (though not proud of it), from the South London suburbs and going somewhere.'[12] The challenge to Englishness in this opening is ironically presented, taking on as it does the pride in Englishness which endeavours to exclude Kureishi's protagonist and which has been prevalent for so long. But the claim is as valid as for any of Kureishi's contemporaries 'born and bred' in England.

It would be possible to focus on any decade after the Second World War for this consideration of what I have termed the 'miasma' of Englishness. I have chosen the 1950s because, after the Second World War, one might be forgiven for thinking that the British Empire's disintegration could no longer be ignored (although, as I have suggested, many managed to see this disintegration as less significant than it was); and some social progress at home did appear to be here to stay (in education and health, for instance). However, as Alan Sinfield has powerfully argued, much remained the same, and the miasma of an Englishness which, importantly, could be taken for granted, did not require definition and continually blurred distinctions of culture, nation, class and race was alive and well.[13] All too often, attitudes to Englishness in the 1950s recall Auden's poem 'Spain', a poem envisaging the Spanish Civil War as a template for future revolution in the world of inherited Englishness. Here, after the 'struggle', he envisages his post-revolutionary world as remarkably like the pre-revolutionary, white middle-class one, but minus all the bits he disapproves of:

> To-morrow, perhaps the future. The research on fatigue
> And the movement of packers; the gradual exploring of all the
>   Octaves of radiation;
> To-morrow the enlarging of consciousness by diet and breathing.
>
> To-morrow the rediscovery of romantic love,
> The photographing of ravens; all the fun under
>   Liberty's masterful shadow;
> To-morrow the hour of the pageant-master and the musician,
>
> The beautiful roar of the chorus under the dome;
> To-morrow the exchanging of tips on the breeding of terriers,
>   The eager election of chairmen
> By the sudden forest of hands ...

---

12 Hanif Kureishi, *The Buddha of Suburbia* (London and Boston: Faber, 1990), p. 3.
13 Alan Sinfield, *Literature, Politics and Culture in Postwar Britain* (Oxford: Blackwell, 1989).

> To-morrow for the young poets exploding like bombs,
> The walks by the lake, the weeks of perfect communion;
>   To-morrow the bicycle races
> Through the suburbs of summer evenings ... [14]

To his credit, Auden would have consigned the poem to oblivion if he could, but while it was written in the 1930s and in terms of revolution rather than evolution, it is all too prophetic as to the 1950s. Kenneth O. Morgan, in his book *The People's Peace* (1990), speaks of the endemic social inequality of post-war Britain, affecting the north/south divide, the Celtic fringe as against the southern 'heartland', wealth and poverty, social class, ethnic minorities and gender.[15] All of these are recognisable ingredients inherited from before the war. Peter Hennessy, in *Never Again* (1992), quotes a report on how, in 1949, Sir Henry Tizard, Chief Scientific Adviser to the Ministry of Defence, warned that '[w]e are not a great power and never will be again. We are a great nation, but if we continue to behave like a Great Power we shall soon cease to be a great nation. Let us take warning from the fate of the Great Powers of the past and not burst ourselves with pride (see Aesop's fable of the frog).'[16] But even Tizard, more perceptive and more courageous than most of his Whitehall colleagues who, according to the record Hennessy quotes, met his words 'with the kind of horror one would expect if one had made a disrespectful remark about the King' – even Tizard cannot entirely shed the epithet 'great'; great power no, great nation yes.[17] And, more importantly, this view of 'greatness' involves the definition of England's role in the world; there is as yet no question of redefining Englishness from within.

All too often, in discussions of Englishness during the 1950s, the 'values' of that nation are defined by the middle class, upper rather than lower. Nancy Mitford's 1955 essay on U and non-U language, a mischievous but subtextually serious piece, revealing among other things how easily choice of vocabulary could 'place' the speaker's class and background, provoked huge attention and sold widely. It caused certain symptoms of anxiety in the utterances of those who wanted to 'get on', to be, as a later generation would put it, upwardly mobile – should they, for instance, refer to 'serviette' or 'napkin', 'lounge' or 'sitting room'?[18] There was no space in this defining of what was to be considered 'correct' English,

---

14 The differences between the text published in 1937, which I quote, and the final revised version published as 'Spain 1937' in *Another Time* (London: Faber, 1940) are listed in *The English Auden: poems, essays and dramatic writings 1927–1939*, ed. Edward Mendelsson (London: Faber, 1977), pp. 210–12, 424–5.

15 Kenneth O. Morgan, *The People's Peace: British history 1945–1989* (Oxford: Oxford University Press, 1990), p. 511.

16 Peter Hennessy, *Never Again: Britain 1945–1951* (London: Jonathan Cape, 1992), p. 431.

17 Margaret Gowing, *Independence and Deterrence: Britain and atomic energy, 1945–52*, vol. 1 (London: Macmillan, 1974), p. 229.

18 See Nancy Mitford, 'The English Aristocracy', *Encounter* (Sept. 1955).

for that part of old Englishness which Alan Sillitoe gave voice to, or the challenge which new Englishness offered in the work of Sam Selvon.

For despite all the conservatism about Englishness endemic in the 1950s, those works of the 1950s which offered subversive readings of that conventional non-definition were already calling for a conscious act of revision. For instance, as I have just suggested, Sillitoe and Selvon are well worth bracketing together. They both resist the miasma of Englishness in the sense that both of them explore Englishness and what it means, not only via their subject matter but via the medium of language itself. They both explore the way the language is spoken and the ideas conveyed by communities other than the one that might be termed the dominant *culture*, which for too long had subsumed nation, race and class (not to mention gender) within its definition of itself. This definition was never spelt out, as I have already argued, because it appeared self-evident to those who accepted it – great nation, great power, great Britain were the essence of that Englishness.

But these qualities were not the essence of Englishness for Sillitoe and Selvon. In *Saturday Night and Sunday Morning* (1958), Sillitoe develops for his narrative and for his protagonist, Arthur, a literary language which conveys something of an element of working-class life in Nottingham, both its perceptions of life and the way it articulates those perceptions.[19] The reader in fact actually watches Sillitoe develop this language as the novel progresses; the first chapter or two take the traditional course, following D. H. Lawrence's example, by using conventional literary English for the narrative, while reserving dialect for speech. But in later chapters, narrative becomes more colloquial, while speech imitates dialect less blatantly, so that the language of the book as a whole is subtly claimed for its working-class characters' priorities and their expression. For instance, this is how Arthur sums up his life at the end of the work:

Born drunk and married blind, misbegotten into a strange and crazy world, dragged-up through the dole and into the war with a gas-mask on your clock, and the sirens rattling into you every night while you rot with scabies in the air-raid shelter. Slung into khaki at eighteen and when they let you out, you sweat again in a factory, grabbing for an extra pint, doing women at the week-end and getting to know whose husbands are on the nightshift, working with rotten guts and an aching spine, and nothing for it but money to drag you back there every Monday morning.[20]

Sweating, 'doing women', working with rotting guts are here articulated as part of Sillitoe's narrative, not as in the majority of other narratives, both previous and contemporary, as confined to the speech alone of the vulgar and uneducated, those inhabiting a world beneath that of the dominant culture.

Two years earlier Sam Selvon, in *The Lonely Londoners* (1956), similarly devised a version of English for his narrative and for his protagonist, Moses, to

19 Alan Sillitoe, *Saturday Night and Sunday Morning* (1958; London: W. H. Allen, 1975).
20 Sillitoe, *Saturday Night and Sunday Morning*, p. 224.

convey something of the life of West Indian incomers and how they articulated their perceptions:

It have a kind of communal feeling with the Working Class and the spades, because when you poor things does level out, it don't have much up and down. A lot of the men get kill in war and leave widow behind, and it have bags of these old geezers who does be pottering about the Harrow Road like if they lost, a look in their eye as if the war happen unexpected and they still can't realise what happen to the old Brit'n.[21]

Throughout his novel, Selvon has devised a syntax and vocabulary which does not directly imitate any of the varieties of Caribbean English, but instead proclaims an Englishness not acknowledged by the traditional literary language. By challenging literary language through uses of language closer to their own usages, both Selvon and Sillitoe strive to avoid the traps which D. H. Lawrence and V. S. Naipaul create for themselves when their narratives obey the rules of so-called 'standard' literary usage, while their dialogue seeks to imitate the language of the people. Lawrence's and Naipaul's practice arguably upholds the 'superiority' of standard English over street norms, whereas what Sillitoe and Selvon celebrate is the richness of other kinds of English, their appropriateness for conveying ideas vastly different from those sold as 'typically' or 'traditionally' English, either implicitly or explicitly, by those writers who were until then seen as the only rightful participants in the canon (whose canon?). In other words, Selvon and Sillitoe expose the perils of the *non*-definition of Englishness – the assumptions, prejudices and exclusions which can go unacknowledged when Englishness is simply accepted for what it says it is: the highest common factor of people in these islands, rather than the province of a dominant culture which simply excludes what it does not practise itself. The assumption of class and racial superiority which this non-definition masks, its roots in a society where an upper class imposes its own standards as if they were common to that society as a whole, its exclusion of the kinds of language used by the bulk of the population on the grounds that such usages are not 'correct' – these are the prejudices, based on the arrogance of a ruling elite, which Sillitoe and Selvon challenge in their writing.

And the narcissism of this approach is infectious: even admirable commentators of lower-class life like Richard Hoggart and Raymond Williams fall into some of the gender, race and language traps of their time. When we really scrutinise literature of the 1950s, how many writers of the period acknowledge any impact on English society of the huge influx of people from abroad during the decade? Very few; not even Doris Lessing, coming as she does at the beginning of the 1950s with a burning sense of the inequities of the colonial regime in Southern Rhodesia. She is indeed aware, as she shows through her character Rose in *In Pursuit of the English* (1960), of the misrepresentation of the working-class in the

---

21 Sam Selvon, *The Lonely Londoners* (London: Alan Wingate, 1956), p. 75.

Ealing film comedies, working people set up, according to Rose, as comedians to amuse the dominant culture:

If it's an American film, well, they make us up all wrong, but it's what you'd expect from them. You don't take it serious. But the British films make me mad. Take the one tonight. It had what they call a cockney in it. I hate seeing cockneys in films. Anyway, what is a cockney? There aren't any, except around Bow Bells, so they say, and I've never been there. And then the barrow-boys, or down in Petticoat Lane. They just put it on to be clever, and sell things if they see an American or a foreigner coming. 'Watcher, cock', and all that talk all over the place. They never say Watcher, cock! unless there's someone stupid around to laugh. Them film people just put it in to be clever, like the barrow-boys, it makes the upper-class people laugh. They think of the working-class as dragged up. Dragged up and ignorant and talking vulgar-ugly.[22]

However, there is no overt black presence in Lessing's England of the 1950s, any more than in the works of that period by Hoggart or Williams.[23] It takes Shelagh Delaney, in her play *A Taste of Honey* (1958), at the end of the decade, to show the diversity behind traditional views of working-class life (and to acknowledge its own exclusions) with a black lover for her young Salford girl.[24] Otherwise, the non-white communities must find their own voices in a country which continues throughout the period to see them as either exotic or unwelcome – certainly as having no impact on Englishness.

In his book *On the Beneficence of Censorship*, Lev Loseff analyses ways in which writers in Russia, under tsarist and Soviet oppression, devised versions of what is termed Aesopian language: that is, language which spells out a tale on one level but sends out signals inviting identification and exploration of a subtext.[25] Arguably, something comparable is going on in works like those of Sillitoe and Selvon in the 1950s, since their experiments, while not in danger from the public censor, challenge the internal psychological censorship of the individual, conditioned as it is by long exposure to the standards imposed as 'correct' by the dominant culture. Sillitoe and Selvon do not waste much time attacking the dominant culture directly, but expose the subtext of traditional literary language usage by their own variations on the medium, just as Lessing's Rose offers an alternative reading of working-class accents and characterisation in Ealing comedies as patronage of one class by another. Such texts encourage the process of undermining authoritative readings of Englishness, of culture, nation, race and class, which have been theorised so eloquently as the century develops. These 1950s writers show, if we need showing, how we become aware of the unjustifiable ways

22 Doris Lessing, *In Pursuit of the English* (1960; London: Granada, 1977), p. 112.
23 Richard Hoggart, *The Uses of Literacy* (London: Chatto & Windus, 1957); Raymond Williams, *The Country and the City* (London: Hogarth Press, 1973).
24 Shelagh Delaney, *A Taste of Honey* (first performed 1958) (London: Methuen, 1959).
25 Lev Loseff, *On the Beneficence of Censorship: Aesopian language in modern Russian literature*, trans. Jane Bobko (Munich: Verlag Otto Sagner, 1984).

in which the dominant culture reads us (as inferior – to what? on whose authority?), how alien that reading can in fact be when we come to question it (why is Englishness all too often seen in relation to a countryside where very few members of the communities that make up the English spend their entire time?), how crucial it is to question propagandist interpretations of Englishness, in so-called peace as well as in war.

And not only at home. In *The Lonely Londoners*, Sam Selvon's Moses recalls the lure of England, of the magic names of places: "'I walked on Waterloo Bridge", "I rendezvoused at Charing Cross", "Piccadilly Circus is my playground", to say these things, to have lived in the great city of London, centre of the world.'[26] 'Centre of the world' is a huge claim, but it is the claim projected by the dominant culture to the colonies and empire, it is the lure recalled by the incomers in Donald Hinds' grim record of immigrant experience in *Journey to an Illusion* (1966), as the reality of life in England destroys their former dreams of belonging. 'Once', says one immigrant, 'I permeated the fabric of life in England, I thought I would be just another English swimmer, tossed along on the same tide, washed up on the same bank as they.'[27] This hope turns to: 'I am no longer troubled about the rigmarole of acceptance and rejection. It matters no more. I no longer have a hand to stretch out in friendship. It has been stretched out too long and has grown weak and tired. But I am indeed grateful to the English. Grateful for rejecting me in order to discover myself.'[28] Again, 'centre of the world' is the lure which corrupts the protagonist in V. S. Naipaul's novel *The Mystic Masseur* (1957), so that he abandons his Indian family name before coming to England, choosing to call himself by a name derived from this island.[29] It is the lure which corrupts and destroys the so-called 'mimic men' in Naipaul's later novel about political sleaze and graft published in 1967.[30]

I use the word 'lure' deliberately, as it seems to me apt: a lure is after all a falconer's bait, used in training, so that even when the hawk is flying free, it returns to the glove as its source of sustenance. And the lure has been used to devastating effect by colonial powers, education and writing being particularly potent in their effect. In Doris Lessing's short story 'The Old Chief Mshlanga', a white child of English parentage, living in the bush of Southern Rhodesia, illustrates this well:

A white child, opening its eyes curiously on a sun-suffused landscape, a gaunt and violent landscape, might be supposed to accept it as her own, to take the msasa trees and the thorn trees as familiars, to feel her blood running free and responsive to the swing of the seasons.

---

26 Selvon, *The Lonely Londoners*, p. 141.
27 Donald Hinds, *Journey to an Illusion: the West Indian in Britain* (London: Heinemann, 1966), p. 1.
28 Hinds, *Journey to an Illusion*, p. 5.
29 V. S. Naipaul, *The Mystic Masseur* (London: André Deutsch, 1957).
30 V. S. Naipaul, *The Mimic Men* (London: André Deutsch, 1967).

This child could not see a msasa tree, or the thorn, for what they were. Her books held tales of alien fairies, her rivers ran slow and peaceful, and she knew the shape of the leaves of an ash or an oak, the names of the little creatures that lived in English streams, when the words 'the veld' meant strangeness, though she could remember nothing else.

Because of this, for many years, it was the veld that seemed unreal; the sun was a foreign sun, and the wind spoke a strange language.[31]

Here is the lure or (to change the image) the miasma of Englishness, keeping the child apart and instilling in her a distorted sense of values by which, as the tale progresses, she is 'superior' to the Africans who live all round her, a sense which she loses as she comes to know the old chief and to understand where she is – only to witness that same sense of superiority asserted by the white policeman, who has the chief's kraal moved because, he alleges, it 'has no right to be there … I'll have a chat to the Native Commissioner next week. I'm going over for tennis on Sunday, anyway.'[32]

This miasma of Englishness abroad is picked up again in Ruth Prawer Jhabvala's *Esmond in India* (1958). Set after Independence, the novel shows how one branch of an Indian family is Anglophile at the expense of their Indian heritage. The father, educated in England, quotes English poems at his gardener, and has mesmerised his daughter (who has never been out of India) into seeing the world through his eyes. As a result, she rejects marriage to the young Indian doctor who has opted to work with the rural poor, a way of life that would have suited her idealistic temperament if only she had not been brain washed. Instead, she falls passionately in love with the Englishman Esmond, who sees India as full of collector's pieces, who had married a wife so as to possess something of this exotic culture and then had been revolted when domestic life did not follow an English pattern. Esmond is a damaged and dangerous relic of the worst of empire, casually certain of his superiority to Indians, careless of the human cost of his complacency in this alien culture which he would own but not share. Shakuntala, however, sees him as the epitome of all that she loves in English literature, which has undermined her hold on the realities of her own culture. The differences between the two young people emerge in their last meeting, when Shakuntala thinks they are to be united as lovers at last, and Esmond is happy because he has decided to leave India, wife and son for England:

One day perhaps he would have another little son, a merry fair-haired little boy (Angels not Angles). He felt so happy and light-hearted that even when a beggar accosted him he drove him away with the greatest good humour.

He found Shakuntala sitting in a shoe-shop … Esmond stood and looked at her, smiling with benevolence. Really, she was quite nice-looking and in a few years' time, when she

---

31 Doris Lessing, 'The Old Chief Mshlanga' (1951 collection) in *Collected African Stories, Vol. 1: This was the Old Chief's Country* (London: Grafton Books 1991), pp. 13–24 (p. 13).

32 Lessing, 'The Old Chief Mshlanga', p. 24.

had been married to everyone's satisfaction and had learned how to dress and be a lady, she would be nicer still ...

'Hello there!' cried Esmond. She looked up and saw him standing in the doorway, smiling and golden. Her Shelley, her Ariel ... [33]

Jhabvala, English-educated, German Jewish by birth, has her Shakuntala seduced by an Aryanism all too reminiscent in its *ubermensch* mentality and physical type of the ideology of Hitler's Nazism.

If we edit out from Queenie Leavis's paper the regrettable equation of human and national concerns, this myopic insistence on an Anglo-Saxon heritage which is, by a kind of unquestioned right, the light of the world, we find the best writers of the 1950s do indeed register what Leavis herself terms 'the characteristic and deeper movements of the life of [their] time'. They possess 'the wisdom and insights which make [them] a warning voice for [their] generation.'[34] However, in the most resonant novels, such as those by Sillitoe and Selvon, Englishness is not being taken for granted; it is being probed, interrogated, broken down, made ready for the creations and fresh dynamisms introduced by writers of different cultures and races as the century has progressed.

In his introduction to Fanon's *Black Skin, White Masks* (1952), Homi Bhabha observes that

in shifting the focus of cultural racism from the politics of nationalism to the politics of narcissism, Fanon opens up a margin of interrogation that causes a subversive slippage of identity and authority ... Nowhere is this slippage more significantly experienced than in the impossibility of inferring from the texts of Fanon a pacific image of 'society' or the 'state' as a homogeneous philosophical or representational unity. The 'social' is always an unresolved ensemble of antagonistic interlocutions between positions of power and poverty, knowledge and oppression, history and fantasy, surveillance and subversion.[35]

The novels I have been exploring demonstrate the centrality of the issues which concern Fanon. What is more, such novels do begin to raise the questions Bhabha suggests we address to Fanon: 'How can the human world live its difference? how can a human being live Other-wise?' – questions which more recent novelists like Kureishi address with increasing urgency as a new century begins. Indeed, as Kureishi urges,

[I]t is the British, the white British, who have to learn that being British isn't what it was. Now it is a more complex thing, involving new elements. So there must be fresh ways of seeing Britain and the choices it faces; and a new way of being British after all this time.

33 Ruth Prawer Jhabvala, *Esmond in India* (1958; Harmondsworth: Penguin, 1980), p. 204.
34 Leavis, 'The Englishness of the English Novel', p. 128.
35 Homi Bhabha, 'Foreword: remembering Fanon', in Frantz Fanon, *Black Skin, White Masks*, trans. Charles Lam Markmann (London: Pluto Press, 1993), pp. xxiv–xxv.

Much thought, discussion and self-examination must go into seeing the necessity for this, what this 'new way of being British' involves and how difficult it may be to attain.

The failure to grasp the opportunity for a revitalised and broader self-definition in the face of a real failure to be human, will be more insularity, schism, bitterness, and catastrophe.[36]

But as yet, the old complacencies and certainties about white English nationhood are all too alive and well. We can only hope.

---

36 Hanif Kureishi, 'London and Karachi', in Samuel (ed.), *Patriotism*, p. 286.

Part II Revising the myth

4 An activity not an attribute: mobilising Englishness

James Wood

It is a welcome sign of this collection that we are all troubled about the use of the word *Englishness*. Like David Gervais, I rebel against the idea of reading texts through their Englishness. We encountered the phrase 'narrating the nation' as if literature can indeed narrate the nation. But literature rarely does this, and rarely wants to do it, for good reason. And we should avoid reading the nation into texts, as John Lucas did in his book about English poetry, *England and Englishness*; by the end of that book, Englishness was anything you wanted it to be.[1]

To read literature as always implicitly about the nation is harmful. There will be times when a novel is about a family, not about a family-as-nation. The family deserves its specificities just as the nation does. The desire to see implication in texts – the implication of nationality – has the odd effect not of honouring the implicit in a work, but coarsening it by allegorising it. The novel's local implications are bruised in the hunt to pluck the golden implication that the book is really about nationhood.

It is partly for this reason that I want to narrow my enquiry and look at books with explicit designs on the nation; books with the epic impulse to cover a nation, to be comprehensive and grand (though not necessarily all-inclusive).

I am interested less in nationhood as an ideology than as an atmosphere, and specifically an atmosphere of place; I am less interested in what nationhood does or doesn't do for us, than in what it does for writers. Writers want to get nationhood and the appeal to nation on their side. By doing this they enlarge their books. Since Englishness often takes the form of an appeal to essence – essence of place, essence of value – writers appealing thus make their own books more essential, more unavoidable.

I want therefore to look first, quite quickly, at the various conventions, tropes and – to use more honest language – tricks, shortcuts and evasions writers use to make their works epic in ambition. Then I want to see what kind of an idea of Englishness emerges once these tricks and shortcuts and conjurings have got to work on it. And finally I want to pluck out three writers – Virginia Woolf, D. H. Lawrence and Alan Hollinghurst – who seem to me to have done something interesting with Englishness.

---

1 John Lucas, *England and Englishness* (London: Hogarth Press, 1989).

'Don't I get an effect out of Folkestone?' This is Henry James, in his notebooks for October 1896, pondering *What Maisie Knew* (1897).[2] This is the A–Z approach in which street and town names are listed in the hope that they give off historical gases. On the one hand, the writer appears to be roaming far and wide; on the other, the names, it is hoped, can be relied on to do their business of ancestral signification. This is a technique that has its roots in the epic lists of classical poetry: it is one of the most familiar methods of tolling the known, and Blake uses it enthusiastically in his epic of how England should be, 'Jerusalem' (1820): 'The Malvern and the Cheviot, the Wolds, Plinlimmon & Snowden'. By 1804, England is so 'chartered' – to use Blake's word from his poem on 'London' – that its meaning is also chartered. We know that these place names mean *something* anterior to their use in the poem, for Blake uses this assumption to strike dissonances off English ones: 'is that / Mild Zion's hill's most ancient promontory, near mournful / Ever weeping Paddington?'[3]

In this century, Eliot, who owed more to Blake than he could admit to, borrowed this technique of epic enlargement, with the difference that London's names – 'Highbury bore me. Richmond and Kew / Undid me' – are played against no biblical grandeur, but its modernist equivalent, literary and cultural grandeur.[4] London Bridge, The Strand, Queen Victoria Street, Lower Thames Street, King William Street – all these are seen not by 'Mild Zion' but by 'Jerusalem Athens Alexandria / Vienna London', by Baudelaire's Paris and Dante's Florence. London is, as it were, the under-achiever in this portfolio of literary stock; though not by the end of the poem, which has essentially made London into *Eliot's* London, and seen its value rise immeasurably on the market.

Individual place names are clearly part of the repertoire of a writer's music of national atmosphere; just as James ponders Folkestone, so Larkin shamelessly uses 'Stoke' in his poem 'Mr Bleaney' ('And Christmas at his sister's house in Stoke') and Ian McEwan makes both the first name Leonard, and the suburb Dollis Hill, where Leonard is from, work very hard for him in *The Innocent* (1990). It is assumed that both Leonard's name and Dollis Hill are saturated in prejudicial meaning.

As well as place names, institutions are appealed to – monuments, sporting events, ceremonies both public and private. A small essay could be written on the importance of tea-drinking – in *Great Expectations* (1860–1), in Lawrence, in Orwell. It is in *Great Expectations*, palpably an epic attempt at the representation of the country, that Dickens brilliantly likens Wemmick's thin, apparently cruel mouth 'to a post office' – meaning the gap through which one posts a letter. In its own right this likeness has an appropriateness; but by appealing to an institution – the

---

2 Henry James, *The Complete Notebooks of Henry James*, ed. Leon Edel and Lyall H. Powers (Oxford: Oxford University Press, 1987), p. 162.

3 William Blake, *Selected Poems*, ed. P. H. Butter (London: J. M. Dent & Sons, 1982), p. 165.

4 T. S. Eliot, 'The Waste Land' in *Collected Poems 1909-1962* (London: Faber, 1963), pp. 63–86 (p. 74).

mail – Wemmick is, as it were, posted to the world to which the other half belongs – Jaggers' cruel 'Little Britain' of law, government, property and other national institutions (Wemmick's gentler half, of course, takes tea and toast with his 'aged P' in Walworth). The mail, like the law, is an easy way to signify a nation because of the mail's own epic ambition to be comprehensive – De Quincy uses the mail to signify nation in this way, and so does Pynchon in *The Crying of Lot 49* (1965), with his evocation of a secret, rival mail service.

Nations are, in part, symbolic structures because enough people believe in symbolic structures like institutions and sporting events. Writers may want to get these institutions on their novel's symbolism, and to make an easier passage. Henry James famously listed the thickness of English life which he felt Hawthorne to be lacking: 'no great Universities nor public schools – no Oxford, nor Eton, nor Harrow ... no Epsom nor Ascot'.[5] In *Mrs Dalloway* (1924), Woolf makes celebrated use of Westminster, Whitehall, the Court, the Prime Minister, an army marching through Whitehall, 'on their faces an expression like the letters of a legend written round the base of a statue praising duty, gratitude, fidelity, love of England', and sporting events: 'The war was over ... It was June. The King and Queen were at the Palace. And everywhere, though it was still so early, there was a beating, a stirring of galloping ponies, tapping of cricket bats; Lords, Ascot, Ranelagh and all the rest of it.'[6] Listing is as much a matter of rhetorical massing as descriptive formation for Woolf; and it still shows its link to the ancient epic lists of the equipment of war, which were indeed statements of militancy. What we have here is the equipment of nationality, intent and typical, massed and sparkling; and this too is the *threat* or *promise* of description rather than description itself. Rhetorical militancy demands that this formation gives a sense of great powers drawn up in reserve but not displayed – as it were, behind front lines. Woolf's coda, 'and all the rest of it', is such a glint.

In Lawrence's novella *St Mawr*, published in 1925, England is both attacked and adored. Lawrence describes the flow of horse-riders in Hyde Park, as 'that regatta-canal of horsemen and horsewomen', the phrase 'regatta-canal' perhaps conjuring a sense of other national pastimes on water. In a marvellous phrase of controlled derision, Lawrence, through his hostile American visitor, Mrs Witt, sees these riders as 'awfully well-groomed papas and tight mamas who looked as though they were going to pour tea between the ears of their horses' – thus linking one public pastime (the regatta of horse-riders) to a private national rite (tea-drinking).[7] And in Alan Hollinghurst's novel *The Folding Star* (1924), Edward, the novel's narrator, remembers a summer ritual that is both private and public –

---

5 Henry James, *Selected Literary Criticism* (London: Penguin, 1963), p. 89.
6 Virginia Woolf, *Mrs. Dalloway* (1924; London: Penguin, 1992), p. 5. All further references to this edition will be given in parentheses in the text.
7 D. H. Lawrence, *St Mawr* (1925; London: Penguin, 1950), p. 16. All further references to this edition will be given in parentheses in the text.

watching the Wimbledon tennis tournament on television with the windows open
and the curtains closed, occasionally hearing 'the sonic wallow of a plane distanc-
ing in slow gusts above'. The moment, Edward recalls, seemed 'an English limbo of
light and shade, near and far, subtly muddled and displaced'.[8]

Although both Englishness and the atmosphere of place are mysteriously
ineffable, this mystery must be seen as a convention like any other literary convention: and it's a surprisingly primitive and unmysterious means by which mystery is evoked. And this is not to sneer at that mystery, nor assume that it does not
exist; just that, like anything in literature, it must be animated. To our quick tax-
onomy of the codes of nationhood, I will add the writer or narrator as traveller or
returnee or exile; and the place – town, home, institution – as microcosm of the
nation. Both conventions are familiar to us, from Defoe's *A Tour through the
Whole Island of Great Britain* (1724–27) to the train from which Edward Thomas
sees England, in his report of 1906, *The Heart of England*. And there are many
more examples. Finally there is the return from absence. One of the – to me –
canonical instances occurs at the end of Dickens' *American Notes* (1842) when
Dickens, sailing back from America, bubbles into lyricism about what he capi-
talises as Home:

The country, by the railroad, seemed, as we rattled through it, like a luxuriant garden. The
beauty of the fields (so small they looked!), the hedgerows, and the trees; the pretty cottages,
the beds of flowers, the old churchyards, the antique houses, and every well-known object;
the exquisite delights of that one journey, crowding in the short compass of a summer's day,
the joy of many years, with the winding up with Home and all that makes it dear, no tongue
nor pen of mine can scribble.[9]

A return from abroad – from India – after five years away is what gives Peter Walsh
in *Mrs Dalloway* his freshened vision of how English society has changed: 'that
shift in the whole pyramidal accumulation which in his youth had seemed
immoveable. On top of them it had pressed; weighed them down, the women
especially' (p. 178).

Writers in general will let us know if their microcosms are stand-ins for
macrocosms, because, it seems, they cannot resist hinting at it. Dickens does this
cheekily in *David Copperfield* (1849–50), when David uses his family to help him
rehearse for his new job as a Parliamentary sketch-writer: 'and night after night, we
had a sort of private Parliament in Buckingham Street'.[10] In a stroke, David's
family becomes the nation. Nearer our own time, Angus Wilson has used in *The
Old Men at the Zoo* (1961) a zoo as an explicit microcosm of England at a time of
emergency. The book imagines a dystopian England in 1971, with Europe on the

8   Alan Hollinghurst, *The Folding Star* (London: Chatto & Windus, 1994), p. 124. All further refer-
    ences to this edition will be given in parentheses in the text.
9   Charles Dickens, *American Notes: a journey* (1842; New York: Fromm International, 1985), p. 20.
10 Charles Dickens, *David Copperfield* (1849–50; London: Penguin, 1966), p. 609.

brink of war. Three years later in what I consider his best novel, *Late Call* (1964), he focuses on the English new town called Carshall as his explicit analogical picture of the nation.

I've almost finished with our codes of English appeal – except to point out the simplest: if all else fails, simply toss in the word 'English'. This strategy is seen most egregiously in A. S. Byatt's novel *Babel Tower* (1996) in which Byatt's Hugh Pink tramps around the fields thus: 'He has a feeling he can't find words for, although it is to do with his poetry. It is a feeling he thinks of as the *English* feeling.'[11] In the text, the word 'English' is italicised – the italic acting as a comically unwitting apology for Byatt's failure to generate meaning: a lather of italics substituting for meaning's true abrasions.

So we have a few of our epic conventions: epic lists, place names, the use of public institution and fixtures, the return home, the explicit microcosm – most of these are familiar to us. But what do these 'effects' effect? One thing they have already suggested to us: that Englishness is indefinable; and further, that this indefinableness rests on a pedestal of certainty. Englishness is unspeakable because what it speaks is so well known. It is like being so rich that you never talk about money. But, on the other hand, this indefinability *can* be spoken about very definitely and at great length, and with great explicitness (as in the Byatt passage). In other words: you are so rich you never talk about money; but, if you want, you may talk a great deal about being rich – as long as you never show a coin or a note, and never give your accounts over to scrutiny. I see, then, in much English writing an odd see-saw between a frustrating reticence about the nation's actualities and an odd, chatty explicitness about that very reticence.

Some of this paradoxical unutterability has to do with late-eighteenth-century and nineteenth-century romanticism, and in particular the romanticism of nationality. But the English mode adds to this, in the late nineteenth century – perhaps from Arnold's 'Thyrsis' onwards – a specifically elegiac tinge. In 'Thyrsis', Arnold elegises his friend, the poet Arthur Clough. But Clough is pastoralised and quickly turned into England: 'where are the mowers, who, as the tiny swell / of our boat passing heaved the river-grass / stood with suspended scythe to see us pass / They are all gone and thou art gone as well.'[12] Englishness in this vision is known and therefore beyond utterance; but Englishness, in this vision, has mysteriously disappeared also, and is being mourned. England, as it were, still has its riches, and about these we do not need to speak; but it has a hole in its pocket and is leaking value; and it will be the writer's task to recoup some of this value.

The tendency toward elegy appears in Edward Thomas, Larkin and William Golding's novel *The Pyramid* (1967). But it is Lily Briscoe in Woolf's *To the Lighthouse* (1927), itself a novel of elegy for a lost generation of the Great War, who gives it a decisive formulation, when she imagines seeing events 'as if everything

---

11 A. S. Byatt, *Babel Tower* (London: Chatto & Windus, 1996), p. 4.
12 Matthew Arnold, 'Thyrsis' in *Selected Poems* (London: Methuen, 1974), p. 128.

was happening for the first time, perhaps for the last time, as a traveller, even though he is half asleep, knows, looking out of the train window, that he must look now, for he will never see that town … again'.[13] It was in this spirit that Edward Thomas set out, in 1906, to elegise England by train. Thomas watched 'that grey land, looking at it from a railway train'. Like Larkin in his poem 'The Whitsun Weddings', Thomas sees a land transformed by new building, 'a land of new streets, and half-built streets and devastated lanes'. Thomas decides that these new streets are impossible to write about, 'so new that we have inherited no certain attitude towards them, of liking or dislike'. But his conclusion suggests that he has indeed invented an attitude towards them: 'An artist who wished to depict the Fall, and some sympathy with it in the fact of a ruined Eden, might have had little to do but copy an acre of the surviving fields.'[14]

I think this assumption, which one finds so much of in English writing, that the writer does not *need* to inscribe meaning because it is already pre-inscribed, has weakened our capacity for epic writing, and encouraged a feebleness of appeal. At its worst, this contradictory unsayable but sayable Englishness produces a preposterous book like *Brideshead Revisited* (1945), which is essentially an anthology of various reference codes, all of which make confident, and therefore inanimate, reference to certain assumptions of Englishness.

To some extent, of course, all literature moves between utterance and unutterability; utterance and talk about unutterability are its North and South Pole. But Englishness excites this tendency. A contemporary example of this vice may help to make my meaning clearer; the example is a story by Julian Barnes called 'Evermore' from his collection *Cross Channel* (1995). In it, Barnes deals with the subject of English remembrance, and it is notable that as he does he slowly surrenders his virtues. Instead of the postmodernist's compound eye – locust-like, it looks around and behind all truths – Barnes' story is weighted around its theme. Barnes' more usual playfulness becomes solemn. In this story we learn of Miss Moss, an elderly lady who makes obsessive visits in her antique Morris Minor to the French war cemetery where her brother lies. She cannot forget him, and has dedicated her life to remembrance. But Barnes turns the story into a tract about the importance of national remembrance; the story becomes unnatural and literary. Miss Moss is given to ask herself the kinds of rhetorical questions, perfectly phrased, that only characters in stories ask themselves, such as: 'was it a vice to have become such a connoisseur of grief?'[15]

The story is themed. It wallows in the explicitness of its own project. The story's own devotion to commemoration does not make clearer Miss Moss's devotion, but drowns it. So it is no surprise that Barnes bursts in at the end and announces: 'if this forgetting of the First World War happened to the individual, would it not also

13   Virginia Woolf, *To the Lighthouse* (1927; London: Penguin, 1966), p. 220.
14   Edward Thomas, *Selected Prose and Poetry* (London: Penguin, 1969), p. 48.
15   Julian Barnes, 'Evermore' in *Cross Channel* (London: Jonathan Cape, 1995), p. 73.

happen on a national scale?'[16] The English theme of remembrance excites in Barnes both a maudlin solemnity towards its mysterious grandeur, and a tiresome explicitness about this solemnity – the story is actually *called* 'Evermore'.

Barnes' story recalls two stories by Kipling on a similar theme – 'The Gardener' and 'Mary Postgate'; this recollection alerts us to the possibility that Englishness, by now, is literary and second-hand in a way that has not yet happened in America. War remembrance, for Barnes, sparks Kipling. Of course, this inevitable literariness of Englishness has not always been unproductive: Ford Madox Ford, whose central character in *The Good Soldier* (1915) is addicted to minor Edwardian poetry, recognised this weakness and mobilised it in that novel; Anthony Powell in his *Dance to the Music of Time* sequence, especially his novel *The Military Philosophers*, makes use of the literariness of Englishness. Sitting in St Paul's Cathedral, at a service of thanksgiving to mark the end of the Second World War, the novel's centre of consciousness Nick Jenkins uses the words of Blake's 'Jerusalem', which the congregation has been singing, to spin off into reflections on English poetry. This would be precious were it not for the insouciance of Jenkins' appropriation, whereby the potentially academic is turned into the gossipy. Jenkins indulges in mental gossip, and the effect is to turn the English poets ('dear old Cowley') into upper-class friends: they are part of high society.[17]

Again, we see the essential unspeakability of England dialectically in relation to a wilful explicitness – the explicitness in this case being the idea that you have only to mention a few 'English Writers' to secure your case. In the passage from A. S. Byatt that I quoted, Hugh Pink decides that 'the *English* feeling' tends to come in this sort of landscape or because generations of his ancestors, thousands and millions of years before towns and cities, and still after, have had this sense in this sort of place. 'There are equally strong feelings in cities', Byatt continues, 'but not this one, which is essentially green, and blue, and grey.' Byatt goes on: 'The thing which can flash into the brain a memory of *this* thing is the repeated reading of words which, like touchstones, are part of the matter of the mind: the "Immortality Ode", say, the "Nightingale", Shakespeare's sonnets.'[18] The thing which is a memory of *this* thing is apparently English Literature, as it is for Peter Ackroyd in his watery, deeply conservative, and desperately explicit tract of 1992, *English Music*.

So we have as a legacy – Englishness as something which cannot be uttered; a paradoxical explicitness about this unutterable Englishness; and Englishness as an inevitably literary or second-hand property created out of impersonation or rebellion against impersonation.

This situation is all very gloomy. It seems that we're trapped. But just as Naipaul and Ishiguro to some extent suggest how this legacy can be manipulated and even escaped, so do three books with which I will close these comments: they

16 Barnes, 'Evermore', p. 76.
17 Anthony Powell, *The Military Philosophers* in *A Dance to the Music of Time* (Chicago: University of Chicago Press, 1995), p. 224.
18 Byatt, *Babel Tower*, p. 4.

are Lawrence's *St Mawr*, Woolf's *Mrs Dalloway*, and Alan Hollinghurst's *The Folding Star*. In all three novels we see a refreshing scepticism about Englishness; Lawrence is actively hostile; Woolf is subtly sceptical; and Hollinghurst is slyly subversive. But all three writers appear to have both a love of and a deep impatience with the rhetoric of English inexpressibility; and all three appear to believe that Englishness can be mobilised, by the application of some stinging ointment. This ointment is a belief in the powers of literalism: not an explicitness about mysterious certainties; but a literalism about definable qualities.

One of the most enjoyable things about Lawrence's very vital novel is that he pulls England out of its metaphysical camouflage, and ascribes – usually negative, though not always – values and qualities to it. He does this through the sharp tongues of his two American visitors, Mrs Witt and her daughter, who become progressively disenchanted with English life and landscape. We have already seen with what darting quickness and subtlety – the image of the English ladies pouring tea into their horse's heads – Lawrence widens his vision to include a culture, without exactly telling us he is doing this. Later in the novel, Mrs Witt mocks two pompous English visitors by giving them tea with immaculate parodic etiquette. When they have gone, she tells her daughter that Mrs Vyner's hat 'looks like a crumpled cup and saucer, and I have been saying to myself ever since: *Dear Mrs Vyner can't I fill your cup!* And then pouring tea into that hat' (p. 88).

England, for American visitors, and for the novel, and for Lawrence, is stifling, fenced-in, hedged, avoiding either the extreme of natural corruption (represented by the Arizona desert) or the extreme of great vitality (represented by the horse St Mawr, and its Welsh name). Mrs Witt loathes England's lukewarmth, and even its inexpressibility: 'And suddenly, she craved again for the more absolute silence of America. English stillness was so soft, like an inaudible murmur of voices, of presences. But the silence in the empty spaces of America was still unutterable, almost cruel' (p. 81). America's unutterability is based, here, on its never having been uttered: it is all pure silence, pure potential. England is not silence but silenced; its unutterability has to do with the presence of voices who have been uttering a great deal in the past.

Lawrence's – and Mrs Witt's – strategy is then to drag England out of its inaudibility and make it speak: give it negative and unpleasant values. Once this has been done, England, in a further paradox, becomes a place of the lukewarm literal, an obstruction to Lawrence's dark fascism of unutterability. Once England has been forced to speak, what is spoken is not worth having because it speaks a whining and mild literalism of the soul. England is the 'nasty, sneaking weak, eunuch civilization' that Lawrence condemns (p. 97); England is the democratic literalist to Lawrence's unspeakable fascism of the blood (symbolised in the horse, St Mawr), and thus must be discarded, must be made to disappear. But to make England disappear, Lawrence must determinedly drag England out of its inaudibility, and point the gun of literalism at its head. And this dragging out of England's qualities is, as we have seen, done with much verve and playfulness as well as hostility and viciousness.

Woolf in *Mrs Dalloway* does nothing less than dissolve Englishness. It is a great epic achievement. First, as we have seen, she enlarges her vision – through appeal to monuments and institutions; and then, like Lawrence, she drags out the terms of Englishness into literal meaning. Like Lawrence again, she literalises Englishness through a series of vivid and spiteful portraits of certain establishment figures. Just as Woolf's descriptions of place radiate outwards, so her characters radiate outwards to include the nation. One of these representative characters is the psychologist, Sir William Bradshaw, who is seen as little more than a suave torturer, paid by the establishment to shut people up: 'worshipping proportion, Sir William not only prospered himself but made England prosper, secluded her lunatics, forbade childbirth, penalised despair' (p. 109). Sir William is continually preaching 'proportion' to his patients, and this is a novel of very precise proportions: it is governed by Big Ben, whose sounds can be heard throughout Westminster; even the time is 'ratified by Greenwich' (p. 84). Sir William shows us the actual disproportion of this supposed proportion. In Woolf's shooting-gallery is the Prime Minister, who turns up to Clarissa Dalloway's party, and whom she thinks dull-looking; and Sir Harry, an old painter who has been churning out 'more bad pictures than any other two academicians in the whole of St John's Wood (they were always of cattle, standing in sunset pools absorbing moisture … all his activities, dining out, racing, were founded on cattle standing absorbing moisture in sunset pools)' (p. 192).

The brilliance of that 'absorbing moisture' speaks for itself; but note how Woolf radiates outwards from Sir Harry's centre – his paintings – to take in all his activities; that centre is, of course, hollow. And this outward radiation is the motion of Woolf's entire novel and its dissolution of Englishness. When Big Ben strikes at the beginning of this novel, it prompts a celebrated line from Woolf: 'The leaden circles dissolved in the air' (p. 4). The phrase is repeated throughout the novel (which is itself patterned on a set of circles) in an incantatory way. These leaden circles are the vibrations of Big Ben's bell; but they are also social circles – the social circles that come to Clarissa Dalloway's party at the end of the book. And they are the radiating outward circles of Sir William's and Sir Harry's lives and they are the radiating outward circles of Woolf's own epic radiations – all the leadenness of monuments, of sporting fixtures, of armies, of pedestals, of Big Ben's own circular clock face: these circles are what the novel establishes and then gorgeously dissolves. This is not a deconstructive reading; this is a deconstructive novel.

I shall be very brief with Alan Hollinghurst's novel. But the middle section of *The Folding Star*, which is called 'Rough Common', is a very beautiful subversion of pastoral Englishness. Rough Common is the fictional name that Hollinghurst gives to the home town of his narrator Edward. It is south of London, both rural and urban. Like Woolf, and as we have seen in the Wimbledon section I have discussed, Hollinghurst uses his novel to make subtle, elegiac radiations from place or family or person to national life. Hollinghurst is wary of explicitness and wary of forcing; he seems to feel that nationality and nation in fiction radiates outward like a medieval town – from a carefully neglected centre.

But Hollinghurst's narrator is gay, and Hollinghurst's subject, to some extent, is homosexuality, and it is this subject matter which forces Englishness out of its soft, hushed inaudibility into voice. Edward recalls as a child going to visit the house of a minor but celebrated pastoral English poet. The poet's decencies and reticence are quietly marked, and mocked by the knowledge of Edward's burgeoning sexuality. At the end of the book, Edward recalls his lost childhood, in classic elegiac form: a memory of 'summer dusks, funny old anecdotes, old embarrassments that still made me burn, boys' cocks and kisses under elms that had died with my boyhood's end' (p. 138). I love Hollinghurst's gentle daring here: the softened syntax and phrasing is shamelessly English – it could be Edward Thomas: 'kisses under elms that had died with my boyhood's end'.[19] But there is 'boy's cocks' in the middle of this elegy – boy's cocks, as it were, inserted into the pastoral bed.

We need to mobilise Englishness as an activity rather than an attribute; and then, as these writers do, if we find that we do not like what we have mobilised, we can dissolve it, modify it, resist it.

---

19 Thomas, *Selected Prose and Poetry*, p. 48.

5 The English and the European: the poetry of Geoffrey Hill[1]

David Gervais

It seems wise to protect the notion of 'Englishness' with quotation marks. It does not always follow from what we think of as English in English poetry. The 'Ode to the West Wind' is a very English poem but it distorts it severely to think of it simply as a manifestation of 'Englishness'. Neither its politics nor its aesthetics are that parochial. Its imagery is as rooted in Dante and Calderon as in Milton or Wordsworth. Similarly, though the *Defence of Poetry* praises the English poets as warmly as anyone has, it offers no grounds for seeing them in a separate category of their own. And if *The Triumph of Life* is – as I believe – Shelley's masterpiece, this is because it is his most completely European poem as well as a deeply English one.

In practice, 'Englishness' and 'Europeanness' are aspects of a single whole. Keats, with his wish to 'be among the English poets', might seem more provincial than Shelley does but his letters – so open to writers like Homer and Dante and Ariosto – are far from Anglocentric. A few decades later, Arnold was to complain that the English Romantics 'did not know enough', that their work was insufficiently part of European Literature: that is he thought them *too* English.[2] He might just as well have said that they were not English *enough*, since England itself is always more than *just* English. The present essay is more Anglo-sceptic than

---

1 A critical essay is no more than a stepping-stone that enables its reader to go further into the subject. Knowing this, my first instinct was to revise this chapter in the light of what Geoffrey Hill has written since the original lecture was delivered from which this chapter was developed. It seemed possible to be more precise and more informed than I could then be. Yet criticism is occasional as well as exploratory (the two things go together) and my original essay was written in the context of a specific debate at a particular point in time. As it has become more accepted for academic study, 'Englishness' has hardened into a sort of category when once it was more fluid and less prescriptive. In this chapter I wanted to keep that sense of it, if I could, the more so because I am now even more chary of using the term than I was. I could therefore only revise the essay by focusing more on the term itself than seems necessary for what is mainly an essay on two recent books of poetry. It was never my intention to offer a view of Hill's career as a whole. Readers can be left to read his most recent books at their own pace. The last ten or so years have been the most prolific in Hill's career and his recent books could not be crammed into a brief coda. I have written on them elsewhere and, in particular, on his relation to his readers (an integral part of his role as an 'English' poet) in 'Geoffrey Hill: A New Direction?', *The Reader*, 11 (autumn/winter 2002), pp. 77–88.

2 Matthew Arnold, 'The Function of Criticism at the Present Time' in *Essays in Criticism* (1865; London: Dent, 1964), p. 13.

Euro-sceptic but it has no truck with the notion that England and Europe constitute a sort of dichotomy. I hope that a political Euro-sceptic might be able to sym-
pathise with my argument as much as a Europhile would.

One could not imagine Hardy describing one of his poems as 'too English'. I
myself enjoy his poems more than his novels but I can't help feeling the novels
have a greater range. Eustacia Vye is as close to Emma Bovary as to George Eliot's
heroines and poor Jude struggles to tune into 'the mind of Europe' but many of the
poems seem to be saying 'This is what it feels like to be English' or 'Look what an
odd lot we English are'. Despite their localness, the novels can never be calibrated
against any standard of 'Englishness': Wessex and England are not synonymous.
Perhaps Hardy's verse has been so influential because it blurs this distinction. One
thinks of the role Larkin and Davie assigned to it. Later poets sometimes give the
impression of trying to be as English as possible.

A few years back I saw a television programme about 'Englishness' presented
by the philosopher Roger Scruton. What you saw was his village retreat in the
Home Counties – all thatch and riding to hounds and cricket on the village green:
a feast of clichés which, he implied, added up to an immemorial way of life that no
English person could fail to be moved by.[3] It would be silly to deny the potency of
such images, or even to deny them a limited historical reality, but it is another
thing to swallow the assumption that such versions of 'Englishness' still come as
naturally to us as breathing. Scruton himself conceded that to some English
people it would seem positively exotic. There is no reason to suppose that being
English means that we know what 'Englishness' is. The idea that there can be some
timeless quintessence of it, which we all have in our grasp may be less potent than
we think. What it reveals is really a fear that we are losing our 'Englishness' and are
anxious to preserve it before it rots. Edward Thomas, who never pretended to have
England in his pocket, said of Rupert Brooke, who did, that '[The w]orst of the
poetry being written today is that it is too deliberately, and not inevitably,
English.'[4] Such inevitability does not come for the asking, as our own 'heritage
industry' makes clear. Whether this collection is itself a similar symptom, as well as
a critique, is not easy to say. We may be tempted to analyse 'Englishness' simply
because we are troubled by the fact that England itself is now a much less
malleable idea, both problematic and unpredictable. Why assume that what is
'English' can always be equated with 'Englishness'?

I ought, at this point, to confess to having written a book about 'Englishness'
myself – or rather a study of various versions of it.[5] I did not assume that these

---

3 Not that Scruton's view is unique to conservatives. Raphael Samuel remarks that "Little
   Englandism" has its plebeian as well as its patrician entrepreneurs, its left-wing as well as its right-
   wing exponents (*New Statesman* (21 Oct. 1988)).

4 Edna Longley (ed.), *A Language Not to be Betrayed: selected prose of Edward Thomas* (Manchester:
   Carcanet, 1981), p. 281.

5 David Gervais, *Literary Englands: versions of 'Englishness' in modern writing* (Cambridge:
   Cambridge University Press, 1993).

different Englands all converged towards one ideal Platonic England. 'Englishness' is a suggestive but treacherous tool for cultural analysis. Nor is it mere iconoclasm that makes one distrust it. My instinct is to add, 'Thank God!' Thank God there is no hard-and-fast, metaphysical 'Englishness' to get in the way of the new. If one is concerned with how English poetry grows and changes one can have no wish to see England mummified. That would be tantamount to trying to neutralise the past.

My main reason for this distrust is that I see no way of distinguishing English literature clearly from the literature of Europe of which it is a part. Where does the one stop and the other start? At any time the course of English poetry may change when some new English poet discovers Montale, say, or Mayakovsky, as it did when Swinburne discovered Baudelaire or Eliot Laforgue. Moreover, poets today write not just in the literary Europe where our poets have always worked but within the Europe in which, whether we like it or not, we all now live. The danger of trusting too much in 'Englishness' is that it tempts us to go on thinking within the structures of the empire even though we are really citizens of the European Community. In other words, to focus too hard on England risks obscuring the English present.

Let me begin from a thought we might agree on. You don't choose your nationality, nor can you rid yourself of it. If you live abroad or take another nationality you still retain the characteristics of your original one. Nationality is involuntary. It operates at a level below morality. Yet nationhood is also the seed-bed of many of our moral attitudes, a built-in yardstick of right and wrong. It enables us to go to war with confidence in the justice of our cause and, in peace-time, to feel satisfaction if our growth rate exceeds that of rival nations (especially if they are our allies) or if we win a gold medal in the Olympics. We make our nationality a guarantor of our deserts. If we are like Mr Podsnap, it helps us to feel superior to the nationality of other countries.

Probably such double-think applies as much to other countries as to England though we may be said to have got it down to a fine art. The trick is to take a quality that is given rather than chosen and then to pretend that it reflects credit on us *as if we had chosen it*. Brooke's 'The Soldier' is a good example: the thought of England helps him to feel a finer person but he is actually being an emotional parasite and England is simply his host. This reaction is understandable in wartime though it has little to do with poetry and it has serious consequences. I will mention three. First, nationhood becomes harnessed to our ego. Milton appeals to such a response in *Areopagitica* (1644) when he seeks to make his readers feel 'noble and puissant' like their country. Secondly, because we soon see that there are other powerful countries in the world, our sense of what we are puts us on the defensive, doomed to prove ourselves to be superior as we want to believe we are. Such anxiety underlies even the most rampant nationalism. Thirdly, because our nationhood is given, not achieved, we have to assume that it was there before us, that our country may once have been more heroic than it is now. An insecurity lurks within all patriotism. Thus, we make fun of cherished institutions

like the monarchy or the English cricket team: we know they can stand criticism.
Patriotic poetry often relies on a veiled rebuke. For instance, Larkin's 'Going,
Going' preens itself on its disillusion:

> And that will be England gone,
> The shadows, the meadows, the lanes,
> The guildhalls, the carved choirs.
> There'll be books; it will linger on
> In galleries; but all that remains
> For us will be concrete and tyres.[6]

Nationality persuades the poet to lay claim to feelings that may not be entirely his
own. I can't myself believe that Larkin cared as passionately about guildhalls and
carved choirs as these lines make out. It certainly doesn't occur to him that he has
any responsibility for England's decline or should be doing anything to stop it.

All these feelings reflect how the English see themselves, all that some English
politicians seem to think about: nationality as a refuge and protection from the
larger world, a sort of sealant. It is even more constricting when it comes to poetry.
How could we imagine Chaucer without Boccaccio, Spenser without Ariosto and
Tasso or Milton without more or less every major European poet before him?
What is native and what foreign? There is no need to proliferate examples, given
that most of our poets in the past knew Latin – and some of them Greek – much
better than most modern English poets know any foreign language. The growth of
'English' as a discipline is much more recent and its mission as an alternative to
'Classics', so crucial to the current obsession with 'Englishness', may have been less
liberating than it was meant to be. It was not necessarily an accident that the rise of
'English' occurred at much the same time as the Georgian anthologies. Perhaps
our modern debate about 'Englishness', which would have seemed introverted
even to a Victorian, is likewise a means of coming to terms with the legacy of the
Great War?

What earlier poets found in European poetry was a basis for comparison, a
means of testing their own language. Doing so opened out their 'Englishness' into
a realm of moral and artistic choice. Arnold's message to the Victorians is not a
new one but I make no apology for quoting it in these un-Arnoldian times:

By the very nature of things, as England is not all the world, much of the best that is known
and thought in the world cannot be of English growth, must be foreign; by the nature of
things, again, it is just this that we are least likely to know, while English thought is stream-
ing in upon us from all sides, and takes excellent care that we shall not be ignorant of its
existence; the English critic, therefore, must dwell much on foreign thought, and with
particular heed on any part of it, which, while significant and fruitful in itself, is for any
reason specially likely to escape him.[7]

---

6 Philip Larkin, *Collected Poems* (London: Faber, 1988), p. 190.
7 Arnold, 'The Function of Criticism', p. 32.

Thus, 'every critic should try and possess one great literature, at least, besides his own; and the more unlike his own, the better'. This inspiration entails more than mere aesthetic tourism, such as we have in plenty ourselves. Foreign literature helps us to understand our own better. Arnold thought his contemporaries were disabled by their insularity. He complained bitterly, for instance, of Wordsworth's lack of interest in Goethe. For him, Europe is 'one great confederation, bound to a joint action and working to a common result'. This ideal may still seem to lie in the far distance. Just as Arnold fell short of it himself when he wrote grudgingly about *Madame Bovary*, so too may we do when we diligently import French thinkers, from Sartre to Barthes and so on, yet show so little curiosity about major French creative writers like Michael Tournier and Yves Bonnefoy. Reading such writers may not safeguard us against provinciality but it can help us to see ourselves better in what we are by reminding us of what we are not.

At one time it looked as if Pound and Eliot might curb our insecurity. Joyce made war on Irish parochialism and everyone admired Cézanne and Wagner, went to the Ballets Russes and read (or claimed to read) Proust. The staunchly English Lawrence turned eagerly to the Continent. A certain cosmopolitanism was intrinsic to the revolt against Victorianism. It now seems as if we have gone back on it. Our most popular poets since the war have been Betjeman and Larkin (and now Heaney). Kingsley Amis made Little Englandism respectable when to Arnold it had seemed benighted. Though we have far greater opportunities to understand Europe our attitudes can be as provincial as those of the Victorians were. We still nurture and flaunt a defensive nostalgia that, despite the watershed of the sixties, remains much the same as Larkin's. Indeed, the more embroiled we get in Europe, the stronger such feelings seem to become. It is this resistance and not just the general negative point itself, which makes me turn now to a poet who does begin to fulfil Arnold's prescriptions for English poetry – Geoffrey Hill. I shall confine myself to two books, *The Mystery of the Charity of Charles Péguy* (1983) and *Canaan* (1996), both of which see England and Europe in conjunction and not in opposition to each other.

Hill's case is a curious one. He has never turned his back on Eliot and Pound and he is held in high (though not unanimous) esteem but he is neither popular nor widely read. His reputation is highest in America where he now works. He has none of the charm of Seamus Heaney and his poetry is too cryptic, allusive and plain 'difficult' to suit tastes formed by the 'poetry circuit'. He is therefore often pigeon-holed as a poet for academics. He is, what is more, too critical, even anguished, on the subject of England to indulge in that comfortable Movement irony it usually attracts. He is, however, also a deeply traditional English poet. *Mercian Hymns* (1971) is one of our most searching explorations of the English identity. Yet in Hill this search goes hand in hand with a twin preoccupation with Europe, not just with Europe as foreign but with Europe as an essential element in the experience of being English. Thus, he celebrates King Offa's alliance with Charlemagne. He would not have made the mistake of thinking of carved Gothic choirs as simply English. He sees no polarity between the English and the

European, the past and the present. English history and landscape, for instance, haunt him in the same way as the Europe of the Holocaust does. In the twenty-first century, the experience of one country may often be interchangeable with that of another. It is possible to write about a foreign country and to be writing about one's own at the same time. None of us lives on a precious stone set in the silver sea, barricaded by a moat. In fact, to write about our own experience fully now we may need to include that of others within it.

Hill's *The Mystery of the Charity of Charles Péguy* concerns the fate of the great French poet who was killed at the Battle of the Marne. A glance at Péguy's poetry, which is expansive, rhetorical and incantatory, reveals how different it is from Hill's own. Coming before modernism, Péguy's derives from Corneille and Hugo. Yet his death in battle has a natural symbolism for Hill. Like the deaths of Thomas and Owen, it marks a watershed between the past and the modern world. Péguy's peculiar left-wing nationalism, his organicism and his militant Catholic faith all make him a mythic figure for Hill. The change he lived through has resonance for the English reader too. The poem is shot through with irony but it also takes us deep into Péguy's very personal French world, so that his patriotism implicates our own and his lost France implies a lost England:

> Landscape is like revelation; it is both
> Singular crystal and the remotest things.
> Cloud-shadows of seasons revisit the earth,
> Odourless myrrh borne by the wandering kings.
>
> Happy are they who, under the gaze of God,
> Die for the 'terre charnelle', marry her blood
> To theirs, and, in strange Christian hope, go down
> Into the darkness of resurrection,
>
> Into sap, ragwort, melancholy thistle,
> Almondy meadowsweet, the freshet-brook
> Rising and running through small wilds of oak,
> Inevitable high summer, richly scarred
>
> With furze and grief; winds drumming the fame
> Of the tin legions lost in haystack and stream.
> Here the lost are blest, the scarred most sacred ... [8]

The emotion here is close to that which many English poets since Hardy have expressed (less ironically) for England. The hint of 'blue remembered hills' is there but not the unrelenting pathos. An elegy for Thomas or Owen would have been too blatant here, a fly-trap for stock responses, but Hill has imagined a foreign land that evokes them as well. Moreover, by seeing the war through the eyes of a French poet, Hill makes it clear that this was a European war and not just an

---

8 Hill is cited from his *Collected Poems* (London: Penguin, 1985) and the *Canaan* (London: Penguin, 1996).

English one. One glimpses this fact only fitfully in the poetry of the 'War Poets' themselves.

Some readers may feel that the lines I have quoted are too nostalgic. I prefer to say that they frankly admit the power of nostalgia, without pretending to be superior to it. But this nostalgia is not an end in itself: it cements a solidarity with the past that transcends the patriotic sort of nostalgia of poets like Brooke and Newbolt, who simply feed off the past. Hill's past is a place of darkness as much as reassurance. Nor is Péguy's Frenchness simply a contrast to our own 'Englishness' or merely a metaphor for it. It is possible to think in terms of 'Europe' as if we actually belonged *within* it. Yet whether younger poets than Hill have been able to build on this breakthrough may seem doubtful. It might, in fact, be argued that it is its very Europeanness that has prevented Hill's poetry from reaching the larger audience it deserves. After all, the 'War Poets' remain as popular as ever in our schools.

The *Mystery* is continuous with other Hill poems that are directly about England – the sonnets in *Tenebrae* (1978), for instance. Hill does not write about Europe *instead of* England but because, in a sense, Europe *is* his nationality. This perspective is less common than one might expect, over twenty years since Britain joined the Common Market. It is not that one wants poets to write about federalism or subsidiarity but, whether we like it or not, we now share a common store of immediate experience with other Europeans, going back at least to 1914, which remains only partly visible in our literature. And it demands more than just poems about the Dordogne or Tuscany after our summer holidays. Europe is no longer 'abroad' as it was to Larkin. I was recently in Amsterdam and found there, to my surprise, an English theatre which performs English plays, in English, every week of the year. We may not know about the Dutch but they know about us. We may not see European television either, though that seldom shakes our steadfast belief in the superiority of the BBC. Nostalgia, which we like to assign to the early part of our century, can eat away at our culture and our politics without our realising it. If we don't want to read Geoffrey Hill, we still need to.

'England', of course, has never been a static entity. Kipling and Forster wrote about it by writing about the empire but that subject has now become the province of the historical novelist. *Little Gidding* (1942) was a wartime poem but Hughes and Hill are post-war poets. In fact, it may well be the loss of empire that has fuelled the appetite for 'Englishness'. The American critic Merle Brown thought of Hill's poetry as a 'return home', bound to the language of a 'world on which the sun never sets' that had been 'precipitously contracted into the language of but one small island'.[9] A period of aftermath may understandably be defensive but that alone can hardly represent any permanent route for English poetry. In opening up other possibilities Hill's work suggests that 'Englishness' of the familiar sort is

9 Merle E. Brown, *Double Lyric: divisiveness and communal creativity in recent English poetry* (London: Routledge & Kegan Paul, 1980), p. 19.

already becoming an exhausted issue for English poetry. The same might be said of this collection itself which has so much the atmosphere of an autopsy: the danger is that it might seem to be doing no more than driving the nails into the coffin. If 'Englishness' ever is defined, as we try to define it, won't it already have ceased to exist?

But it is not for me to peer into the future. Critics are always in the position of trying to catch up. Let me simply say that I do not mean to set Hill against every-one else. Other poets, like James Fenton, grapple with Europe too, sometimes in more contemporary ways. Peter Reading ruthlessly anatomises 'Englishness'. Hughes soon moved from writing about England to writing about the land itself, as opposed to the nation: in 'Pike', for instance, the pond is said to be 'as deep as England' which is a way of saying that it is distinct from it. These poets inhabit a larger world than Housman did. They make it possible for other poets to write something more than the mere vacationist's poem about Europe that reinforces the distinction between the Europe we visit and the Europe we live in. Yet the new never comes easily. 'Englishness' can still get in the way. We may still have no more readily available language for our experience of Europe than Arnold's generation had. And, in the meantime, we have lost the basis in the classics which confirmed our European roots. The odd thing is that Europe is central to our politics but seems almost optional to our experience.

By contrast, Charles Tomlinson celebrated his retirement from Bristol University with a book called *Jubilation* (1995) (in Spanish 'jubilation' means retirement). In the 1950s Tomlinson was often seen as a cosmopolitan maverick and cold-shouldered by the Movement. He is not one iota less English for that. He simply knows that good poetry makes a country of its own, where Shelley and Octavio Paz are citizens together. As the title poem of *Jubilation* puts it:

> I signal back my depth of inspiration,
>   The piece I'm finishing for *Poetry Nation*
> (What nation, as a nation, ever cared
>   A bad peseta of a dry goose turd
> For poetry?) Our Shelley's right, of course,
>   You can't spur on a spavined Pegasus ... [10]

This perception enables Tomlinson to write about 'abroad' without writing tourist poems. His humanity is subject to the same joys and griefs in Tokyo as in the Cotswolds. He knows the difference between writing *about* Europe and writing within it. He also knows that only the latter can suggest what it means to be English in the modern world. Being English in England is no longer enough. Nor is it simply a result of our joining the European Community. It would be just as true if we were to leave it. When were our best poets ever simply 'English'? There is

10   Charles Tomlinson, *Jubilation* (Oxford: Oxford University Press, 1995).

a sense in which Victor Hugo was being perfectly reasonable when he proclaimed that Shakespeare was a French writer.[11]

Turning over the books I get sent from the Poetry Book Society I am struck by the prevalence of a sort of stubborn regionalism in many of them. The poems may be accomplished and sensitive, even moving, and yet they seem to come from a small world – a world unlike the one revealed by my daily newspaper. Sometimes the effect seems navel-contemplating English, often communicating a pleasure that seems to rely too much on its own lacunae. I enjoyed, for instance, Alice Oswald's first book, *The Thing in the Gap-Stone Stile* (1996), but wondered at the dust-jacket's reference to her classical culture; how did this classical (European) grounding come through in these poems about English people and English land-scapes? Such sources are no longer as easy to draw on as they once were or as the England of *A Shropshire Lad* (1896) still seems to be. Of course, there are exceptions too – most obviously Tony Harrison. He understands very well that to write about England you have to write about things like the Gulf War too, not just the English landscape. But Harrison tends to write either about Yorkshire *or* the world and that, however exciting, may involve other evasions. I want to turn instead to Geoffrey Hill's book *Canaan*, because it explores the native and the foreign together, not through contrast but as parts of a continuous experience.

It may seem presumptuous to write about a book published relatively recently, more so such a 'difficult' book (I prefer the word *different*). I say this not because of its arcane allusions (which can be looked up) but for its elusive broken music which most reviewers seemed to miss. Teasing out individual lines matters less than responding to the instinct for coherent form that Hill's concentrations often mask. He is a natural epigrammatist and it takes time to see that his gift for the right original word is not an end in itself but part of a larger music. Yet I cannot resist discussing *Canaan* because it is such a natural sequel to the *Mystery*. It confirms my feeling that Hill writes differently about England from most of his contemporaries, much less as if 'Englishness' were a thing in itself.

The Canaan of the title evokes a familiar biblical paradox; a land that promises redemption but that has been desecrated by the faithlessness of the faithful. The book's epigraph, from the Geneva Bible, makes this plain: the Israelites 'offered unto the idols of Canaan, and the land was defiled with blood. Thus were they stained with their own works …'. Such staining, the consequence of past actions, is almost an obsession in Hill's poetry. His Clark Lectures, *The Enemy's Country* (1991), are an intricate meditation on its workings when one poet inherits a language from another. Writers are shaped not simply by their past but by the way they choose to understand it: history is fashioned, not given. The process amounts to more than mere determinism. History always includes the possibility that its

---

11 In the preface to his son's great translation of Shakespeare (1864) Hugo states that, 'Traduire un poète étranger, c'est accroître la poésie nationale'. He also thought the English needed a translation of Voltaire.

forces can be re-channelled. Hence Hill's fascination with von Stauffenberg's plot
against Hitler, as in his magnificent sequence 'De Jure Belli ac Pacis'.

'Canaan' itself has three parts: the first concerns self righteous Protestant
soldiers (presumably in the Thirty Years War?), the second the violence of
'Fourier's children' and the third 'Moloch his ovens' (the Holocaust). Put like this,
it might seem that Hill is simply lamenting the fact that history repeats itself but
that is only partly the point. What is most frightening about the violence the poem
evokes is that it cannot be disentangled from impulses we might otherwise value:

> They march at God's
> Pleasure through Flanders
>   With machine-pistols,
> chorales, cannon
>   of obese bronze,
> with groaning pushcarts,
>   to topple Baal.

The chorales belong with the cannon. The second section moves without warning
from 'corpse-gas' to:

>   immemorial
> sightings in Canaan:
>   fig trees and planted vines ...

Such a studied absence of transitions is characteristic of Hill. A poet can live in two
worlds at once. Heaven and hell are not opposites; they belong together.[12]

If Hill's Canaan symbolises England (and the Europe it is part of) 'Canaan'
itself is interestingly vague about nationality. It goes from the English (and
perhaps the Dutch or the Germans) to the French and then culminates in Nazi
Germany. Yet these may all imply a single experience. The juxtapositions invite us
into a Europe in which a common drama is played out by separate nations interchangeably. Nationality itself is a side-issue. One sees this in the way the book itself
is organised, in sequences which are not quite sequential. It begins and ends with
poems from an intermittent sequence entitled 'To the High Court Parliament' and
there are other sequences in it ('Mysticism and Democracy', 'Dark-Land') which
run less consecutively than one expects them to. A poem on Wesley follows hard
on one about Stefan Georg; just as we are settling into a meditation on England we
meet a sequence on Aleksandr Blok's Russia. Such a cutting is clearly deliberate
and, indeed, something we are prepared for every time we turn on the *Ten O'Clock
News*. It may be the only exact way that Hill can broach the subject of England at
all. Nationality has to be related to other nationalities. Anyway it interests him not
so much as a set of specific characteristics, as in *Henry V*, but for the inevitable
discrepancy that exists between what we want our country to be and what we

---

12   There are many signs in *Canaan* of Hill's debt to Blake. A related debt to Milton goes with it.

actually see it to be. Thus, the poems on Parliament are all subtitled 'November, 1994', the time when the cash-for-questions scandal broke, and they all veer alarmingly from the lofty to the scathing. Loving a country may mean berating it. Hill will have found better precedents for such mixed feelings in Milton and Wordsworth than in Rupert Brooke. Modern poets have often preferred to keep their feelings about England unmixed. In either case, though, a country is never an entirely actual thing. Nor can it ever be circumscribed by its geographical boundaries. This is therefore the place to mention how tangibly present Latin civilisation is in Hill's Europe – more so, to my mind, than it was in Eliot's. In a poem about Constable, who is so often vulgarised into an icon of 'Englishness', he says:

> the ancient words suffice,
> Latin or English, worn channels for the rain …

Yet what is 'worn' to Hill may seem worn out to some of his readers. So too may his exact and exacting biblical references. What makes him a 'difficult' poet is that he holds faith with these traditional sources of English poetry when other poets have turned away from them. The more contemporary we think ourselves, the more he will seem old-fashioned. Yet in many ways his apparent pedantry confirms one's sense of him as a European poet, one who, just like Virgil or Goethe, can distinguish the essential from the ephemeral.

'To the High Court of Parliament' may seem to give itself airs. Hill speaks as an 'unacknowledged legislator', not as a leader-writer. The poem attributes dignity to his own voice as well as to Parliament. It cherishes a whiff of the archaic, provides the poet with a platform from which to reprove such local scandals as the sale of Westminster cemetery to developers. Yet this tone is not mere pomposity. It is also a way of implying that such tawdriness is simply a part of the long, continuing history that *is* Parliament. The year 1994 has to seem both significant and yet only an episode. Otherwise, the indignation would sound shrill, transient itself. This paradox will be familiar to readers of Hill's earlier books, particularly *Mercian Hymns*, dwelling as they do both on our discontinuity from the past and our habit of repeating it. In the first poem of *Canaan* Hill adjures England to 'let her wounds weep / into the lens of oblivion'. It is a lens that can easily seem only a blank but it may nonetheless shape us as deeply as more obvious sources do. England is more than just its external landscape. It is a process, not a scene. Like Hill, we all possess some inner image of Parliament that comes to more than just the appearance of Barry and Pugin's building or the chiming of Big Ben. England is something that, in Wordsworth's phrase, we half-create and half-perceive. But for this potential in it we would be left with little but pictures, private versions of a public world.

Canaan could be described as an intense conversation which the poet is having with himself, rather than as a direct address from poet to reader. The tone feels oblique, even uncertain, but this is not 'reflective' poetry of the sort where the poet muses aloud and simply invites the reader to eavesdrop on his musings. Hill himself often seems surprised (surprise is one of his strengths) when his thoughts

open out before some sudden abyss of blackness or at unsuspected hints of plenitude. As one poem has it:

> but by occasion
> visions of truth or dreams
> as they arise -
> to terms of grace
> where grace has surprised us -
> the unsustaining
> wondrously sustained.

Opposites yoked to a point where they cease to be opposites are a hallmark of
Hill's poetry. The emotion is fraught in a religious way, though in no sense didactic
as Hopkins sometimes is. England always stands for a common human condition,
beyond and beneath its own particularities. The Holocaust can be seen through
the Wars of the Roses. Just so, England's present can divulge its past. Not for Hill
the far-off sadness of 'blue remembered hills'. In one 'Dark-Land' poem, where he
castigates England's 'inane Midas-like hunger', he evokes not only the National
Lottery but also the England of Wesley and Bunyan (the phrase 'Dark-Land' is
from Mr Valiant-for-Truth). Such greed is no mere symptom of Thatcherism and
the poet's anger subsides into an older sadness. The present revives the past even
when it seems to have betrayed it.

In 'Respublica' (which republic is not stated) the past returns not as a warm
feeling but like a sharp admonition:

> Respublica
> Brokenly recalled,
> Its archaic laws
> And hymnody
>
> And destroyed hope
> That so many times
> Is brought with triumph
> Back from the dead.

To contemplate this past requires active moral energy, not nostalgia of the usual
sort. Some poets seem almost pleased, even relieved, that the past is past, out of
harm's way, as if England's history were no more than an evocative memory of
ruffs and crinolines. For Hill, as Faulkner said about the South, the past isn't yet
past here.[13] Through his immersion in history he works towards an idea of
'England' as potently present, too alive to be sighed after. It is never clear or settled
enough to develop the ideal aura of an 'England, my England'.

As he states in *The Enemy's Country*, Hill follows instead 'a track of peculiar
virtue – English – which so often deceives us by the way'. He has little time for

---

13 Nor would Hill share the current vogue for the word 'new' as a sort of synonym of 'good'.

Wordsworth's England of past heroes. Most of his English people – the martyrs and poets aside – are forgotten, ordinary people, the bit players and victims of history, whose voices have long since been silenced. 'Churchill's Funeral', for instance, pointedly dwells on the anonymous crowd of mourners rather than on Churchill's catafalque or the dignitaries who follow it so publicly:[14]

> Who is to judge
> Who can judge of this?
> Maestros of the world
> Not you not them.

In the same way Hill writes of a common Europe, a *Europa hetaera*. The common past has to be saved from the official pieties of history. To the French generals Péguy was just another statistic; to Hill he supplies a link which goes back to the peasant-born Joan of Arc. Hence, his unwillingness to sweep the horrors of twentieth-century Europe under the carpet. Like Constable at Dedham, he thinks of even the church, that fulcrum of 'Merrie England', as wounded:

> the English
> Church as it must be
> Charred in its own standing.

So Europe stands. Unless it is so seen, only part of it, the picturesque surface, can be seen at all. Hill's Europe, unlike that of Brussels, is continuous and admits its past without trying to exorcise it. Tradition entails the suffering and labour of 'common' people as well as artists and statesmen. In this respect Hill's view of it goes further than Eliot's. In 'The Laurel Axe' in *Tenebrae*, for instance, it is quite clear that the English country house in question owed its existence to far more than just 'high culture'. There is darkness in it as well as light.

All this needs to be emphasised because it is still common to find Hill caricatured as a pompous votary of 'high culture'. His passionate anger at privilege gets missed. So too does his sympathy for poets like Hopkins and Gurney who, like Péguy, worked outside the bounds of the establishment of their day. In particular, Hill has always been drawn to those whose religion resisted the currents of their time: St Robert Southwell, Bunyan, Wesley, Péguy, Bonhoeffer. A religion can be a kind of nation within the nation and, in *Canaan*, Hill draws more deeply than ever before on Christianity, like a postulant seeking succour from it. The new poems are religious in the sense that they see the world from beyond the world as well as from within it. Thus the constant tension in them between hints of grace and passages of unflinching tragic realism. It is too soon to judge how well Hill brings off this heady combination but clear enough that his England and his Europe are both completely impregnated in Christianity. If this emphasis seems off-putting to

---

14 The epigraphs to 'Churchill's Funeral' are all drawn from people outside the magic circle of power – Elgar, Ruskin and Blake (though Hill can't forgive Elgar his Edwardian nobilities).

some readers, one might add that, given their history, it is bound to be. To deny it would be an evasion. But though Hill is not afraid to sound out of key it is harder to be a Christian poet (and a poet of Christian polity) today than it was for Milton or even for Hopkins. We no longer think of our politics as a branch of our religion. Hill's position sometimes seems Blakean but Blake, though a modern hero, is really foreign to the way most of us think of England. Those who dislike Hill's poetry will still see it as the last breath of a vanishing world, even more so after *Canaan*. The poetry's answer to their objections is simply that such worlds *never* vanish, however much we try to erase them. If they did, it would diminish ourselves. Sometimes it can be evasive to deny one's nostalgia.

Canaan ends with a final 'Parliament' poem, full of pained indignation, seeming almost pleased at getting on its high horse. It invokes Marvell, Milton and Gillray but no modern politicians. It also turns out to be more in sorrow than in anger:

> None the less amazing: Barry's and Pugin's grand
> dark-lantern above the incumbent Thames.
> You: as by custom unillumined
>   masters of servile counsel.
> Who can now speak for despoiled merit,
>   the fouled catchments of Demos,
> as 'thy' high lamp presides with sovereign
> equity, over against us, across this
> densely reflective, long-drawn, procession of waters?

Though to my ear 'masters of servile counsel' sounds mannered, too self-consciously dated, rereading suggests that the elaborate diction is a way of reining back anger. The sense of Parliament we end on is not black and white but shifting. A sort of anxious wonder takes over the poem's tone. It is not easy to say if a word like 'sovereign' is just ironic or whether it still retains some of its positive sense. The 'long-drawn, procession of waters' reflects something both murky and venerable. The strange building, famous yet unknown, shimmers in the river, whether for good or ill it seems impossible to tell. Yet the more one listens to the poem the more its cadences seem to sound together, however jarring its feelings might be. Whatever it is, it is not merely a political broadside.

In a way a poem like this one is unlike Hill's earlier work. *Mercian Hymns* and *Tenebrae* construct their idea of England from specific past lives but, in *Canaan*, England is seen more frontally, almost as if it were an abstract idea or itself a character. This perspective seems to me characteristic of the expatriate and I can't help remarking that most of the poems in this book have been written since Hill went to work in Boston in 1988. One's country looks different from abroad and being abroad encourages us to see it, whether ideally or balefully, as an entity. Fellow Americans who met Eliot in London often resented his blanket judgements on his homeland; the further Lawrence went from England, the easier he found it to sum it up. Perhaps something similar applies to Hill. At all events, I myself remember that it was only when I lived abroad that I really realised that I was English. Until then, my 'Englishness' had been only an unconscious assumption. In England, there was nothing to compare England with. In a similar way, Henry James used to compare his own cosmopolitan stance with the simpler certainties of more native Americans like Emerson and Thoreau. If he saw what he lacked he also saw what he gained as a result. He was less likely to confuse the national with the universal than they were and more alert to a sense of Europe as a tangible whole (more so, to my mind, than was the cosmopolitan Joyce, who used it as a slogan). I would conjecture that, in the same way, expatriation has deepened Hill's sense of England as an integral part of Europe and not, as for many of its recent poets, led him to focus on what is exclusive in its story. His Europe may at times seem like a vast network of battlefields, a Babel of quarrelling tongues and contending nationalisms, but nationality is not its essence. In *Canaan* it figures not as special or specific but as an epitome for human life in general. Its politics, that is, is inseparable from the book's religion.

I realise that these speculations may seem impertinent. I have no direct knowledge of what expatriation has meant to Hill. Yet this worries me less than it would worry me to argue that his poetry expresses some quintessential 'Englishness'. His true subjects are loss and guilt and hope, mortality and grace, and one could hardly suppose that the English, or anyone else, have any copyright in them. To claim him as an English poet means recognising when his poetry ceases to be *simply* English. It is because he has understood how Europe makes his idea of England whole that he can write so well about them both. Only a jingoist could, in any case, wish to see them as opposites.

But perhaps even this claim is a parochial way to end. As a sometime student of Marshall McLuhan I can't forget that Europe is simply our most immediate manifestation of the 'global village'. One would not want it to block that other world from us as England often blocks off Europe from us today. Seen in the wrong way Europe could become almost as insular. Is history really 'now and England' as Eliot wanted to think? I turn instead to the globe-trotting Lawrence, who loved England but also saw how dangerous the idea of 'Englishness' is, how easily it can sanction a retreat from experience that masquerades as a commitment to it. There is a passage in *Women in Love* where Gudrun asks Birkin if there is still hope for England:

'Any hope of England's becoming real? God knows. It's a great actual unreality now, an aggregation into unreality. It might be real if there were no Englishmen.'
     'You think the English will have to disappear?' persisted Gudrun ...
     'Well – what else is in front of them but disappearance? They've got to disappear from their own special brand of Englishness, anyhow.'[15]

We need not endorse everything Birkin says as long as we recognise that he speaks not cynically but out of a painful hope that a living, evolving 'Englishness' is still a

---

15   D. H. Lawrence, *Women in Love* (1917; London: Penguin, 1996), p. 142.

possibility. England is a process, not a congenial fall-back position for jaded patri-
ots like Gerald Crich. The passage seems prescient, more so than much that has
been written on the subject in recent years. Hill's own approach may be very
different but I believe he shares Lawrence's refusal to re-tell a tale that has already
been told in the same terms. It is for this reason that *Canaan* is important – too
important, perhaps, to confine it further within the present debate about
'Englishness'.

6 A case of red herrings: Englishness in the poetry of Philip Larkin and Ted Hughes

Antony Rowland

Some 17 per cent of Yorkshire people would rather canonise the Hollywood star George Clooney than celebrate the obscure aspirations of a fourth-century dragon-slayer. The same (dubious) poll, published in the *Guardian*, observed that only a third of those questioned knew that St George's Day is 23 April.[1] Yet England and St George are inseparable in Shakespeare's rallying cry for Henry V, an inextricability which is undercut by the saint's origins in Capadocia (now part of Turkey), a far cry from Blake's pleasant pastures. Alleged to have dispatched an errant dragon terrorising a pagan town in Libya, George appeared (rather conveniently) to Richard the Lionheart during the Crusades, encouraging him to murder as many infidels as possible. A mythical progenitor of genocide and a depoliticised 'Jerusalem' thus form two possible adjuncts to the slippery signifier known as 'Englishness'. The '-ness' suggests an essential identity, rather than a proliferation, and rewriting, of identities, but when W. H. Auden claimed that 'The pleasures of the English nation' are 'Copotomy and sodulation', he presumably did not intend his aphoristic spoonerism to indicate that the rest of the world was devoid of such amorous activity.[2]

Christopher Byrant has recently distinguished between four constructions of England: Anglo-British England, Little England, English England and Cosmopolitan England.[3] Whilst avoiding essentialism, Bryant concedes that the categories overlap, and that they are not definitive.[4] They often merge in a single

---

1 www.guardian.co.uk.
2 Quoted in Charles Osborne, *W. H. Auden: the life of a poet* (London: Michael O'Mara, 1979), p. 81.
3 Christopher G. A. Bryant, 'These Englands, or Where Does Devolution Leave the English?', *Nations and Nationalism*, 9:3 (2003), pp. 393–412. Anglo-British England is the England of the former empire, in which the divisions between Britishness and Englishness are elided. Little England is the England that attempts to ignore overseas developments: this originated in left-wing resistance to colonialism, but is now located more commonly in right-wing responses to the European Union. English England is the attempt, as in Hughes's work, to define that which is quintessentially English. Cosmopolitan England, unlike Larkin's, is more open to cultural diversity and European developments than any of the preceding categories. Bryant champions the latter, but a worry remains that a definition of Englishness based on openness does not provide a satisfactory exposition of what it means to be English.
4 Instead of categorising different aspects of Englishness or Britishness at the beginning of 'Nation and Empire: English and British national identity in comparative perspective', Krishan Kumar argues that the character of the United Kingdom is 'a conceptual hole' (*Theory and Society*, 29

literary text: in the novel *The Franchise Affair* (1949), Robert Blair's Little England of the late 1940s, unchanged for Blair since the Wars of the Roses (the recent world war is not mentioned), is subverted by the dissolution of the formerly aristocratic house called The Franchise, a vision of what David Gervais has termed 'post-England', where the decent house guests mourn the decline of fine palates, nice upholstery and horse-copers.[5]

Such instances of mourning underline the fact that national identities may be read as something of a red herring, the products of nationalist ideologies, the preserves of the ruling class, or a set of unstable signifiers given meaning through fantasy. Nevertheless, they are tenacious: even if identity is ultimately impossible, the paradox is that 'there can be no escape from identity'.[6] Even so, most contemporary poets in Britain appear to avoid being drawn into discussions about Englishness, rejecting it as a chimera rather than a culturally unifying force; responses could be summarised as displaying bafflement, suspicion or hostility. For example, England is rarely referred to in the poetry of Paul Muldoon, Simon Armitage, Carol Ann Duffy and Tony Harrison: for Harrison and Armitage, identity politics are bound up with the northern working classes rather than English nationalism. Perhaps the visibility of Welsh and Scottish nationalism in recent times might have incited poets to define Englishness more exactly, beyond the vague icons of a literary elite, the dragon-slayer, the football hooligan and the beer belly. Yet Duffy does not so much revise tenets of Englishness as betray puzzlement that they ever existed. For this poet England can only be represented properly *in extremis*. In 'Mrs Skinner, North Street', the xenophobic old woman is clearly meant to be dismissed by the reader as regurgitating outdated notions of Englishness, but the fact that there is nothing offered to replace her views means that the category risks redundancy. Mrs Skinner stays in her house, which may symbolise the political impotence of jingoistic versions of English national identity. Englishness has become so intangible in Duffy's work that it can be defined only from the outside as it is in Harrison's early monologues written from the perspective of a louche colonial in Africa. Hence the speaker in 'Translating the English' luxuriates in England as a country of warm beer and lovely royals. The irony that the taxi driver has arrived in England only recently highlights the superficiality of the icons he has learnt to indulge. Simon Armitage's rejection of England as a topic suitable for study can be evidenced from his prose collection *All*

(2000), pp. 575–608 (p. 575). Kumar claims that this gap resulted from colonialism and concludes, along with the seventeenth report of *British Social Attitudes* (London: Sage, 2000), that since devolution the 'English are for the first time having to confront seriously the question faced previously by many nations: who are we?' (p.593).

5 Josephine Tey, *The Franchise Affair* (1949; London: Arrow Books, 2003); David Gervais, *Literary Englands: versions of 'Englishness' in modern writing* (Cambridge: Cambridge University Press, 1993), p. 200. Gervais defines Larkin's England as post-England: the poetry displays 'a sense of *something that was absent*: a sense of what was left when the older England was "gone"'.

6 Jacques Derrida, quoted in Antony Easthope, *Englishness and National Culture* (London and New York: Routledge, 1999), p. 24.

Points North: similar to Harrison, little points south, and certainly not towards the mythic unity of Ted Hughes's England; instead, Armitage uncovers the provincial difficulty of bats communicating across the boundary of Yorkshire and Lancashire.

In contrast, Duffy does engage with England's intangibility: when a speaker asks in *The Other Country* where a character is from, the response is hesitation. When Philip Larkin passes Coventry in 'I Remember, I Remember', the exuberant sense of the *heimlich* ('"I was born here"') is undercut ten lines later when the friend asks if he has his 'roots' there: the narrator wishes to reply that his childhood was merely 'unspent' in the Midlands.[7] This lack of identification goes a step further in *The Other Country*: rather than challenge the concept of a sense of origins, the post-structuralist poet appears confused as to how it could have existed in the first place. For Duffy and many other contemporary writers, to reply 'Scotland' or 'England' to the question 'where are your roots?' would risk a nonsensical response. Contemporary poets today are more likely to write about a mixture of regional identities than attempt to demystify abstract categories of Englishness. Despite the fact that 'devolution and European integration are prompting fresh discussions about English identity', Englishness itself in contemporary poetry appears to have become a red herring.[8]

This chapter will examine two earlier modern poets' positions with regard to this dismissal of Englishness as red herring. It will analyse their responses to the polysemy of Englishness, contrasting the England of a mobilising myth of an integrated community in the poetry of Ted Hughes with a resistance to constructions of national and regional identities in the poetry of Philip Larkin. In *Englishness and National Culture*, Antony Easthope argues that Hughes and Larkin form part of an empiricist tradition in English poetry which eschews the modernist concept of fractured subjectivity, and promotes the belief that all art is basically mimetic.[9] This essay turns Easthope's thesis on its head by arguing that Hughes seeks Englishness in the metaphysics of myth, rather than empiricism, and that Larkin attempts to reject identity politics in the symbolist endings to many of his poems.

Larkin has been upheld as a champion of Englishness, whereas poems such as 'Here' signal a retreat into stubborn provincialism and private epiphany: Gervais argues that he 'simply could not find *enough* to explore in the idea of England'.[10] In *The Post-Colonial Critic*,[11] Spivak notes that one learns about one's place from

---

7   Philip Larkin, *Collected Poems* (London: Faber, 1988), p. 81.
8   Raphaël Ingelbien, *Misreading England: poetry and nationhood since the Second World War* (Amsterdam: Rodopi, 2002), p. 1.
9   Easthope, *Englishness and National Culture*, p. 178.
10 Gervais, *Literary Englands*, p. 215. Larkin's desire for Little England could be adduced from the famous photograph of him sitting on the sign for 'England' on the Scottish border. He had urinated on it just before the picture was taken.
11 Gayatri Chakravorty Spivak, *The Post-Colonial Critic: interviews, strategies, dialogues* (London: Routledge, 1990).

other people: whereas this might be true for the England commuted in Carol Ann Duffy's 'Translating the English' through the voice of the taxi driver, it is not the impetus for Larkin's *œuvre*. As James Booth has argued in *New Larkins for Old*, 'Larkin cuts a most implausible figure as a hoarder and shover of Englishness ... His poetry ... does not dig beneath a flag'.[12]

The Ted Hughes archives – recently opened at Emory University in Atlanta, Georgia – reveal in contrast that the Yorkshire writer became increasingly attracted to this 'flag', and the legend of St George, during his period as Poet Laureate. The reason for this attraction appears to be a desire to unite the people of England within a mythic schema, a poetic trajectory which Larkin, with his famous distaste for the 'myth kitty', would no doubt have deplored.[13] In two Emory letters from 1988 and 1992, Hughes discourses on St George at length, and points out that an old ballad forms an English version of the legend, which conveniently elides George's Capadocian origins. The son of Lord Albert of Coventry, this George was stolen and brought up by a wild woman of the woods, and trained to be a warrior.[14] He bore three marks on his body: a dragon on his breast, a garter on his leg and a blood-red cross on one arm. Whilst fighting the Saracens, he met a dragon, which demanded to eat fresh maidens every day. Following the pro-aristocratic narrative thrust of many folk tales, it was only when it was the turn of the king's daughter Sabra that George intervened and killed the dragon, whilst making the sign of the cross. Sabra then followed him (inexplicably) to Coventry, Larkin's birthplace, where they lived happily ever after.[15] In the other version of the myth, George's tendency towards cross-dressing fulfils its symbolic potential when he puts a girdle around the dragon's neck, and brings it to the terrorised city; the inhabitants were so terrified that they all converted to Christianity.

'Rain-Charm for the Duchy', Hughes's first major Laureate poem, was published first in the *Observer* (23 December 1984), and can be read alongside this interest in St George as an attempt to find a metaphysical linchpin that might unite the English.[16] The royal family form, along with the George legends, possible 'hubs' for Englishness. In an Emory letter to Alan Ross (15 March 1988), Hughes writes that the 'Royalty's relationship to the people is primarily to the hub centre of their psychic life, as representatives of the sacred axle – that's why people invent

12 James Booth (ed.), *New Larkins for Old: critical essays* (Basingstoke and New York: Macmillan, 2000), p. 203.
13 Larkin argues that 'As a guiding principle I believe that every poem must be its own sole freshly created universe, and therefore have no belief in "tradition" or a common myth-kitty' (quoted in Philip Larkin, *Required Writing: miscellaneous pieces 1955–1982* (London: Faber, 1983), p. 69).
14 Letters to a 'David' and 'Dear Sir' (6 Apr. 1988 and 25 Apr. 1992).
15 Sabra's choice is opposed to Larkin's version of Coventry in 'I Remember, I Remember', where the town stands for the supposed nothingness and boredom that typified the poet's youth (*Collected Poems*, pp. 81–2).
16 Ted Hughes, 'Rain-Charm for the Duchy', *Observer* (23 Dec. 1984), p. 7.

them in the first place. Laureate's relationship [*sic*] ideally should be the same.' In 'Rain-Charm for the Duchy', as at the end of 'The Whitsun Weddings', the 'hub' joining all the English proves to be rain: all subjects of the 'sacred axle' enjoy a tumultuous downpour to celebrate the christening of Prince Harry. Rain itself, of course, cannot form a definitive sign of Englishness (rain, like copotomy, can happen elsewhere), and yet both poets connect it with the 'hub centre' of their poems. For Larkin, this is procreation, for Hughes, the royal family: 'Big, sudden thunderdrops' on Cranmere's 'cracked heath-tinder' form a symbolic nexus in Hughes's poem with the water poured on Harry's head. The sacred nature of this act for Hughes draws all of England together in a 'Blessed, Devout Drench', as the subtitle would have it.

To use the context of 'Englishness' to begin to outline connections between these two poets might seem to be controversial: Alvarez's introduction to *The New Poetry* anthology – written in 1960 – has often been cited as the key influence in polarising the work of Larkin and Hughes. Such a critical stance cannot account for the connections between the writers in terms of their occasional engagement with each other's work, and the unpublished correspondence held at Emory University. 'Rain-Charm for the Duchy' can be read as a partial rewriting of 'The Whitsun Weddings' and another Larkin poem, 'Water'. The rain that ends 'The Whitsun Weddings', and the 'sousing' in 'Water', reappear as the downpour to celebrate the christening of Prince Harry.[17] Specific phrases from 'The Whitsun Weddings' appear in both texts, such as the 'bunting-dressed, / Coach-party annexes' which become the 'tourist bunting' in Hughes's poem.[18] But whereas the 'we' in Larkin's text remains a more abstract plurality, Hughes's 'bunting' attempts to ensnare 'us' in a specific, public, 'civic event': the christening of a royal. Other connections are evident between the two poems: swelling at the end of 'The Whitsun Weddings' indicates the possibility of future procreation for the wedding couples; this becomes the 'tors' in Hughes's poem. 'Tor', a hill or rocky peak, originates from the Latin 'torus', a 'swelling', 'bulge' or 'cushion'. This is connected with the 'girl in high heels' in 'Rain-Charm for the Duchy', who is 'cuffed' by surf in an image of insemination, adding sexual piquancy to Larkin's image in 'Water' of a 'fording' congregation. Even the 'squares of wheat' in 'The Whitsun Weddings' make a displaced appearance here, in the guise of Hughes's companion's cry: 'Think of the barley!'[19] Fecundity is then conveyed through the images of rivers as attractive, pregnant women.

Larkin's poem is perhaps the more complex piece due, in part, to the ambiguity of the images of procreation. In an unpublished letter to James Sutton held in the Brynmor Jones Library (which I have discussed elsewhere), 'swelling' denotes both the working-class couple's predilection for children, and their obesity: they

---

17 Larkin, *Collected Poems*, p. 93.
18 Larkin, *Collected Poems*, p. 115.
19 Larkin, *Collected Poems*, p. 116.

'swell, say, and die. PAH!'[20] Indeed, this letter's depiction of marriage as a 'tawdry' affair uncannily anticipates the doubleness of 'The Whitsun Weddings' in its celebration and simultaneous denigration of the nuptial: the gaudy purple cushion in the missive forms a precursor of the distasteful mauve clothes of the girls in the poem. In contrast, the fugacious rise and fall of the rivers in Hughes's poem allows for no such psychic unease in the author's view of procreation, nor in its depiction of the grounded nature of national identity: the 'clay vaults' of the Tamar tumble out the 'rusty knights' of both dispersed soil and mythic English heroes. In a sense, 'Rain-Charm for the Duchy' celebrates that 'somewhere' that ends 'The Whitsun Weddings', a pastoral space that remains both indescribable and ineluctable for the urbanite Larkin. Hughes fills that metaphysical gap with wet salmon. In the Sutton letter the working-class couple 'spawn'; in Hughes's poem, the fish 'stir' as they begin, perhaps, to move upriver in order to spawn.

Rather than celebrating an England of frisky salmon and St George-like figures, however, the poem perhaps unwittingly celebrates regional diversity. Although the narrative unfolds in the south-west, it rejoices in diversity in that Hughes's West Yorkshire vowels resonate through the piece, such as in the echo rhyme of 'Mole', 'choked', 'Oak', 'Yeo', 'commotion', 'smoke' and 'Lowering'. Indeed, the diction as a whole reveals an etymological 'drench' of linguistic plenitude. '[R]iddle', a kind of sieve, from the Old English *hriddel*, complements 'cinders', from the Old English *sinder*, in the memorable image of what the Hull poet Peter Didsbury has referred to as rain that bounces back off the pavement.[21] Here, 'The pavements danced, like cinders in a riddle': 'Siling it down', a northern phrase employed by Didsbury to describe this phenomenon, originates from Old Norse; similarly, the derivation of specific words in 'Rain-Charm for the Duchy' evince not so much an insular English language as one of semantic invasion. Another Hughes poem, 'Thistles', mirrors this process: the thistles/warriors that return after being mown down are not the English after all, but Viking invaders.

As if to register the poem's debt to the Hull librarian, when it was first published in the *Observer* in 1984, 'Rain-Charm for the Duchy' included a subtle reference to Larkin. 'A Blessed, Devout Drench for the Christening of Prince Harry' is clearly an allusion to 'A furious devout drench' in 'Water'.[22] This disappeared mysteriously in the version published in Hughes's *New Selected Poems 1957-1994* in 1995, and was replaced with the terse epigraph, 'for H.R.H. Prince Harry'.[23] One possible reason for this disappearance can be adduced from the Emory letters, Thwaite letters and Motion biography. The poets corresponded

---

20 See Antony Rowland, '"All is not Dead": Philip Larkin, humanism and class', *Critical Survey*, 10:2 (1998), pp. 1–14 (pp. 9–10).

21 *OED* 2nd edn. Peter Didsbury, 'The Hailstone' in *The Classical Farm* (Newcastle upon Tyne: Bloodaxe, 1987), pp. 60–1 (p. 60).

22 I must thank Professor Neil Roberts from the University of Sheffield for pointing this connection out to me.

23 Ted Hughes, *New Selected Poems 1957–1994* (London: Faber, 1995), p. 285.

occasionally; the uncollected letters from Larkin in Atlanta reveal a much more amiable relationship than has been acknowledged. Polite envy runs through Larkin's first missive to Hughes (13 June 1975): asking Hughes how the Ilkley Literature Festival went, Larkin adds 'I hope all these stories about young girls fainting in the aisles are not exaggerated'. In the next letter, Larkin apparently responds to a Hughes letter praising 'Aubade': he thanks Hughes for his 'kind words', and states, 'Since writing it I stopped being afraid of death for a few months, but it is beginning to creep back now'.

Of course, these initial letters display a different private attitude towards Hughes than that recounted in the Thwaite letters and Motion biography: the latter reveals that Larkin framed a picture of Hughes in his toilet; in a letter to Kingsley Amis (3 June 1967), he laments that 'Ted's no good at all. Not at all. Not a single solitary bit of good'.[24] Perhaps the first signs of a more public rift between the two writers occurred in 1980, when they disagreed over an entry to the Arvon Poetry Competition. In a letter to Judy Egerton (10 December 1980), Larkin expresses his regret that he became involved in the event, and declaims an 'extraordinary parody of Pope called "The Rape of the Cock"'.[25] Wendy Cope parodied the clash of poetic styles involved in the judging panel in 'God and the Jolly Bored Bog-Mouse' from *Making Cocoa for Kingsley Amis* (1986); what Cope could not have known in the early 1980s was that 'The Rape of the Cock' was about a woman having sex with a baboon.[26]

Hughes was fond of the thirty-five-page parody; in a letter to David Ross (December 1980) held at Emory, he explains that it was 'a wild marvellous obscene lament for the glorious passion between a beautiful woman and a baboon in a night-club'. Seamus Heaney quite liked the poem too. Charles Causley's reaction remains unrecorded, but Hughes notes that 'Larkin said if it got the prize he'd have to dissociate himself publicly from the judging panel'. Nevertheless, the poets continued to correspond after the event. Larkin appears to have been similarly unimpressed by the eventual winner, Andrew Motion: 'When I see him', he writes to Hughes (30 January 1981), 'I will ask him what the poem means.' He adds dryly, 'Charles [Monteith] has just rejected his next collection of poems, so the situation is full of inconsistencies.' A few days earlier he expressed a more strident view to Amis (11 January 1981): 'to think that someone is going to get FIVE THOUSAND POUNDS for some utter ballocks [*sic*] makes me want to do damage'.[27]

Hughes remained relatively unaware of Larkin's reservations about his poetic taste and acumen, for the present. On one occasion he even sent Larkin his horoscope. Larkin replies in an Emory letter (8 November 1982) by stating:

---

24 Anthony Thwaite (ed.), *The Selected Letters of Philip Larkin* (London: Faber, 1992), p. 396.
25 Thwaite (ed.), *The Selected Letters of Philip Larkin*, p. 632.
26 Wendy Cope, *Making Cocoa for Kingsley Amis* (London: Faber, 1986), p. 55.
27 Thwaite (ed.), *The Selected Letters of Philip Larkin*, p. 636.

'Thank you for taking the trouble to send me my horoscope which I shall carefully preserve, though I don't know whether it is supposed to help me or frighten
me … I never thought to ask what time of day I was born, and the information by
now is gone beyond recall. I should guess about opening-time.' Such tongue-in-
cheek geniality continues in the next letter (19 December 1984), when he con-
gratulates Hughes on the Laureateship: 'Much as I admired JB [John Betjamin], I
believe the job needs a different kind of imagination now, and I'm sure you can
supply it. Hope you survive!' Whether this 'imagination' includes creating a
'sacred axle' for the English is left open. Four days later, Larkin wrote to Robert
Conquest (23 December 1984), calling Hughes a 'boring old monolith', and
accepting that 'he'll do the job all right except for writing anything readable'.[28]
This was penned on the same day that 'Rain-Charm for the Duchy' was published
in the *Observer*; the critic can only surmise whether Larkin wrote the letter after
coming across the supposedly unreadable piece. Nevertheless, Larkin continued
to correspond with Hughes, and in the last letter held at Emory (7 August 1985)
he touchingly complains that 'any journey further than Leeds seems to me fraught
with danger'. In a bizarre letter to Larkin just before he died of cancer (21
November 1985), Hughes offers the services of a local faith healer. In a later letter
to Monica Jones (8 December 1985), Hughes is appalled by the prospect that
Larkin might have read the letter just before he died.

Despite this genial relationship recorded in the Emory letters, Hughes's suspicions that Larkin was less than enamoured by his poetic output begin to increase
after 1985. In a letter to Alan Ross (15 March 1988), Hughes contends that he
always stated publicly that he would have preferred Charles Causley to be the new
Laureate, a more 'obvious natural choice', because he thought Larkin too 'obviously right wing, too much in himself a right-wing icon'. Hughes's reading of
Larkin as Conservative, and promoting a version of Englishness based on insularity and humdrum banality, is complemented by Thom Gunn's comment in an
Emory letter to Hughes (3 February 1990) that 'Larkin was a malign influence' on
English poets, 'encouraging a kind of pusillanimity that takes from them any
chance of the imagination'. Hughes was then piqued at his depiction by Larkin in
the selected letters. In a letter to Douglas Dunn in 1993, he records that he spotted
the proofs at Faber's:

No, I shan't read Philip's letters. When I saw the proofs lying there in Daphne Tagg's office at
Faber's I said: I don't expect I come out of that looking very clean. And she suddenly froze,
in a My-God-we-completely-forgot-to-ask-him-whether-he'd-mind sort of posture. I
could see her real alarm there, for a moment. So I reassured her. I told her from my experience they'd be blamed far more [for] what they cut out than for what they leave in. And no
matter how bad his remarks might be, if they're cut out everybody will assume they were far
worse. And who cares. (11 January 1993)

---

28   Thwaite (ed.), *The Selected Letters of Philip Larkin*, p. 726.

Hughes 'cared' in a sense, though, since he appears, as a retort, to have deposited a blank postcard of Bobby Charlton into the back of the Larkin file at Emory: the resemblance between the former Manchester United player and the Hull poet (in terms of their bald pates) is remarkable. Hughes's increasing antagonism towards the deceased poet after coming across the proofs may have also resulted in Larkin's final excision from 'Rain-Charm for the Duchy', a poem which, ironically, was originally designed to highlight a literary genealogy between the poets' views of a united England.

More seriously, in 1992, Hughes almost accused Larkin of plagiarism. In an intriguing letter to Alice Quinn (6 October 1992), Hughes contends that 'Two of Larkin's poems Larkinise (to my mind) two early poems of mine that I never republished (though he certainly saw them). One of them is one of his best.' Any clear charge of plagiarism appears to be absent: 'to Larkinise' seems to suggest that the texts in question form, at best, a pastiche of Hughes's originals. As Phillipa Gregory has pointed out in relation to eighteenth-century novelists, the appropriation, rather than copying, of content cannot be sullied with the charge of plagiarism, since authors 'simply poached whole scenes or motifs from their colleagues, thus converting rivals into unwilling collaborators'; she uses the example of the party in *The Card*, a novel by John Hidgell, which was reimagined by Smollett, Richardson, Fielding and Haywood.[29]

Which poems, then, does Larkin poach 'scenes' or 'motifs' from? If 'One of them is one of his best', can a previously unknown source be uncovered for one of his most canonical pieces? 'Mayday on Holderness' and 'Here' share a remarkably similar subject matter: even though the shadow of Gallipoli and the 'Cordite oozings' broach the Mexborough marvel's palate as he contemplates the Humber estuary – as opposed to the *seemingly* more conventional version of English pastoral in 'Here' – both poems share a stubborn provinciality.[30] For Hughes, Sheffield, the 'inert North', the North Sea and the Humber represent the national effort at Gallipoli rather than England as a whole (his Yorkshire father was one of the few survivors of his regiment). For Larkin, the villages around Goole form buffer zones to the postal districts of London in 'The Whitsun Weddings'; as he once wryly remarked, tourists would much rather travel northwards to visit Basil Bunting than change at Doncaster to bother him, and the landscape of 'Here'. James Booth has argued persuasively that Larkin's poetry as a whole espouses parochialism rather than provincialism. Instead of celebrating particular landmarks in East Yorkshire, he contends, Larkin attempts through the lyric form to transcend essentialist notions of place (unlike Seamus Heaney).[31] Booth's chapter in *New Larkins for Old* is set against Heaney's seminal, but much maligned, essay 'Englands of the Mind', in which he argues that Larkin, Hughes and Geoffrey

---

29 Phillipa Gregory, 'Beware of Imitations', *Sunday Times* (8 Nov. 1992), p. 9.
30 Hughes, *New Selected Poems 1957–1994*, p. 24.
31 James Booth, 'From Here to Bogland: Larkin, Heaney and the poetry of place' in *New Larkins for Old*, pp. 190–212.

Hill share a provincialism which stands for a covert Englishness, accompanying the era of decolonisation.[32] Raphaël Ingelbien similarly points out the flaws in Heaney's thesis in '"England and Nowhere": contestations of Englishness in Philip Larkin and Graham Swift'.[33] For Ingelbien, a contradiction exists between postcolonial and post-imperial views of provincialism. Larkin's work can be interpreted as both a post-imperial lament for the loss of the colonies, and a postcolonial reclamation of the provincial as a progressive sign of national identity. As Ingelbien notes, 'Here' has been read as both a defiant Hull poem (by Robert Crawford), and a text in which Larkin speaks for the nation (by Tom Paulin).[34] 'If it ultimately proves impossible to associate their [Larkin and Graham Swift's] Englands with either conservative of [sic] radical politics', he concludes, 'the reason is that they tend to do away with England altogether.'[35]

Typical symbolist moments in Larkin's poems complicate political readings: at the closure of 'Here', East Yorkshire has given way to 'unfenced existence' beyond Spurn Point, joining the signified 'nowheres', 'anywheres' and 'elsewheres' which predominate elsewhere in his verse.[36] Booth and Ingelbien concur on this point, and it certainly allows a distinction between 'Here' and 'Mayday on Holderness'; the latter ends with the microcosmic 'nightlong frenzy of shrews' rather than the macrocosmic metaphysics of an existence 'out of reach'. The titles of the poems emphasise this difference: the more abstract 'Here' vies with the particularity of Holderness at a specific time of year. Nevertheless, 'Here' evinces particularity as much as abstraction: the title may refer to the villages around the A1 and (or) the symbolist ending. Even though Ingelbien argues that the poem functions as a 'degraded version of classical pastoral' due to the paltry meadows and 'harsh-named halt', Larkin's subversive tendency is balanced by the repetition of 'swerving'.[37] Whatever the drawbacks of 'Here', the movement of the poem is at least still 'swerving' from 'there', the A1 and the metropolis to the south. Hence, for this critic, the two poems *can* be compared as espousing a stubborn provincialism that goes beyond authorial intention, however compromised it might be in the Larkin piece, as opposed to the specific landmarks in Hughes's poem. However, the conceptual leap Heaney makes between these vaguely anti-southern poems and a pro-English, provincial ideology at the level of authorial intention is an entirely different matter. Neither poem convinces as an example of the writers treating 'England as a region – or … their region as England'.[38]

---

32 Seamus Heaney, 'Englands of the Mind' in *Preoccupations: Selected Prose 1968–1978* (London: Faber, 1980), pp. 150–69.

33 Raphaël Ingelbien, '"England and Nowhere": contestations of Englishness in Philip Larkin and Graham Swift', *English*, 48:190 (Spring 1999), pp. 33–48.

34 Ingelbien, '"England and Nowhere"', p. 38.

35 Ingelbien, '"England and Nowhere"', p. 45.

36 Larkin, *Collected Poems*, p. 136.

37 Ingelbien, '"England and Nowhere"', p. 37.

38 Heaney, *Preoccupations*, p. 150.

Despite the similarities in terms of their provinciality, however, 'Mayday on Holderness' can be discounted as a precursor of 'Here' on Hughes's own terms: the former was published in *Lupercal* in 1960, and was reprinted in the *New Selected Poems 1957–1994* in 1995. Hughes's comment in the letter to Alice Quinn needs to placed in two contexts: his reaction to the publication of Larkin's selected letters (noted previously), and a sense – which can be adduced from reading the Emory letters as a whole – that he was increasingly aware that these missives would be read by future scholars. After Keith Sagar struggled to make sense of the vast collection in the early 1990s, Hughes himself took over the process of selecting material for the archives. Hence the – perhaps offhand – comment in 1992 could be regarded as the epistolary equivalent of the Bobby Charlton postcard: a red herring to confuse literary scholars, and another jibe at a contemporary who had proved less than generous towards him in his letters.[39] To Larkinise a piece of writing might only produce an instance of intertexuality, or, more broadly, influence. Following Hughes's logic, 'Rain-Charm for the Duchy' must be regarded as a 'Hughesinising' of 'The Whitsun Weddings' and 'Water'. Hughes's vocabulary still has repercussions for literary revisions of Englishness, since if the Hughes and Larkin poems in question both deploy similar (sometimes identical) signifiers of national identity, as I shall argue, then the process of rewriting signs of Englishness is indistinct from stealing. After all, T. S. Eliot famously remarked that the best poets do not borrow from their predecessors, but steal. Rather than plagiarising Hughes in particular, perhaps Larkin could be said to be stealing, and then altering, potential images of national identity from a series of intertexts ripe for all writers to pilfer: David Gervais argues that every exposition of England 'predicates a slightly different England'.[40]

To try and ascertain whether Hughes's comment is indeed a red herring, I have consulted Hughes's early poems which were never published in a full collection.[41] Hughes's assertion that the culprits appertain to 'early' poems poses one of the major problems in detecting the originals: the pieces above date until 1964, by which time Hughes had published two major collections, *The Hawk in the Rain* and *Lupercal*. Two poems published before 1960 might be expected, and yet one piece from 1968 does bear comparison with a Larkin poem dated October 1969 in the *Selected Poems*; in the analysis to follow, however, the late 1960s must be regarded as an 'early' part of a career which ended thirty years later in 1998.

---

39 In 1992 Hughes may have also been particularly sensitive to issues surrounding authors' intentions and critical interpretations in relation to the Plath Estate. Jacqueline Rose's controversial study *The Haunting of Sylvia Plath* was published in 1991: numerous Emory letters register Hughes's disapproval of the feminist's analyses.

40 Gervais, *Literary Englands*, p. 1.

41 Since the completion of this chapter, Hughes's Collected Poems has been published, which has made the tracking of the (possibly) 'Larkinised' poems much easier. Two other possibilities, apart from the poem discussed here, are "Poem to Robert Graves Perhaps' and 'Gibralter': these may have influenced 'Sad Steps' and Homage to a Government'. I discuss these texts in an essay due to be published in HJEAS.

'Dog Days on the Black Sea' and '?' appeared in the tenth anniversary special of *Critical Quarterly*, which comprised the spring and summer issues of 1968.[42] It might be tempting to suspect a connection between the 'see-saw' brains of '?' and the slide of 'High Windows', were it not for the fact that Larkin's poem appears in the same issue (p. 55). Nevertheless, Larkin would perhaps, if not 'certainly', have read this edition of *Critical Quarterly*, precisely because it contained one of his poems. Larkin's interest in the journal can be proved with respect to the material held in the Brian Cox and Critical Quarterly Archives at the John Rylands Library in Manchester. Letters dating from 1968 to 1974 betray Larkin's close friendship with Brian (or C. B.) Cox, his self-promoted 'English' insularity, his homoerotic interest in George Best and a potential male partner at dancing, and a proclivity for pork pies. In a letter to Cox (30 July 1968), Larkin agrees to visit Manchester and watch United, at the same time as he makes it clear that he is refusing all invitations to speak formally. 'If I once start to give way', Larkin writes, 'my life won't be worth living.' 'Of course, it isn't worth living as it is', he continues, 'but you know what I mean.' In another letter dated 4 October 1968 he contends that 'Drinking to me was a fearful experience, like playing squash'; in a missive to Jean Cox (23 November 1969) he reports that he 'ploughed [his] solitary way back to Hull [from Manchester], much fortified by the pork pie'. (Said pie obviously had a less deleterious effect than the one consumed at Sheffield in 'Dockery & Son'.) In the Jean Cox letter he also apologises for not dancing 'with that old boy', and then intriguingly adds that 'I can't get it into my head that it isn't illegal any more'.

If these letters indicate that Larkin might have read the tenth anniversary special of *Critical Quarterly*, they provide no clues as to which poem might be a Larkinised version of 'Dog Days on the Black Sea' or '?'. *A Concordance to the Poetry of Philip Larkin* might prove helpful to the detection of the copies: if he poached a whole scene or motif, the iteration of at least the odd word might be expected.[43] Only the most abstract or common words from '?' are employed in Larkin's work: 'time' has seventy-four occurrences, 'see' fifty-one, 'second' twelve and 'everything' ten; none of the texts in question appear relevant. As Brian Cox related to me in a private letter, 'Dog Days on the Black Sea' reads as 'very much a Hughes poem'. There are no equivalents in Larkin, as one might expect, for 'space-ditch', 'sombrero' (nothing could be less Larkinesque than the image of him wearing a sombrero in a space-ditch), 'lizards', 'massacre', 'lurch', 'prehistory', 'thunderhead', 'soft-bellied', 'baskers', 'thunder-blue' or 'boomerang'. Nor are there for the perhaps less Hughesian 'perspiration', 'eyebrow', 'slogs', 'burden', 'fleeing' or 'pendulum'.

However, 'beach', 'towels' and 'summer' are an entirely different matter. There are five examples of 'beach': 'Midsummer Night, 1940', 'Lift through the Breaking

---

42 'Dog Days on the Black Sea' and '?', *Critical Quarterly Tenth Anniversary Number*, (spring–summer 1968), pp. 107–8.
43 R. Hildesheim (ed.), *Philip Larkin: a concordance to the poetry of Philip Larkin* (Olms-Weidmann, 1995).

Day', 'Many Famous Feet have Trod', 'Here' and 'To the Sea'; the first three can be discounted, as they were composed too early in Larkin's career. 'Summer' lists five poems: 'To the Sea', 'Cut Grass', 'Going, Going', 'Show Saturday' and 'Bridge for the Living'. 'Towels' has only one listing, as has 'surf': 'To the Sea'. With four 'hits', is it possible that 'To the Sea' can be tentatively identified as a Larkinisation of 'Dog Days on the Black Sea'? If this is the case, it is intriguing that a piece about the Black Sea metamorphoses into a text that epitomises the Englishness some readers detect in Larkin's work. It also uncannily mirrors the way in which the symbol of England, St George, was lifted from his origins in Capadocia, and appropriated for an English ballad, as Hughes recounts, as the son of Lord Albert of Coventry.

'Towels', 'surf', 'summer' and 'beach' are signifiers that one might expect to find in the scenarios depicted by the poets; any similarity between the two pieces may be entirely coincidental. If the Hughes letter does refer to this poem, however, then Larkin subverts his depiction of the beach as a site of primeval activity, and transforms it into an elegiac piece which tentatively celebrates holiday rites. Nevertheless, the poems share similarities: both pit human insufficiency against the natural world. Dog days in the Hughes piece – the hottest days of the year, reckoned in antiquity by the heliacal rising of the Dog Star – render the writer hopeless as he sweats helplessly; in 'To the Sea', the humanist 'we' in Larkin's verse falls 'short' of the 'flawless weather'. However, compensatory activity does then differ. In Larkin's poem, sunbathing on the beach is 'half an annual pleasure, half a rite'.[44] '[R]ite' emphasises the cultural, as much as essential, pleasure, whereas Hughes portrays the process as purely biological, in which the humans creep like helpless lizards towards the beach in an unknowing lament for their fishy ancestors.

In both poems, the writers remain slightly aloof from such shenanigans. Hughes remains in stasis, and yet still manages the Blakean moment in which the famous grain of sand metamorphoses into the 'bead of perspiration' that hangs like the whole world – instead of eternity – 'In the writer's eyebrow'. The poetic 'I' in 'To the Sea' separates the narrator from the mass on the beach in the first three stanzas, but, unlike in 'The Whitsun Weddings', only just, since the poem also recalls the biographical incident in which Larkin's parents met in a shelter whilst on holiday; it also records his foraging for cigarette cards in the sand as a child. '[O]ur' in the final stanza then merges the 'I' and 'they', but only until the next line, where 'these' marks the holidaymakers out as perhaps superior to the poet, since they teach their children on the sand, and look after the elderly. Since 'To the Sea' was based on a holiday enjoyed with his mother, the only way in which Larkin might be displaying a concomitant irony or bitterness here would be if the final word 'ought' contains a pun: 'ort' (or, more usually, 'orts') means refuse; this view of parental obligation would be more in line with that depicted in 'The Old Fools'. In contrast, Hughes sets himself the task of word-chipping before dusk to 'balance' the 'soft-bellied baskers'.

---

44 Larkin, *Collected Poems*, p. 174.

Perhaps the Black Sea location inevitably alienates the Yorkshire poet: the river merges with local fare, as it is 'slow as honey'; it is so hot that the writer can only 'slog' on under his sombrero. In contradistinction, the 'flawless' English weather paradoxically contains its own imperfection: 'Like breathed-on glass / The sunlight has turned milky'. Whereas for Hughes the heat feels like a fever, the seaside for Larkin remains uncannily familiar: the world beyond the low wall appears like an apparition from the past, 'something known long before'. Any sense of the *heimlich* is supported by Larkin's familiar listing technique: the steep beach, blue water, towels, bathing caps. The next list in stanza three undercuts this sense: in an echo of Larkin's surreal, metonymic half-line from 'The Whitsun Weddings' ('and then the perms'), the delicate trebles at the sea's edge are sullied by the half-line, 'and then the cheap cigars', followed by chocolate papers, tea-leaves, rusting soup-tins.[45] None of the items in this list are definitive signs of Englishness, yet, despite the abstract title – 'Sea' rather than 'Prestatyn' – they cohere as a whole to emphasise the particularity of the scene summed up as the 'miniature gaiety of seasides'. For Hughes, any such potential signs of Englishness merely remind the poet of his extreme circumstances: the land is compared to a 'big rose', but rather than place the Black Sea landscape in the context of the familiar English flower, Hughes reminds the reader that it is, like St George, a foreign invader, and was shipped over from Persia only during the medieval period. Even the form of the two pieces emphasises the contrasting landscape: whereas the benign beach is rendered in the tradition of the ode for Larkin, Hughes writes in his characteristic free verse, the stylistics of which may have encouraged Larkin's comment that he was not one iota of good as a writer. Does Larkin ultimately domesticate the text of this supposedly useless poet in 'Dog Days on the Black Sea', replacing barbaric lizards with frilled children to create, in Hughes's words 'one of his best pieces'? The answer is indeterminate: this tentative comparison between the two pieces openly shows that foraging for these Larkinised texts might turn up not cigarette cards in the sand, but red herrings.

---

45 Larkin, *Collected Poems*, p. 115.

7 The love that dares not speak its name: Englishness and suburbia

Vesna Goldsworthy

> It's not their fault they do not know
> The birdsong from the radio,
> It's not their fault they often go
> To Maidenhead
>
> And talk of sport and makes of cars
> In various bogus-Tudor bars
> And daren't look up to see the stars
> But belch instead.
>
> (JOHN BETJEMAN, 'SLOUGH')

Introduction: what, if not cricket?

In the early 1980s I moved from Yugoslavia, a federal state which no longer exists, to the United Kingdom, a union which still holds together. Having grown up in a country which comprised a mosaic of nationalities and in which only 10 per cent of the people, some two million, claimed Yugoslav identity, I'd developed a heightened awareness of the complexities of national identification. My acquisition of dual citizenship of two such states opened up a broad range of possible definitions of my own nationality. From one census to the next, from one equal opportunities form to another, I have difficulties in remembering how I described myself last time. 'Hyphenated' identities may increasingly be the norm, but my description seems to warrant a trio or even a quartet of hyphens. I am Serbian, but I am also Montenegrin and Herzegovinian, and I have become so thoroughly 'Anglicised' that I dream in English most of the time.

Should I describe myself as an Anglo-Montenegrin-Herzegovinian-Serb, a Serbo-Herzegovinian-Montenegrin-Englishwoman, or should I just adhere to the 'British-Yugoslav' tag for the sake of simplicity, even if the bloody break-up of the Yugoslav federation in the 1990s has rendered my Yugoslav identity meaningless, and my Britishness is in fact almost entirely English? Or should I – and this seems the most practical solution, although the census forms do not recognise it – simply say that I am a Londoner? Regardless of the number of hyphens I choose, there are so many like me in London. In fact, if one adhered to old-fashioned notions of Englishness, England's capital is in many ways already only tentatively English. It is certainly the European city which is closest to the vision of a post-national age.

I've lost count of the number of times I've been told that I would one day be British but never English. From personal experience, therefore, it would appear that one *becomes* British but one can only be *born* English. Britishness follows the principle of residence and territory, the *ius soli*, whereas Englishness is conferred by parentage and blood – *ius sanguinis* – irrespective of whether one grows up in Buenos Aires, Bombay or Brighton.[1] Britishness, like American, Canadian, Yugoslav or Spanish identities, is based on the civic idea of nationality, and characterised by inclusion. It can, in theory, be acquired by anyone who resides in the country for a set number of years. It is still the nationality inscribed in our passports. Englishness – like Serbianness or Castilianness – is based on ethnicity and descent, and therefore tends to be seen as exclusive. It is defined in terms of genetic inheritance and ultimately race. Only 'true-born Englishmen' are seen as really English.

In practice, this means that immigrants continue to be reluctant to describe themselves as English (or Scottish or Welsh, for that matter), even if their experience of any part of the United Kingdom other than the one they reside in may be negligible. A foreign name, a foreign accent, different skin colour, all seem to imply 'hyphenated' Britishness. However, life in this country often shapes immigrant identities in ways which render that Britishness relatively abstract. In so far as I have *become* anything, I've become an Englishwoman, without necessarily losing my Southern Slav identity. I've visited other parts of the United Kingdom (except Northern Ireland – a trait I share with many English people) and my interest in their affairs is comparable to that of an English person. In fact, if nationality were to be judged according to the terms of the Conservative politician Norman Tebbit's 'cricket test' (that is by the loyalty to a particular national team) as set out nearly fourteen years ago, and if I could understand the laws of cricket, I would have no reason to support any other country over England. Conveniently, given that they don't play cricket where I come from, I would pass the Tebbit test of Englishness with flying colours. Passing that test, however, would not erase my hyphens, nor would I want them erased. If not cricket, what makes one person English and another a British-Yugoslav?

If English descent and parentage were all that mattered, the *revisions* of this book's title would be largely meaningless. It would have been more appropriate to invite contributions from geneticists rather than English literature scholars such as me who tend to believe, with Benedict Anderson, that nationality is primarily a matter of imagined communities.[2] Against the backdrop of devolution and large-scale immigration in this country, however, it seems that the notions of Englishness are slowly expanding, from embracing those 'ethnically' English to accommodating a variety of 'others' who claim England as their home, whatever their parents' nation-

---

1 For a discussion of different definitions of nationality and nationalism, see Philip Spencer and Howard Wollman, *Nationalism: a critical introduction* (London: Sage, 2002).
2 Benedict Anderson discusses the nation as a construct in *Imagined Communities: reflections on the origins and spread of nationalism*, rev. edn (London: Verso, 1991).

ality. In a reflection of that shift, Labour MP Barbara Roche recently pointed out that her own school in East London once 'used to teach little Jews how to be English and now teaches little English boys and girls how to be Jewish'.[3] At the same time, as the Union devolves, fewer and fewer of us find the idea of Britishness sufficiently mean-ingful when the last repositories of British identity seem to be immigrant communi-ties and the monarchy itself of sturdy immigrant stock.

I've seen similar realignments in my former homeland, even if they may have happened more abruptly and sometimes at the point of a gun. Some two million Yugoslavs of all persuasions 'chose' narrower identities in the early 1990s. They became Croats, Serbs, Bosniaks, etc., according to the place of residence, religious affiliation, favourite parent, the sound of their surname or the location of the refugee camp they happened to end up in. Only ten years after its break-up, Yugoslavia seems more fictitious as a country than it ever appeared to be in the eighty-odd years of its existence. It is conceivable that a process of adjustment to devolution, albeit entirely peaceful, will in a similar way drain Britishness of any residual meaning.

In his book *Nations and Nationalism*, Ernest Gellner offers the following, and very masculine, provisional definitions of nationality: cultural, in which 'two men are of the same nation if and only if they share the same culture'; and voluntaristic, in which 'two men are of the same nation if and only if they *recognize each other* as belonging to the same culture'.[4] My putative Englishness might be questionable not so much under the former as under the latter definition. Simply claiming that I have become English rather than British does not mean that I will be 'recognised' as such if the dominant perceptions of Englishness are ethnic and not civic.

If, according to the 2001 census, England accounts for 83.6 per cent of the total population of Britain, it is also home to by far the largest proportion of immi-grants who have settled in this country. According to the same census, 9 per cent of the total population of England is non-white – with almost half of those living in London – compared to only 2 per cent in Scotland and Wales and less than 1 per cent in Northern Ireland. The think tank Migration Watch UK, which is sceptical about the benefits of immigration, claims that three-quarters of all immigrants to Britain in fact remain in the south-east of England.[5] Nevertheless, immigrant communities continue to be shy about asserting their Englishness. According to the Office of National Statistics, two-thirds (67 per cent) of all Bangladeshis living in this country say that they are British and only 6 per cent define themselves as English, Scottish, Welsh or Irish.[6] The statistics for other immigrant communities

3 Barbara Roche was speaking in favour of the motion 'Britain needs more immigrants' at the *Intelligence Squared* debate, Royal Geographical Society, London, 22 Jan. 2004.
4 Ernest Gellner, *Nations and Nationalism* (Ithaca: Cornell University Press, 1983), pp. 6–7 (emphasis added).
5 www.migrationwatchUK.org (accessed, 26 Jan. 2004).
6 John Carvel, 'Tebbit's Cricket Loyalty Test Hit for Six', *Guardian* (9 Jan. 2004), p. 6.

are similar: they are a result of habit and cultural conditioning, rather than a preference for Britishness over Englishness.

Yet, such conditioning neglects the fact that Englishness itself is nothing if not hybrid. As Daniel Defoe observed in 1701, in *The True-Born Englishman: a satyr*, 'A true-born Englishman's a contradiction: / In speech an irony, in fact a fiction.' Like any other national identity, Englishness has always implied a range of disparate cultural elements and groupings:

> Thus from a mixture of all kinds began
> That het'rogeneous thing, an Englishman:
> In eager rapes, and furious lust begot,
> Betwixt a painted Britain and a Scot.[7]

Englishness, hybridity and the city

In an echo of common patterns of settlement and assimilation in this country, my own sense of belonging has been shaped by London. Initially, I based myself in the capital not only because it offered better job opportunities, but also because it seemed to provide a sheltered habitat for someone who did not wish to be a visible (or, in my case, audible) other, 'a stranger in a strange land'.[8] As those familiar with the themes of nineteenth-century gothic fiction will know, the hidden, invisible stranger is often perceived to be the ultimate threat to the native inhabitant: the seducer and the enemy at the same time. However, the 'visibly alien' is just as often seen as a lonely, melancholy creature, 'uprooted' from the native soil and 'out of place'.

If nothing else, London provides that indifference which – in Julia Kristeva's terms – 'is the carapace of the stranger'.[9] Like other global megalopolises, this city is both of its country and no one's. I have a connection to the rest of the country through my marriage and my work, but many of my fellow immigrants lead happy lives within the confines of the M25, the orbital motorway and the 'conceptual haha' which marks 'the boundary of whatever can be called London'.[10] They do not venture much further than the nearest airport and do not need to speak English for days on end. Does that necessarily imply that they are not English?

It is often said that 'London is not England'. Indeed, I've met people who have lived in London for many years while maintaining a vague, quasi-mythical set of notions about what English people 'typically do', like a Croatian friend of mine who pushed away a piece of suet pudding with as much distaste as could be

---

7 Daniel Defoe, *The True-Born Englishman: a satyr* (London, 1701). Quoted from: http://eir.library. utoronto.ca/rpo/display/poem627.html (accessed 24 Jan. 2004).
8 Exodus 2:22.
9 Julia Kristeva, *Étrangers à nous-mêmes* (Paris: Gallimard, 1988), p. 17 (my translation).
10 Iain Sinclair, *London Orbital: a walk around the M25* (London and New York: Granta, 2002), p. 3.

summoned by waving a fork, having just discovered after a decade in this country that the English 'make cakes with beef fat'. Paradoxically, however, if we adopt the cultural definition of nationality, my friend is certainly much more English than Croatian. She has an MA from an English university, has worked for an English employer for many years, is an avid follower of English celebrity gossip, sees every play and film Alan Rickman and Jeremy Irons ever appear in, can tell you all there is to know about the comparative virtues of individual supermarket chains and has spent many a happy Sunday immersed in DIY. These are but a few ways in which she embraces English culture, and some of them would baffle the average Croatian.

However, it is through the very act of claiming London for herself – by living, working and socialising in its centre – that my friend, together with many other immigrants, has so far conspicuously refused to share one of the most important traits of Englishness. It is the ideal of country life. In fact, recent immigrants often dwell in an inner city which has been abandoned by the 'aboriginal' English inhabitants in pursuit of a rural dream. They do so sometimes by default – because of poverty – but often by choice, having arrived in this country with a system of values which rates city-centre living over rural and suburban lifestyles. In London, the French 'colony' in South Kensington and the Arab-inhabited streets of Bayswater are notable examples of choice rather than necessity. Immigrants often feel highly conspicuous in the countryside which they perceive as 'white' and alien, and visit it so rarely that the Department for Environment, Food and Rural Affairs has just instructed the Countryside Agency to investigate how to boost the number of people from the ethnic minorities who visit rural Britain.[11]

It is the ideal of country living, like perhaps no other aspect of Englishness, which separates the English both from other Europeans, and from England's immigrant communities. In practice, however, the rural ideal gives way to the more viable suburban reality. So, paradoxically, the very English desire to affect the ways of living in the country without actually working the land, coupled with the high population density, has led to large-scale suburbanisation which now represents the most familiar feature of the English portion of the 'scepter'd Isle'. This is particularly the case with the South-East which increasingly resembles, to borrow Deyan Sudjic's phrase, 'the hundred-mile city'.[12]

The lament for the disappearing countryside, as expressed, for example, in Philip Larkin's poem 'Going, Going' ('I thought it would last my time – / The sense that, beyond the town, / There would always be fields and farms'), is a frequent theme both in English writing and in political life.[13] Greater anxieties about the countryside distinguish England from Scotland, Wales and Northern Ireland. Indeed, such is the emotional hold the countryside exerts that proposals for meas-

11   Raekha Prasad, 'Countryside Retreat', *Guardian*, Society (28 Jan. 2004), pp. 2–3.
12   Deyan Sudjic, *The 100 Mile City* (New York: Harcourt, 1993).
13   Philip Larkin, *Collected Poems* (London: Faber, 1988), p. 189.

ures to protect what remains of 'nature' rarely meet anything but a cross-party consensus.

With the population density of 378 per square mile (425 in the South-East), compared to 227 in Germany and 105 in France, and with so many people whose main lifestyle-ideal seems to be the ownership of a piece of garden, it is hardly surprising that suburbia represents the most typical face of the English land-scape.[14] It is in many ways paradoxical that right-wing politicians tend to blame immigration for the overcrowding and hence suburbanisation of England, when immigrants represent just about the only large group in this society prepared to enjoy family life in urban centres and in high-rise dwellings.

Idealised representations of England have traditionally been shaped by the countryside, from Shakespeare's 'other Eden, demi-paradise', Blake's 'green and pleasant land' and Housman's 'blue remembered hills', to the paintings of Constable and Gainsborough, and everything that the country house and the country church have come to stand for.[15] (Is there a poem more 'English' than Thomas Gray's 'An Elegy Written in a Country Church-Yard'?) When asked to point out the most beautiful parts of their city, English people often single out particular 'villages' within it. Similarly, England's writers and painters have often portrayed the urban landscape as curiously pastoral and rural, as though – with the brief modernist interlude as the most notable exception – they have never quite come to terms with the beauty of the man-made cityscape.

Some of the most famous descriptions of London, such as William Wordsworth's sonnet 'Upon Westminster Bridge' (1802), offer evidence of the way in which rural ideals of beauty are superimposed on the cityscape. London is represented as silent and smokeless, a city opening 'unto the fields':

> The City now doth like a garment wear
> The beauty of the morning; silent, bare,
> Ships, towers, domes, theatres, and temples lie
> Open unto the fields, and to the sky;
> All bright and glittering in the smokeless air.[16]

Since at least the Industrial Revolution, when the middle classes began to expect their own piece of the countryside as a birthright, the very English Wordsworthian dream of a silent city which opens 'unto the fields' has resulted in waves of suburban development. England may no longer be a 'nation of

---

14 Source: www.migrationwatchUK.org (accessed 24 Jan. 2004).

15 I cite some of the most famous rhetorical evocations of idealised England, from Shakespeare's *Richard II* ('This England' speech in Act 2 Scene 1), Blake's 'Jerusalem' (1820) and Housman's *A Shropshire Lad* (1896), XL. Paradoxically, the 'This England' speech and 'Jerusalem' also contain much darker images of England. Housman's poem, written in near-exile in London, evokes the lost world of childhood innocence through remembered landscape.

16 Thomas Hutchison (ed.), *The Poetical Works of William Wordsworth* (Oxford: Oxford University Press, 1917), p. 269.

shop-keepers', but – with recent surveys showing that only 4 per cent of us would choose to live in the city centre – it has become a nation of suburbanites. An apparently reluctant 'suburbanness' born out of the love for the countryside which has, since the days of the Romantics at least, exercised such a tight hold over the English imagination, is in many ways a *differentia specifica* of Englishness. Oscar Wilde's poetic suggestion that 'each man kills the thing he loves' would certainly hold true in relation to the open country, which is shrinking much faster in England than anywhere else in Europe, in spite – or very likely because – of being the subject of such adulation. In the demise of the countryside, Philip Larkin sees the death of England:

> And that will be England gone,
> The shadows, the meadows, the lanes,
> The guildhalls, the carved choirs.
> There'll be books; it will linger on
> In galleries; but all that remains
> For us will be concrete and tyres.[17]

The guilty secret: Englishness and suburbia

Just what is it about the idea of suburbia in England that makes the choice of suburban life 'the love that dares not speak its name'? We profess to hate the suburbs but we want our gardens secluded, our parking off-street and our shops and post offices close by – but not to the point of living above them. When it comes to choosing a home, most of us have traditionally found Clifton, Edgbaston and Ealing preferable to the centres of their respective cities. Over the past two centuries at least, we have enjoyed nothing so much as discussing the Hogarthian depravities of inner London from a safe distance in Middlesex or Surrey. Moreover, this is a way of life which the 'mother country' seems to have passed on to the English-speaking world as a whole, from the 'hundred-mile', polynucleal cities of North America to the quarter-acre plots of Sydney and Melbourne. The vast majority of English-speaking people continue to find individual homes with a garden more appealing than flats in the city centre, in spite of the fundamental unsustainability of this type of development. As Swiss urban historian André Corboz has suggested, 'the ideal of the individual home is both quintessentially petit-bourgeois and excessively expensive to service'.[18]

While urban planners do their best to promote a range of lifestyle choices, and the media devote disproportionate amounts of space to trendy urbanites in minimalist warehouse apartments, most English people continue to choose very

17 Larkin, *Collected Poems*, p. 190.
18 André Corboz, *Looking for a City in America: down these mean streets a man must go* (Los Angeles: Getty Center for the Humanities, 1992), p. 14.

traditional housing either in the suburbs themselves or in the many quasi-sub-
urban areas which are becoming the dominant models of both town and country
living. The aspiration to own a house you can walk around, embodied in the
notion that 'an Englishman's home is his castle' is particularly problematic in the
south of England, which – according to government data – will need one million
new homes in the coming decades to accommodate population growth. How
much easier to build one million flats than one million houses each with its own
minute piece of land, but for the fact that so few people in England (other than
recent immigrants, of course) see flats as suitable long-term – and certainly family
– accommodation.

At the same time, and in the face of a wholesale flight to suburbia, books, films
and media in general tend to represent the suburb as a place one escapes from
rather than to. Patronising the suburbanite seems acceptable even in these politically correct days. Phrases such as 'suburban values' or 'suburban lifestyles'
continue to sound at best like a joke and at worst a reactionary conceit. However,
while the suburbs are culturally derided, in politics – where demographic choices
impact more directly – they are often flattered and pandered to just as uncritically.
In an era in which suburban focus groups determine political priorities, the
gnomes of Esher are definitely much more important than Harold Wilson's
'gnomes of Zurich'. We are all suburban now, our successive prime ministers seem
to say.

With her Finchley constituency and her purchase of a never-lived-in Barratt
home in Dulwich, Margaret Thatcher was hardly alone among recent leaders in
affecting an espousal of the lifestyle choices of the suburbanite majority who hide
behind the name of Middle England (never Middle Britain). Their patron saint,
surely, was Thatcher's successor John Major, a leader vanquished by the invincible
green suburbs of which he so lovingly spoke. John Major chose a curiously
protean self-image, in what David Gilbert and Rebecca Preston describe as a
'double myth of origin', trying to be both the inner-city Brixton boy and the
Honest John of the 'deep suburban heartlands of South West London'.[19] John
Major's suburbs looked not so much to the city centre as towards the Ruritanian
country shires. 'Fifty years from now', he told fellow Conservatives in 1993, 'Britain
will still be the country of long shadows on county grounds, warm beer, invincible
green suburbs, dog lovers and pools fillers and – as George Orwell said – "old
maids bicycling to holy communion through the morning mist"'.[20]

John Major epitomised safe, middle-of-the road choices which are so often
seen as the essence of suburbanness; an image which his reactions to revelations of

19 David Gilbert and Rebecca Preston, 'From Margo and Tom to Margaret and John (and Tony too):
    suburban rhetoric and imagery in late-twentieth century British politics', paper delivered at the
    'Good Life' conference, Centre for Suburban Studies, Kingston University, Sept. 2004.
20 Quoted from 'Huntingdon's Invincible Green Shadows', at: http://news.bbc.co.uk/vote2001/
    hi/english/features/newsid_1362000/1362285.stm.

his extra-marital affair have only reinforced. Tony Blair and Cherie Booth (she perhaps more than him) may project themselves as Islington urbanites, but although they are – unusually for a prosperous family – bringing up their children in an inner-city flat, their consumer choices, from the toy-strewn magnolia interiors to the people carrier, seem designed to appeal to the suburban majority.

How can it be otherwise, when so many of their voters live in the necklaces of neo-Georgian and neo-Victorian developments which garland the wide commuter belt around London? These dwellings offer telling evidence of the suburban preference, not for the open country, but for the *rus in urbe*. They combine a pastiche of the countryside away from the unpleasant aspects of country dwelling, and a pastiche of a historic house without the discomforts of old buildings. Built in an architectural vernacular which is often an expression of the lowest common aesthetic denominator, they offer housing designed primarily to be inoffensive.

Much of the new building in England represents the architectural equivalent of the national preference for magnolia wall-paint. Countless interior decoration programmes on British television might lead one to a conclusion that we are developing more adventurous tastes, but the buying team at B&Q confirms that magnolia continues to outsell any other colour. When it comes to architecture, our preferences remain similarly bland and vaguely Oedipal. The houses the English most want are like the ones their fathers built. The towns they desire are villages. Even in the heart of the inner city, gated communities of 'suburban-style' villas often express a nostalgic longing for a prelapsarian country idyll rather than any easy urbanity. In fact, although geographically in the city centre, they speak eloquently of a nation uncomfortable with whatever urban life is supposed to represent. I often wonder how boring the working day must be for all those dozens of architects commissioned to devise an endless variation on the themes of pastoral Arcadia or historical pastiche – the 'Meadow Views' without meadows and 'King's Closes' without kings – which are the feature of so much new building in this country.

According to research published in August 2003 by the Royal Institution of Chartered Surveyors, 77 per cent of British people would never want to live in a flat, and almost half of these claim that absolutely nothing would make them change their mind. An equal proportion (77 per cent) of new property-buyers in England would prefer to live on non-through roads.[21] We don't seem to like our cities very much but we are apparently not quite ready to acknowledge our love affair with the suburbs. We continue to move to them *en masse* but react badly to being called suburban, preferring instead to pretend that it is a piece of the countryside we are after. In this respect, as Gail Cunningham writes in 'The Riddle of Suburbia', little has changed since 1782 when William Cowper wrote:

---

21 Popular Housing Forum data, cited at: http://www.odpm.gov.uk/stellent/groups/odpm_planning/documents/page/odpm_plan_606194-05.hcsp.

Suburban villas, highwayside retreats,
That dread encroachment of our growing streets,
Tight boxes, neatly sashed and in a blaze,
With all the July's sun collected rays,
Delight the citizen, who, gasping there,
Breathes clouds of dust and calls it country air.[10]

Given the emotional investment which, at least since the days of the Romantics, has gone into the worship of ever shrinking areas of countryside, few of us seem ready to face the fact that we love the suburbs exactly for what they are. Many of the contemporary commentators who most snobbishly decry English 'suburbanness' do so in the spirit of middle-class self-loathing, speaking from their own piece of yesterday's leafy suburbs on the edge of the genteel heaths of Hampstead, Richmond and Wimbledon, or atop fashionable London 'Hills' such as Primrose or Notting. As one *Guardian* columnist recently pointed out, all sorts of politically incorrect feelings can be conveniently hidden by the notion of 'leafiness'. In politics, 'green' very often stands for 'white'.

In fact, there is little meaningful debate about contemporary suburbia and the implications of our suburban lifestyle choices. The dominant cultural images of suburban life are largely negative and outdated. Epitomised by the white, heterosexual Surbiton of the BBC's *Good Life* (1975), the mind-numbing routine of commuter existence in *The Fall and Rise of Reginald Perrin* (1976), or the cringe-making, claustrophobic version of the suburban soirée imprinted in the collective memory by Mike Leigh's wonderful and unbearable *Abigail's Party* (1977), the suburbs of our imagination seem forever stuck in the 1970s. Many of these depictions of white, middle-class English suburbia evince self-loathing and are patronising about the aspirations they depict. They represent the suburbs as prison-houses of freedom and imagination. From Mr and Mrs Pooter of *The Diary of a Nobody* (1892), to Beverly and Laurence of *Abigail's Party*, there is a long cultural tradition of exposing the suburban dwellers as boring, pretentious, uncreative and frustrated.

It is in itself a very middle-class idea that suburban pleasure somehow contradicts artistic creativity and intellectual achievement. For every happily suburban J. G. Ballard there are dozens of writers who seem to believe that the muses do not visit suburban postcodes. In that most bourgeois of films, *The Hours* (2002), Virginia Woolf's line 'If the choice is between Richmond and death, I choose death' inspired a considerable number of column inches in metropolitan newspapers.[23] The debate focused mainly on whether or not Richmond could be considered suburban. Woolf's choice seemed to touch a raw nerve among the media

---

22 Quoted from Gail Cunningham, 'The Riddle of Suburbia: suburban fictions at the Victorian *fin de siècle*' in *Expanding Suburbia: reviewing suburban narratives*, ed. Roger Webster (New York and Oxford: Berghahn Books, 2000), pp. 51–70.
23 Adapted from Michael Cunningham's novel, *The Hours* (1998; London: Fourth Estate, 1999).

pundits who, in the same situation, opt to reside in Richmond in preference to Bloomsbury every time. One wonders whether the film's scriptwriter, the playwright David Hare, himself a resident of London's 'leafy' inner suburb of Hampstead, was aware of the irony.

The Hours is a celebration of urbanity whose heroines struggle to escape the 'living anaesthetic of suburbia' at enormous personal cost. The film and the novel seem to argue – against all statistical evidence – that no woman would actually choose suburban life, even if it offered the best chance of a room of one's own. Virginia Woolf's *Mrs Dalloway* (1924), the novel which inspired *The Hours*, represents one of the high marks of the modernist movement, a celebration of London which effectively covers a few square miles around Bond Street and Regent's Park. This narrative of female *flânerie* was a very English response to the masculine celebration of Dublin in James Joyce's *Ulysses* (1922). Both novels richly exemplify high urbanism, as well as one of the conflicts which produced modernism, identified by John Carey in *The Intellectuals and the Masses* (1992) as the tension between an intellectual elite and the recently educated masses.

The modernist movement celebrated the urban and man-made just as much as romanticism looked for unspoilt nature in its sublime majesty. The two worldviews they represented continue to coexist alongside each other in the public debate. In this country, the romantics easily outnumber the modernists, even if the latter tend to be, on balance, a bit louder. Seen as multiply marginal, suburbia has few public supporters.

Indeed, some of the best-known 'suburban' works, such as John Betjeman's poem 'Slough' (1937) – 'Come friendly bombs and fall on Slough! / It isn't fit for humans now, / There isn't grass to graze a cow' – seem to call for a wholesale destruction of the suburbs.[24] Despite christening many suburban architectural styles, in 1939 Osbert Lancaster noted on a walk through 'bypass variegated suburbs', that 'the anticipation of their obliteration is an eventuality that does much to reconcile one with the prospect of aerial bombardment'.[25] Such 'unashamedly elitist' pronouncements on matters suburban are quoted as evidence of their authors' sense of humour, in spite of the realities of the aerial bombardment which followed so soon after these works were first published.

Far from being prisons of creativity, the original garden suburbs of London – places like Bedford Park and Hampstead Garden Suburb – were in fact its hothouses. They provided models for a particular type of suburban development which was fitfully emulated throughout Europe as well as in the Anglophone 'New World'. I grew up in a suburb of Belgrade which was a distinct descendant of William Morris's vision of *rus in urbe*, and in which 'English villas' were surrounded by 'English lawns' in a version of Euro-Edwardiana apparently satisfied

24 John Betjeman, 'Slough' in *The Best of Betjeman*, Selected by John Guest (London: Penguin, 1978), p. 24.
25 Osbert Lancaster, *Homes, Sweet Homes* (London: John Murray, 1939), p. 24.

by the belief that the best possible (sub)urban lifestyle was that devised by London builders on the eve of the First World War.

The Continentals, however, have perhaps always been too fond of city-centre living to adopt the English model as anything other than an experiment, an exception to the aspirational rule. The European cities have tended to retain a footprint which is the reverse of London's. In Paris, for example, the suburbs are by and large seen as undesirable. Bourgeois apartments cluster in central *arrondissements* while the modernist Corbusian *cités* of the poor occupy the suburban space beyond the *Périphérique*. Even the word 'suburban' does not seem fully translatable into European languages. The French *banlieu* or German *Vorort* suggest topography rather than insults. Few translations of 'suburban' can quite convey the condescension with which one might use the label in British English.

In spite (or perhaps because) of the wholesale flight to the suburbs, suburbia continues to occupy an ambiguous space in our public discourse. Writers and commentators – most of whom tend to project themselves either as urban sophisticates or wholesome country-lovers – tend to use the language of gothic fiction to describe the suburbs which the majority of their readers, and often they themselves, inhabit. The suburbs sprawl and devour. They are uncontrollable, aggressive mutants which spread like cancer tissue. They destroy the heart of the city by their siren calls and the countryside by obliterating it. To accept the suburban choice as a true preference of the majority of English people seems to be very difficult indeed.

8 'Dying of England': melancholic Englishness in Adam Thorpe's *Still*

Ingrid Gunby

When Adam Thorpe's first novel, *Ulverton*, was published in 1992, reviewers greeted it as 'the most interesting first novel I have read these last years', 'one of the finest novels to have come out of England in a long time', even 'a masterpiece'.[1] Expectations of Thorpe's second novel were, accordingly, high, and the disappointed bemusement when it appeared was considerable. *Still* (1995), it seemed, abandoned sensuous concreteness for a deadly load of literary and cinematic allusion, and a multitude of voices ranging across 350 years for just one: that of Ricky Thornby, failed English film director and 'the worst imaginable kind of bore'.[2] What, reviewers wanted to know, could Thorpe have been thinking? Could this dangerous flirtation with artistic failure and the reader's boredom threshold possibly have been intentional? And what connections might there be between *Still* and *Ulverton*?

With the subsequent publication of three more novels, another collection of poetry and one of short stories, however, continuities have become more obvious. The legacies of colonialism and war, the partial histories conveyed in fractured, even pathological, narratives, and the vitality – or otherwise – of modernism in late-twentieth- and early-twenty-first-century culture have emerged as key preoccupations in his work. Just as significant, however, is its complex and conflicted engagement with forms of twentieth-century Englishness. Having begun, in the anti-pastoral of *Ulverton*, by reworking that dominant site of English cultural memory, the South Country, to reveal the violence and loss on which it is founded, Thorpe provides in *Still* an anatomy of a late-twentieth-century Englishness constructed around a melancholic attachment to the 'Edwardian summer' and the fate of the Great War's 'doomed youth'.[3]

Still purports to be the life's masterwork of the twice-married expatriate Thornby, who in the course of the novel is dumped by his girlfriend and 'retired

---

1 John Fowles, 'Thank the Gods for Bloody Mindedness', *Guardian* (28 May 1992), p. 25; John Banville, 'Big News from Small Worlds', *New York Review of Books* (8 Apr. 1993), pp. 22–4 (p. 24); Peter Kemp, 'A Hamlet's Ghosts', *Sunday Times* (10 May 1992), Section 7, p. 4.

2 Derwent May, 'And Thus Spake on that Ancient Film Buff', *The Times* (27 Apr. 1995), p. 35.

3 Wilfred Owen, 'Anthem for Doomed Youth', in *The Complete Poems and Fragments*, ed. Jon Stallworthy (London: Chatto &Windus, Hogarth and Oxford University Press, 1983), vol. 1: *The Poems*, p. 99. On *Ulverton* and the South Country, see my 'History in Rags: Adam Thorpe's reworking of England's national past', *Contemporary Literature*, 44:1 (2003), pp. 46–72.

early without honours' from his job teaching European Cinema in Houston to
students who write with their tongues sticking out. The film consists entirely of
text that will be exhibited at his Thames-side sixtieth birthday party as the new
millennium dawns.[4] Its subject, ostensibly, is the lives of Ricky's grandparents,
great-aunt and great-uncle between 1913 and 1918, the period when, having
started out with such promise, the twentieth century went wrong. But as the novel
goes on ('progresses' might be too strong a word), it becomes increasingly clear
that this film is playing only in 'the Enfield Ritz or maybe ... the Biograph mat-
inée of [Ricky's] skull' (p. 77). Furthermore, the text is disrupted by the intrusion
of Ricky's own life in the present of the 'film's' composition, and indeed by his
own reluctance, or inability, to get to the point. The result is a work of rampant
prolixity and incompletion that left Tom Shippey, reviewing the book for the
Times Literary Supplement, wondering about the 'incurable inferiority complex'
that afflicts 'so many characters of the English novel from Powell to Williamson'
(surely not a very comprehensive range). 'Why', he asked,

should a clever, tricky writer like the author of *Ulverton* spend so much time imagining
such a dreary, introspective whinger as Thornby? There has to be a reason for it: something
that haunts the English psyche still and makes its victims at once so arrogant and so inse-
cure. An answer, I have no doubt, is buried somewhere in the 584 pages, though there is
something characteristic in Thornby's final cry, 'You missed it'.[5]

Something characteristic indeed. Ricky and his career could have been conceived
as a lengthy illustration of Pauline Kael's contention, made in 1968, that 'the
English can write and they can act (or at least *speak* beautifully ...), but they can't
direct movies. ... Compared with the motion picture art of Sweden or Italy or
Japan or France or pre-Nazi Germany, English films have always been a sad joke'.[6]
Riven by his insecurities, his desire for and fear of England, his anxieties about
class – as an Enfield boy, Ricky certainly does not 'speak beautifully', in Kael's terms
– his admiration for the great European directors, and his loathing of America,
Ricky's masterwork *is* something of a 'sad joke'. More dangerously, *Still* itself
invites a similar dismissal, although a few, including Nicola Barker, found Ricky
'wild and woozy and hilarious'.[7] Ricky's style of anxious wit is not a universal taste,
and Thorpe never quite manages to establish a critical perspective on his narrator's ramblings. But despite the fact that one suspects Ricky's reading of England's
twentieth century is, substantially, Thorpe's, the novel offers an intriguing study of
artistic failure as the marker of a thoroughly melancholic relationship to history:

4 Adam Thorpe, *Still* (London: Secker & Warburg, 1995), pp. 15, 49. Further references will be given
   in parentheses in the text.
5 Tom Shippey, 'English Accents', *Times Literary Supplement* (21 Apr. 1995), p. 21.
6 In Lez Cooke, 'British Cinema: Class, Culture and Consensus, 1930–55' in *Literature and Culture in
   Modern Britain,* vol. 2: *1930–1955,* ed. Gary Day (London: Longman, 1997), pp. 163–90 (p. 164).
7 Nicola Barker, 'Speeding with Ricky', *Observer* (23 Apr. 1995), Review Section, p. 16.

of a late-twentieth-century Englishness unable to confront its relationship to its past, even at the cost of consigning itself to death.

In exploring *Still*'s Englishness as a melancholic formation I am, up to a point, following a path mapped out by other recent literary and social critics. Ian Baucom is amongst the most explicit of these, arguing that 'the melancholy discourses of nostalgia' have been crucial to constructions of Englishness over the past 300 years, and that, given the persistence of this attitude and indeed its intensification after the end of empire, we might conclude that to be English is 'to be a member of a cult of the dead, or, at the very least, a member of a cult of ruin'.[8] My reading of *Still*, however, depends on two qualifications of this analysis of Englishness. In the first place, it seems to be important both to allow room, in discussions of melancholia and nostalgia, for a distinction between, as Geoffrey Hill has put it, being nostalgic and 'trying to draw the graph of nostalgia', and also to acknowledge that a text may do both.[9] Literary explorations of nostalgia and melancholia inevitably risk reproducing or reinforcing these attitudes, but may also, and simultaneously, manage a critical engagement with them. This first caveat is underpinned by my second, which is to note that more recent thinking on 'healthy' mourning and melancholia suggests that the two are not as easily distinguished as Freud's original paper on the subject – the basis of Baucom's reading, for example – would like to argue. All mourning, it is suggested, involves a degree of ambivalence and of narcissistic identification with the lost person or object – characteristics, according to Freud, of melancholia – and mourning rarely ends with the clean severance of all affective ties to what has been lost. Consequently, all mourning has aspects of the melancholic, and rather than seeing it as, ideally, a methodical cutting of ties to the lost object, we might instead talk of a process of weaving the threads of connection into a new pattern – though not without a good deal of repetitive, and ambivalent, unweaving and reweaving on the way.[10]

---

8 Ian Baucom, *Out of Place: Englishness, Empire, and the locations of identity* (Princeton: Princeton University Press, 1999), p. 175. David Gervais has gone so far as to ask whether, without nostalgia, there would be any literary versions of England at all (*Literary Englands: versions of 'Englishness' in modern writing* (Cambridge: Cambridge University Press, 1993), p. 4). For other representative discussions of English nostalgia, see Antony Easthope, *Englishness and National Culture* (London: Routledge, 1999); Robert Hewison, *The Heritage Industry: Britain in a climate of decline* (London: Methuen, 1987); Martin J. Wiener, *English Culture and the Decline of the Industrial Spirit, 1850–1980* (Cambridge: Cambridge University Press, 1981); and Patrick Wright, *On Living in an Old Country: the national past in contemporary Britain* (London: Verso, 1985). Although Hewison's and Wright's titles refer to Britain, it is really the English 'national past' with which they are concerned.

9 Cited in Raphaël Ingelbien, *Misreading England: poetry and nationhood since the Second World War* (Amsterdam: Rodopi, 2002), p. 67.

10 See Sigmund Freud, 'Mourning and Melancholia' in *The Standard Edition of the Complete Psychological Works of Sigmund Freud*, ed. and trans. James Strachey, 24 vols (London: Hogarth Press and Institute of Psychoanalysis, 1953–74), vol. 24 (1957), pp. 237–60; and Jean Laplanche, 'Time and the Other', trans. Luke Thurston, in Laplanche, *Essays on Otherness* (London: Routledge, 1999), pp. 234–59.

Interestingly, these recent re-examinations of mourning have emphasised the connections between mourning and creativity, suggesting that successful mourning involves the creation of 'something – whether it be a memory, a dream, a story, a poem, a response to a poem – that begins to meet, to be equal to, the full complexity of our relationship to what has been lost and to the experience of loss itself'.[11] Here we seem to be approaching the territory explored by Peter Brooks in his formulation of a psychoanalytic theory of narrative as a process of working through or binding the disruptive or painful energies that stimulate the desire for narration in the first place: desire, we might recall, being a response to a sense of loss or lack. What narrative provides, Brooks argues, is a 'space of retard, postponement, error, and partial revelation', where repetition, and 'vacillation between illumination and blindness', enable that working-through to take place, and a reconciliation with the death that is the end of narrative to be reached at the proper time.[12] The problematisation, or even collapse, of plot in a novel such as *Still* corresponds, on this analysis, to an unwillingness or inability to work through the loss or lack impelling the narrative – a response to the loss that is more strongly melancholic than that of the classic nineteenth-century fiction on which Brooks's discussion is focused.

Like Naipaul's *The Enigma of Arrival* (1987) – Baucom's case study of Englishness, nostalgia and melancholia – Thorpe's work has its melancholic aspects, not only in *Ulverton*'s evocation of a rural landscape under threat, for example, or *Pieces of Light*'s longing for a lost West African childhood, but also in its formal structures, such as *Ulverton*'s violent refusal of closure, its return of its fragmentary materials to history's rag-and-bone yard. His fiction enacts from within an anatomy of end-of-the-century English melancholia and a complicated, ambivalent work of mourning for ideas of England that it cannot not want. In the case of *Still*, however, this work is complicated to the point of paralysis: as I will argue, a commitment to tracking English melancholia – even with the object of loosening its grip – fatally ensnares the text in the repetition, the 'vacillation between illumination and blindness', that it sets out to explore.

The apparent object of Ricky Thornby's melancholic remembrance is the Edwardian summer – or, more properly, the Georgian summer – before, as what Samuel Hynes calls the 'Myth of the [Great] War' would have it, everything changed.[13] His narrative is suffused with regret for innocence lost, or betrayed: the key element of the myth as defined in the work of the trench poets and in the war memoirs and novels of the 1920s and 1930s, and repeated ever since in what inevitably reads as a version of Englishness as a cult of ruin. Ricky sees the war as

---

11 Thomas H. Ogden, 'Borges and the Art of Mourning', *Psychoanalytic Dialogues*, 10:1 (2000), pp. 65–88 (p. 65).
12 Peter Brooks, *Reading for the Plot: design and intention in narrative* (Oxford: Clarendon Press, 1984),
    pp. 92, 96, 101, 103.
13 Samuel Hynes, *A War Imagined: the First World War and English culture* (London: Bodley Head,

responsible for his personal misery and his artistic impotence: England, in his account of it, is still in the Great War's grip, a waste land, all 'meanness and lemon cheesecake' (p. 527), its modernity gone sour.[14] It may seem rather difficult to credit Ricky's attribution of the fear-ridden banality of life on the 'septic isle' (p. 303) to the lingering effects of the First World War, but he is certainly not alone in the post-war period – post-Second World War, that is – in seeing it as 'number one national ghost'.[15] Indeed, Thorpe himself shares his narrator's sense that '1914 was the point at which this century went wrong', and that England is still in the grip of 'the war and the conservative forces it released'.[16]

The family history Ricky screens in his film/text attempts to consolidate this view of the war by personalising it. His great-uncle Willo and great-aunt Agatha, who die within a week of each other in November 1918 (Willo at the front and Agatha of influenza) personify England's unrealised 'great age': they represent, respectively, its contribution to the future of twentieth-century European painting and the New Woman.[17] They are destroyed, while their conventional, unimaginative brother Giles survives – although blinded – and their mother, the toxic Mrs Trevelyan, presides over a house that is still in deep mourning in the 1940s, seemingly untouched by any history since November 1918. Ricky himself is presented to her annually, dressed, he tells us, in knickerbockers and frilly collar and cuffs to impersonate Willo. This traumatic memory is offered towards the end of the novel as if it is the key to his, and England's, condition: the moment in which familial and social pathology is transmitted to the next generation. But we cannot take Ricky's primal scene at face value. His analyst suspects that his memory of it is taken from an Ealing chiller (p. 536), and it appears to draw heavily on films that Ricky would have seen in the 1940s, particularly David Lean's *Great Expectations* (1946) – a ticket for which is given to him as a reward for his performance as Willo (pp. 582–3). And in more general terms, Ricky's focus on Agatha, Willo, Giles and their maid, Milly – who turns out to be his grandmother, having been seduced, or raped, by Giles – seems to screen one history in order to screen off another. Ricky's obsession with a mythical moment

———1990), p. ix.

14 See p. 280, where Ricky lists the 'really incredible' things going on in 1913, 'like Cubism and Old Age Pensions and Militant Feminism and National Insurance and the Modernist Novel', and wonders 'where it could have got to' if the war had not intervened.

15 Ted Hughes, *Winter Pollen: occasional prose*, ed. by William Scammell (London: Faber, 1994), p. 70.

16 In Barker, 'Speeding with Ricky'. Thorpe is not the only recent writer to endorse this reading of the war's impact. In his discussion of twentieth-century English thought's 'deep seated intellectual and moral aversion to modernism, mass culture, and mass democracy', Iain Chambers has commented that 'apart from the brief period of Vorticism just before the First World War … the modern avant-garde as it developed in Cubism, Futurism and Surrealism largely remained an extraneous experience for twentieth-century Britain' (*Border Dialogues: journeys in postmodernity* (London: Comedia/Routledge, 1990), pp. 17, 31).

17 In 1937, Wyndham Lewis wrote that he and his generation were '*the first men of a Future that has not materialised. We belong to a "great age" that has not "come off"*' (quoted in Hynes, *A War Imagined*, p. 464; emphasis in original).

when the (Eliotic) 'Shadow' fell, and with justifying his own failure as a version of
the doom visited on the youth of 1914, reads as a way of avoiding coming to
terms with his own life and with the history through which he has lived.[18]

Two cinematic metaphors embedded in psychoanalytic theories of memory
and narrative are clearly operative here, and, I suggest, are at least as important in
Still's play with film as the history of interaction between cinema and literature.
Most obviously, Ricky's film/text illustrates Freud's arguments about the revision
of memory in 'Screen Memories'. Memories, Freud contends, do not 'arise simultaneously with an experience', to be retrieved at a later date, but are formed through
the operation of a range of motives on unconscious 'memory-traces' at the time
when they are apparently retrieved. All memories, therefore, are subject to revision: 'people often construct [their memories] unconsciously – almost like works
of fiction'. Ricky's own memories are clearly permeable to such unconscious
reworking, and his account of the years from 1913 to 1918 functions very like a
special instance of this process, which Freud calls 'screen memory': a memory that
'owes its value as a memory not to its own content but to the relation existing
between that content and some other, that has been suppressed'. Screen memories,
in other words, simultaneously screen off that other content and display it in
refracted, displaced form.[19] If what passes for Ricky's family history can be interpreted as a product of these processes of revision and screening, it is also a work of
projection: an account of his dead relations' lives composed from unacknowledged aspects of his own. There is a suspicious similarity, for example, between
Agatha and his girlfriend Zelda, and Ricky notes that he keeps 'screwing the
action', recounting his analyst's opinion that he has a 'projective personality' (p.
168). At crucial points in the narrative, such as when his mother is about to be
conceived, he worries about his 'projector' overheating or blowing up (pp. 98,
525), and at the end of the novel he imagines his audience tipping it over in its
rush to leave (p. 584). He cannot quite allow himself to recognise how much of his
narrative is projection, however, insisting 'THIS IS THE TRUTH' (p. 375) – even if he
has to 'read between the lines' (p. 392).

Understanding *Still* as a projective screen memory helps to illuminate the relationship between Ricky's film and the unnarrated history that haunts it. Ricky's
identification with Georgian England is a compensation for, and an evasion of, the
very history that, if confronted, might give his work more than parasitic, voyeuristic significance: the Second World War and post-war world of which he, the grammar school boy and son of a Mosleyite costermonger, is much more directly a
product. But this England is pushed to the margins by his sense that the true
England is elsewhere, in 'deepest most profound and forgotten Sussex', with roses
and 'a teapot with a stand and mauve cups Thomas Hardy handed on and a stand
of elms and a sun-hat that once sheltered Saxon Sydney-Turner from the Dorset

---

18 See T. S. Eliot, 'The Hollow Men', in *Collected Poems 1909–1962* (London: Faber, 1974), pp. 87–92.
19 Freud, 'Screen Memories' in *Standard Edition*, vol. 3 (1962), pp. 299–322 (pp. 321–2, 315, 320).

sun in 1910': the England where he had tea with Quentin Bell in 1968 to discuss a (never made) biopic of Virginia Woolf (p. 271). His clothes betray his fraudulent claim to 'belong' to this true England, however: his leather jacket 'with the biggest lapels in Christendom, … smelling of diesel and nicotine and BR [British Rail] lavatories' (p. 271) marks him as a product of the post-war Welfare State, inimical to great art – of the world of Larkin's railway journey in 'The Whitsun Weddings', perhaps – rather than of 'deep' England (p. 378).[20] His desire to 'belong' to Bell's England, which drives his evocation of England at its 'peak' (p. 377), when 'you [couldn't] see the hayricks for boaters and blazers and their impossibly lovely cousins in embroidered lawn' (p. 384), is complicated, however, by the awareness that this England depends on his own marginality, and on the labour of those like his mother and grandmother; their doomed youth – doomed not by war on the horizon but by the inevitability of an adolescence spent in service – is not what is at issue in the 'Poppy Day' version of the national past.[21] Thus England is both the subject of his narrative and a 'Black Hole' or 'bunker' (p. 271) into which that narrative threatens to collapse under the pressure of the ambivalence that suffuses its melancholic romance with the past.

Ricky's identification with Willo and Agatha is crucial to avoiding a confrontation with this ambivalence. Because they died young and because, as he is gradually forced to admit, he knows almost nothing about them – his mother maintained near-total silence about her family (p. 33), and his access to the Trevelyan family archive is very limited – he can represent them as innocent of the 'crime without attenuating [*sic*] circumstances' (p. 511) that is twentieth-century history after 1914 and, equally, of implication in the painful history of class conflict *before* 1914. The very scarcity of their material traces makes them perfect screens for Ricky's melancholic identification with England's doomed youth.

The 'deep' England evoked in the passage dealing with Quentin Bell, and elsewhere (see pp. 378–9), can itself be understood as a form of melancholic mourning, an attempt to bind the disturbing energies released by not one but two world wars, as well as the transformations occasioned by empire and its disintegration. Initially an invention of the late nineteenth century, a vision of the beauties of the English countryside as testimony to historical continuity, stability and tranquillity

---

20 Philip Larkin, 'The Whitsun Weddings' in *Collected Poems* (London: Marvell and Faber, 1988), pp. 114–16. The idea of 'deep' England comes from Patrick Wright's *On Living in an Old Country*, and, as I have argued elsewhere, the concept clearly informs both *Still* and *Ulverton* (Gunby, 'History in Rags', pp. 53–4). For accounts of the widespread sense that post-war Britain was not conducive to great art, see Alan Sinfield, *Literature, Politics and Culture in Postwar Britain*, 2nd edn. (London: Athlone, 1997), pp. 13–19; D. J. Taylor, *After the War: the novel and English society since 1945* (London: Chatto & Windus, 1993), especially pp. 26–7, and Ingelbien, *Misreading England*, pp. 62–5, 86, 98, 105–6.

21 On '"Poppy Day" nationalism', see Margaretta Jolly, 'After Feminism: Pat Barker, Penelope Lively and the Contemporary Novel' in *British Culture of the Postwar: an introduction to literature and society 1945–1999*, ed. Alistair Davies and Alan Sinfield (London: Routledge, 2000), pp. 58–82 (p. 75).

(including the absence of class conflict), but also as threatened by change and decay, this version of England was popularised in the wake of the Great War, as part of a shift away from imperialist modes of Englishness towards others that, as Alison Light has argued, were 'more inward-looking, more domestic and more private – and, in terms of pre-war standards, more "feminine"'.[22] The inter-war rise of a domestic and a green England can, as Light suggests, be understood as a compensatory and perhaps a healing response to the trauma of the Great War, an attempt to reconcile past and present, tradition and modernity. It also worked, however, to cover over the gap between the idea of Englishness as stability and tranquillity and the realities of the British state that the war had revealed, and it could harden, as Light goes on to say, into an evasion of history and the present: a 'fixation' on home and a 'wilful denial' not merely of imperial ambitions, but of 'any notion of wider social involvements or place'.[23]

In the Second World War, the symbolic load carried by this 'green' England, and the gap between the vision of Englishness it enshrined and the experience to which it was a response, increased further. The stresses of total war prompted a widespread investment in an 'island dream' of England that melded pastoral domesticity, (defensive) heroism and social harmony, and encouraged imaginative detachment from the war beyond Britain's shores.[24] The consequences of this insular imaginary are worth pondering in relation to Ricky's sense of the fraudulence of his own artistic response to the twentieth century. Bernard Bergonzi has written of an 'anaesthetized or evasive response' to the wider meaning and experience of the war, and Adam Piette has suggested that a willingness to take the rhetoric of the miraculous island at face value accompanied a reluctance to investigate the 'private stories' of the war and the broken backed culture it left behind: the 'broken minds, anaesthetized feelings, deep depression and loss of any sense of value'.[25] Evasiveness and a dependence on wartime myths could certainly be said to characterise Ricky's response to the war: he refers to it as 'the to-do that had recently finished' (p. 533), and offers an account of his birth during an air raid in January 1940 (p. 26) that cannot be accurate, as there were no raids on London until August of that year. We might also note, moreover, that Second World War and post-war writers continued the habit established in the inter-war years of looking to the period before the First World War in an effort to identify when, and more tentatively how, everything went wrong: Larkin's 'MCMXIV', with its

---

22 Alison Light, *Forever England: femininity, literature and conservatism between the wars* (London: Routledge, 1991), p. 8. On the countryside between the wars, see David Matless, *Landscape and Englishness* (London: Reaktion, 1998), and Alex Potts, '"Constable Country" between the Wars', in *Patriotism: the making and unmaking of British national identity*, ed. Raphael Samuel (London: Routledge, 1989), vol. 3: *National fictions*, pp. 160–86.

23 Light, *Forever England*, p. 46.

24 See Adam Piette, *Imagination at War: British fiction and poetry 1939–1945* (London: Papermac, 1995), pp. 255–72.

25 Bernard Bergonzi, *Wartime and Aftermath: English literature and its background 1939–1960* (Oxford: Oxford University Press, 1993), p. 206, and Piette, *Imagination at War*, pp. 1, 5–6.

photographic descriptions of lines of 'moustached archaic faces' and of country 'place-names all hazed over / With flowering grasses', and its bald concluding assessment, 'Never such innocence again', is emblematic of the place of the Great War in the post-war English imagination, and clearly a source for *Still*'s treatment of this material.[26]

There are moments in *Still* when even Ricky is – almost – forced to acknowledge the consequences of this imaginative evasion of post-1918 history. A striking instance can be found in his musings on the question of when, as he puts it, 'everyone's eyes changed' (p. 122). As he says, 'there's a lot about eyes in this film' (p. 60), and his reflections on a portrait of 'Honeydew' Philips – a humane housemaster at Giles and Willo's public school – make clear what is at stake in this preoccupation. According to Ricky, this portrait, *circa* 1910, shows not only that Mr Philips's eyes are of different colours, but that they are different from people's eyes at the century's end: 'His eyeballs are kind of rubbed up, like they've been spat on and polished.' 'Maybe they cried more', Ricky speculates. 'Maybe for them the storms always cleared. There was a lustre to the grey light, the sun was out, their eyes were awash with rain but it was going to be a fine day.' He interprets the light in Mr Philips's eyes as 'the kindness and civility … that went generally from the world' (p. 123), and seems to want to locate this change – or, we might say, the moment when 'the Shadow' fell – during the Great War, when Mr Philips's eyes were literally changed, his green one lost.[27] But as he later acknowledges, 'Shadows' do not 'fall once only' (p. 204), and he goes on to say that 'between Mr Philips and us there's someone signalling he's really interested in this fact about [Mr Philips's] eyes. It's Dr Mengele.' Referring to Mengele's experiments on 'the Romany girl with eyes of a different hue in Birkenau', Ricky continues:

That's our century, for Christ's sake. It's not prehistory, it's not the time of the dinosaurs or the Crusades or the invention of the steam-press. I was alive, I was up and walking, I was arsing about with my mother's pinny as Dr Mengele padded up to her. The Romany girl, I mean. Whoever she was.

Hey, wake up. How do I talk to Mr Philips, Samaritan Man, about kindness and civility and oyster-coloured light after storms with that guy stood between us, waving his little cut-throat?

How do we talk to anyone after that?

Really, I'm serious. (pp. 124–5)

---

26 Larkin, 'MCMXIV' in *Collected Poems*, pp. 127–8.

27 As Martin Jay has argued, twentieth-century art and thought has often figured a crisis of understanding, of the intelligibility and communicability of experience, as a crisis of vision. In particular, the blinded or mutilated eye has been used as a symbol of this crisis: these eyes, writes Gerald Eager, 'are not moist or movable, they are not alive and do not suggest the power to look back and see … So the individual or divine spark of contact does not exist in the missing or mutilated eye. In place of contact there is rejection; instead of sight, there is complete blindness' (Martin Jay, *Downcast Eyes: the denigration of vision in twentieth-century French thought* (Berkeley: University of California Press, 1993), p. 260).

The shift from the First to the Second World War here, and the nagging sense that he is being histrionic, encapsulate Ricky's problem. He wants to represent the Great War as the definitive end of 'kindness and civility', but that leaves him with no way of representing the century's later history other than as an echo of 1914–18. As a consequence, Ricky is haunted by the sense that his account of the century is little more than voyeuristic, myth-ridden grandstanding, and his attempt to produce a millennial masterwork collapses into bathos.

Ultimately, Ricky's melancholic investment in England's doomed youth is more comfortable and more pleasurable than a confrontation with his compli-cated, conflicted relationship with post-Second World War England as fact and idea. Hence his fantasy of himself as Hylas, the young boy kidnapped from Hercules by nymphs and dragged down to the bottom of their spring: 'dying of England', escaping from his own history in a reunion with the lost object(s) of his love (p. 143; see also pp. 136–7, 151, 583). Indeed, even his decision to illustrate his film with stills speaks of this melancholic mourning. He tells us that 'the film [is] never as good as the stills' (p. 47), referring to the scope they allow him to invent a narrative around them. But we might also suspect that, like Roland Barthes in *Camera Lucida* (1980), Ricky is drawn to the stills that illustrate his film/text because photographs allow him to dwell on *'what has been'* and on its loss – with the many 'holes in the world' (p. 486). As Barthes notes, whereas film flows past 'like life', a photograph is the sign of a catastrophe that cannot be worked through, but instead clings like a 'specter': 'when [a photograph] is painful, nothing in it can transform grief into mourning'.[28]

Brooding over his stills, Ricky prolongs his narrative indefinitely, never reaching the 'Amazing Truth' that he promises will be revealed in the last few frames (p. 530), and finally evading an ending. He initially leads us to believe that Milly's rape, and thus the question of his own origins, will be the crux of his narrative, but as he approaches this point he shifts the focus to more conventional traumas: Giles's blinding by gas, and – promised but never delivered – Willo's death on the Western Front and Agatha's funeral. Returning to Brooks's account of narrative, we might suggest that Ricky's inability to find a proper plot, or a proper end, for his narrative, signals a reluctance to confront both his ambivalence about England and the fact that his narrative of the Edwardian summer and the Great War cannot account for his contemporary condition. Like Pip in *Great Expectations* (1860–1), which as I have already noted is a significant influence on his account of his relations with the Trevelyan family, Ricky has been misreading – or miswriting – the plot of his life.[29] But unlike Pip, Ricky has not renounced this plot at the novel's end. Nor has he reevaluated the mythic account of twentieth-century Englishness that underlies it.

---

28 Roland Barthes, *Camera Lucida: reflections on photography*, trans. Richard Howard (London: Vintage, 1993), pp. 85, 89–90; emphasis in original. For a discussion of this point, see Jay, *Downcast Eyes*, pp. 454–6.

29 On *Great Expectations* and the misreading of plots, see Brooks, *Reading for the Plot*, pp. 113–42.

In order to gauge the impact of this melancholic evasion, it is instructive to compare *Still* with Beckett's late work 'Still' (1973), with which Thorpe's novel shares not only its name but its setting: that named in *Krapp's Last Tape* (1958) as 'a late evening in the future'.[30] Michael Wood has described this setting as 'a spatialization of the unseeable mind', a limbo-like 'domain just off the edge of life' – descriptions that are appropriate enough, too, for the sickeningly awful party taking place in Ricky's head. Beckett's 'Still' allows only the slightest delay and digression on the way to its end, thus suggesting, as Wood argues, 'how little we can say, … since whatever we say turns out to be excessive, a form of hubris, an extravagant claim on the unclaimable'.[31] But if Beckett's texts of stillness and silence can be read as situated *in* the abyss of twentieth-century history, where plot has collapsed and there is almost nothing to delay the death which is the end of narrative, Ricky's avoids this 'hole in the world' through its overstuffed wordiness and its refusal to come to an end. The 'stillness' of the history to which his narrative testifies – its persistent, ambiguous, untameable and wounding presence – is what he must at all costs avoid. Instead of Beckett's 'all quite still head in hand listening for a sound' we are given nearly 600 pages of 'retard, postponement, error, and partial revelation', of unresolved 'vacillation between illumination and blindness', that climax in an image of possibly blinded eyes sinking into the darkness and a taunting 'listen, dumbos. You missed it' (pp. 583–4).[32]

By offering us as Ricky's would-be millennial masterwork a text concerned above all to avoid confronting its own meaning while appearing to have left nothing, not even the most mundane detail, untold, *Still* suggests that late-twentieth-century Englishness is a melancholic misreading of its own history. But if Ricky's narrative is comprehensively melancholic, then we must ask to what extent Thorpe succeeds in simultaneously acting out and 'drawing the graph' of that melancholia, or, to put it another way, to what extent *Still*'s representation of Englishness as melancholic misreading moves, through repetition, towards some form of working-through. Here, I think, Thorpe's execution falls somewhat short of his conception.

Still clearly attempts to articulate the matter of England in terms of the European literary and cinematic traditions which for Ricky and, one feels, Thorpe himself, represent an authentic engagement with the twentieth century, and thus also seeks to reconnect Englishness with the progressive modernity that the Great War supposedly nipped in the bud – at least in Britain. Unfortunately, however, this strategy combined with the fact that, apart from a few nods to the Second World War, to the 'early fuck-all Fifties' (p. 24) and to 1968, *Still* is largely silent on

30 Samuel Beckett, 'Still' in *For to End Yet Again* (London: Calder, 1999), pp. 17–21, and 'Krapp's Last Tape' in *'Krapp's Last Tape' and 'Embers'* (London: Faber, 1965), pp. 9–20 (p. 9).
31 Michael Wood, *Children of Silence: studies in contemporary fiction* (London: Pimlico, 1998), pp. 33–4.
32 Beckett, 'Still', p. 21.

English history after 1918, means that the work of reimagining millennial Englishness through a more comprehensive understanding of its history is left undone. It may be unreasonable to demand that *Still* should do more than anatomise the desire to 'die of England'. But *Ulverton*'s signal achievement is to combine a fidelity to nostalgia and melancholia with a deployment of melancholia's impulse to fragmentation and destruction against itself. Its fragmentary aesthetic – borrowed from that great melancholic Walter Benjamin – both mourns the way that the violence of English history bars any simple celebration of its 'cultural treasures', and returns those treasures to the matrix of history, thus opening up space for alternative, and complex, revisions of Englishness.[33] *Still*, on the other hand, seems too committed to the myth of Englishness it takes as its subject, and too unable to imagine an alternative reading of England in the post-war period, to manage such a double manoeuvre. Perhaps this is why in the two novels that followed it, Thorpe returned twice more to the period from the Great War to the Second World War, attempting through more detailed revisitings of its cultural forms to understand its continuing legacy for post-war versions of Englishness.

---

33 See Walter Benjamin, 'Theses on the Philosophy of History' in *Illuminations*, ed. Hannah Arendt, trans. Harry Zorn (London: Pimlico, 1999), pp. 245–55 (p. 248).

Part III New Englands

9 *Bhaji on the Beach*: South Asian femininity at 'home' on the 'English' seaside

Bilkis Malek

Endearing 'Olde England'

'Race' as a marker for defining English identity can be traced back to the history of empire.[1] But, as Ian Baucom points out, only in the late twentieth century, marked specifically by Enoch Powell's theories on British immigration and the 1981 British Nationality Act passed under Margaret Thatcher's government, was a racial narrative of English identity rendered hegemonic. Both Powell's rhetoric and the policies of the Thatcher government portrayed the presence of immigrants as an 'invasion' on Englishness, and in doing so located English identity 'in the moment of its vanishing, as whiteness, a command of the English language, and a certain kind of domestic space'.[2] Such a vision of Englishness narrates a particular 'construction' of England which has come to occupy the official public image of Britain excluding 'other possibilities, other versions of Britain'.[3] In Stuart Hall's words, 'only by dint of excluding or absorbing all the differences that constituted Englishness, the multitude of different regions, peoples, classes, genders that composed the people gathered together in the Act of Union' is such an Englishness able to 'stand for everybody in the British Isles'.[4]

With the processes of globalisation creating ever increasing international economic and social interdependence, a condensed notion of Englishness, as Hall observes, is becoming increasingly hard to sustain. In the present moment the intensity with which the fates of the world's populations are interlinked has perhaps never been made more stark than by the events now commonly referred to as '9/11'. Yet, instead of a complex response sensitive to the intricate interrelations between nations and 'races', the political response to the 'terrorist' acts on the

---

1 See, for example, Jonathan Rutherford, *Forever England: reflections on masculinity and Empire* (London: Lawrence & Wishart, 1997), and Ian Baucom, *Out of Place: Englishness, Empire and the locations of identity* (Princeton: Princeton University Press, 1999).
2 Baucom, *Out of Place*, p. 15.
3 Ken Lunn, 'Reconsidering "Britishness"' in *Nation and Identity in Contemporary Europe*, ed. B. Jenkins and S. A. Sofos (London: Routledge, 1996), p. 87.
4 Stuart Hall, 'The Local and the Global' in *Culture, Globalization and the World-System: contemporary conditions for the representation of identity*, ed. A. D. King (London: Macmillan, 1991), p. 22.

United States being pursued by governments on both sides of the Atlantic has further polarised racial boundaries. This has been specifically relayed, in the political addresses of Tony Blair and George Bush, through a heavy reliance on mutually exclusive conceptions such as 'them' and 'us', 'good' and 'evil', the 'civilised' and 'uncivilised', and 'superior' and 'inferior' cultures. In Britain, the 'War on Terror' has doubled as a concern with protecting the nation's integrity from pollution by 'outsiders'. It has been seized upon by the New Labour government to give renewed vigour to Powell's conception of a superior English identity through the introduction of 'citizenship tests' announced by the Home Secretary, David Blunkett. The tests, due to be introduced in 2004, will make it compulsory for immigrants wanting to become UK citizens to undertake an exam to illustrate proficiency in the English language as well as a formal oath or 'citizens' pledge' affirming that the individual will embrace 'British' laws and customs. Of course there is no open rejection of the right of immigrants to naturalise as UK citizens, as in Powell's case, but there is an underlying supposition that 'outsiders' have an inferior outlook and way of life and so must be subjected to 'citizenship tests' to make them acceptable citizens.[5] Thus, implicit in the measures announced by David Blunkett is a celebration of a notion of Englishness that is static, free of impurities and in need of protection from foreign elements. Englishness is, in effect, absolved of any responsibility for ongoing racial divisions and tensions.

The political impasse in engaging more complex, racially and culturally fragmented notions of national identity has had to be confronted and challenged by black Britons themselves in order simply to 'survive'. Homi Bhabha puts this succinctly when he argues that the migrant's survival is dependent on the 'newness of cultural translation' which 'desacralizes the transparent assumptions of cultural supremacy'.[6] It is in this context that the work of several black British film-makers has been recognised as making a significant contribution.[7] These film-makers, with varying degrees of success, have been engaged in the struggle to develop a counter-discourse to racially pure, homogeneous notions of Englishness and English national identity. Producing images from the position of the 'other', narrating 'other' histories, 'other' experiences of living in England, they have introduced new perspectives on what it means to be English. For example, texts such as

---

5 It is worth noting, as some commentators have pointed out, that many indigenous British people would find it difficult to answer correctly some of the questions on British national institutions and history to be included in the citizenship tests. See for example, Gary Younge's article 'The Wrong Way Round' in the *Guardian* (8 Sept. 2003).

6 Homi Bhabha, 'How Newness Enters the World' in *The Location of Culture* (London: Routledge, 1994), p. 228. See also Paul Gilroy, *The Black Atlantic: the cultural politics of race and nation* (London: Verso, 1993), and Kobena Mercer, 'Diaspora Culture and the Dialogic Imagination' in *Welcome to the Jungle: new positions in black cultural studies* (London: Routledge, 1994), pp. 53–66.

7 See, for example, Stuart Hall, 'New Ethnicities' in *Black Film, British Cinema*, ed. K. Mercer (London: ICA Documents 7, 1989), pp. 27–31, and Kobena Mercer, 'Recoding Narratives of Race and Nation' in *Welcome to The Jungle*, pp. 69–96.

Passion of Remembrance (1986) and *My Beautiful Launderette* (1985) have ventured noticeably into the complex dynamics between race, sexuality, and gender to draw attention to the dialogic, fluid features of England, its people and culture. It is within this context of destabilising the earlier more secure definitions of Englishness that I introduce and consider the film *Bhaji on the Beach* (1994). More specifically my aim is to consider in what ways *Bhaji*, within the confines of its subject matter, contests the ideal of 'Olde England' and its superior position in relation to 'other' cultures, replacing it with a more inclusive and fluid construct that no longer resists racial difference and change or holds them in constant tension.

Narrating from the perspectives of South Asian women, *Bhaji* gives voice to 'other' female subjectivities, offering a fresh angle on themes central to 'official' constructions of a superior, racially exclusive English identity. As Nira Yuval-Davis has argued, not only do 'women often come to symbolise the national collectivity, its roots, its spirit, its national project. ... Women's culturally "appropriate behaviour" ... can also signify ethnic and cultural boundaries'.[8] In this regard, the shy, subordinate, passive South Asian woman has for so long been constructed in direct opposition to white English femininity.[9] Thus, to disrupt such an equation would be to unsettle one of the central bases on which conventional notions of Englishness have laid claim to an irrefutably superior status. To establish, in more detail, the exclusion of South Asian femininity from 'official' representations of Englishness, but also by way of constructing a theoretical framework for examining *Bhaji*, I begin my analysis by describing dominant discourses on 'race' and their specific impact on popular perceptions of the position occupied by South Asian women in England. In order to illustrate how the cultural distance and mutually exclusive status of white English and South Asian femininities is reflected in the national imagination, I provide a comparative critique of domestic reactions to the overseas murder convictions of four British women – Louise Woodward, Deborah Parry, Lucille MacLaughlan and Manjit Basuta. My analysis underlines the persistence of a racialised discourse pervading dominant attitudes and representations of South Asian women which I then use as a framework for assessing *Bhaji*'s ability to disrupt the 'official race relations narrative' and project a more inclusive vision of England.[10]

---

8 Nira Yuval-Davis, 'Gender and Nation', *Ethnic and Racial Studies*, 16:4, (Oct. 1993), p. 627.

9 See Parminder Bhachu, 'Identities Constructed and Reconstructed: representations of Asian women in Britain' in *Migrant Women: crossing boundaries and changing identities*, ed. Gina Buijs (Oxford: Berg, 1993), pp. 99–117, and Pratibha Parmar, 'Gender, Race and Class: Asian women in resistance' in *The Empire Strikes Back: race and racism in 70s Britain*, Centre for Contemporary Cultural Studies (London: Hutchinson, 1982), pp. 236–75.

10 Jim Pines coins this phrase to refer to dominant discourses and assumptions of 'race'. See his essay 'The Cultural Context of Black British Cinema' in *Blackframes: critical perspectives on black independent cinema*, ed. M. Cham and C. A.Watkins (Boston: Celebration of Black Cinema and MIT Press, 1988).

'Official race relations narrative'

Referring to such examples as Enoch Powell's 'rivers of blood' speech and Lord
Scarman's identification of the 'herd instinct' as the cause of the Brixton riots, a
number of theorists have documented how a theory linking 'race' and nation
governs contemporary racist discourses of British society.[11] They have shown how
this theory purports to explain race relations in Britain within the framework of a
'culture clash' thesis, and exposed how it represents a mode of thinking that legit-
imises racial prejudice – not on the grounds of belonging to a superior or inferior
'race', but on the basis that it is human nature to feel threatened by the alienness of
'newcomers'. In other words, humans instinctively defend and want to preserve
their culture, traditions and way of life. This way of thinking has been termed as
'common sense' racism or the 'new' racism and has been described as representing
a marked shift from eighteenth- and nineteenth-century ideologies of 'race' which
stressed biological differences. A key reference point for explaining the logic
underlying 'common sense' racism has been the work of Antonio Gramsci, which
is worth summarising briefly.

In his *Prison Notebooks* Gramsci differentiates between 'good sense' and
'common sense'. He defines 'good sense' as those commonly held beliefs and taken-
for-granted assumptions that are practically and empirically viable. 'Common
sense' shares a characteristic of 'good sense' in that it also signifies a set of ideas and
beliefs that are, in the main, unquestioningly accepted by the 'masses' and through
which people make sense of their everyday lives. However, Gramsci argues that,
unlike 'good sense', 'common sense' does not manifest itself as a single, static body
of knowledge. Instead, it functions in complex and contradictory ways:

Common sense is not something rigid and immobile, but is continually transforming itself,
enriching itself with scientific ideas and philosophical opinions which have entered ordinary life. Common sense is the folklore of philosophy, and is always half way between folklore properly speaking and the philosophy, science, and economics of the specialists.
Common sense creates the folklore of the future, that is as a relatively rigid phase of popular
knowledge at a given place and time.[12]

Using Gramsci's ideas of 'common sense', cultural theorists have demonstrated
how socially constructed notions of 'race' become naturalised truths. Further,
although proponents of 'common sense' race ideologies claim to distance themselves from notions of racial superiority, this distance is, as Errol Lawrence points

---

11 See, for example, Martin Barker, *The New Racism* (London: Junction Books, 1981); Stuart Hall,
'The Whites of their Eyes' in *Silver Linings: some strategies for the eighties*, ed. G. Bridges and R.
Brunt (London: Lawrence & Wishart, 1981); Errol Lawrence, 'Just Plain Common Sense: the
"roots" of racism' in *The Empire Strikes*, pp. 47–94; and Paul Gilroy, *'There Ain't No Black in the
Union Jack': the cultural politics of race and nation* (London: Routledge, 1987).
12 Q. Hoare and G. Nowell-Smith, *Antonio Gramsci: selections from prison notebooks* (London:
Lawrence & Wishart, 1971), p. 326.

out, 'seldom explicit in their arguments. At one level such lack of explicitness occurs because such talk is not necessary. Once the argument has been couched in terms of "alien" cultures, "common sense" racism can be relied upon to provide the missing inflexions'.[13]

It is impossible to discuss in detail here the complex and sometimes contradictory nature in which the 'new' racism functions. Suffice it to say, however, that it is a mode of thinking which seeks to explain race relations and the subordinate position of black people in England as a direct outcome of 'inherent qualities' peculiar to each racial group, as opposed to the institutional and everyday racism. Thus, for example, the high number of small businesses owned and run by South Asian families is seen as a result of the propensity of South Asian families to stick together and nothing to do with the limited job or career opportunities available to them. Further, by regarding English culture as more progressive and offering more freedom of choice than the cultures of black people, it is deemed 'common sense' that members of the black British population (especially the young) are torn between two cultures. Thus, at the heart of the 'new' racism is the idea that British (or English) and Asian/African-Caribbean cultures (or that of any other settler group) are mutually exclusive and incompatible. The only routes out of this unhappy conjuncture are presented as assimilation or repatriation.

With specific reference to the position of South Asian women, on which *Bhaji*'s narrative focuses, Pratibha Parmar has highlighted how dominant discourses have tended to construct and articulate their sexuality and femininity with reference to the assumption that their lives are controlled by religious and cultural traditions.[14] The practices of purdah, arranged marriages and extended families are the most frequently cited characteristics when interpreting and understanding the position of South Asian women in England. Faced with a taste of the freedom supposedly offered by Western society, 'new' racist discourses have perceived South Asian women as yearning to adopt the culture enjoyed by their white English counterparts. Thus, demonstrations by South Asian women of a degree of independence and autonomy have often been ascribed to their adoption of Western values.

As Parmar argues, however, such perceptions are problematic.[15] They not only ignore events in which South Asian women in Britain have clearly and determinedly resisted the racist and sexist treatment they face, both at work (as demonstrated in the strikes at Grunwick and Imperial Typewriters) and at home (through organising their own women's groups), but they also fail to acknowledge that such resistance, along with economic activity, is not new to migrant women. Parmar goes on to describe the various struggles and campaigns South Asian

---

13 Lawrence, 'Just Plain Common Sense, p. 82.
14 Pratibha Parmar, 'Hateful Contraries' in *Critical Decade: black British photography in the 80s*, ed. D. A. Bailey and S. Hall (London: Ten 8, 1992), pp. 50–7.
15 Parmar, 'Gender, Race and Class', pp. 236–75.

women have initiated and contributed to in their countries of origin. She asserts that 'to assume that these women have no history of struggle and are only politically "born" when they arrive in the metropolis, is to deny their historical experience of fighting back, and to devalue anti-imperialist struggles as a whole'.[16]

The language of 'common sense' racism thus speaks of culture as a fixed, static entity. It presents English culture as constituting the most progressive way of life and, by speaking of culture in this way, maintains racial boundaries through cultural differences. But, as Hall and Lunn point out, maintaining a homogeneous national identity, particularly in the face of global economic and mass migration processes, is not an effortless achievement. In Lunn's words, 'in order for the English swan to glide serenely across the water, a considerable amount of beneath-the-surface paddling is required'.[17] Within the policies of the New Labour government, for example, this 'beneath-the-surface paddling' is encapsulated by the fact that whilst New Labour has been quick to denounce the so-called Tory 'race card', it is also responsible for the introduction of 'citizenship tests' (noted above) to ensure that immigrants know how to be, in Blunkett's words, 'good neighbours'.[18]

To illustrate how the intricate and subtle ways in which British politics has maintained the older notions of Englishness are manifested in the imaginations of large sections of the indigenous population, I want to turn my attention to consider reactions to the murder convictions of nurses Deborah Parry and Lucille MacLaughlan in Saudi Arabia, and nannies Louise Woodward and Manjit Basuta in the United States. The respective reactions are highly revealing of, on the one hand, how an innocent notion of white English femininity is central to superior conceptions of Englishness, and, on the other, how maintaining such a marker of Englishness essentially rests on a complex and contradictory process through which the many manifestations and negotiations of race and gender are denied, by the social imaginary, as being integral to the unfolding of English identity.

Defending a purveyor of 'innocence' – white English femininity

The narrative interlinking the lives of Deborah Parry, Lucille MacLaughlan, Louise Woodward and Manjit Basuta is that, between 1997 and 1999, they were all British citizens living and working abroad when they were accused and convicted of murder. For the purposes of discussion here what is interesting is that the 'beneath-the-surface paddling' that Lunn identifies as necessary for maintaining an untainted superior conception of Englishness can be located in the selective

---

16 Parmar, 'Gender, Race and Class', p. 249.
17 Lunn, 'Reconsidering "Britishness"', p. 87.
18 In this regard, as I've argued elsewhere, it should be noted that the more outspoken racist rhetoric of individuals like Norman Tebbit is becoming increasingly isolated even on the political right. See Bilkis Malek, 'Not Such Tolerant Times', *Soundings*, 6 (1997), pp. 140–51.

and inconsistent manner in which the respective cases captured the public's support and imagination. In the cases of Parry, MacLaughlan and Woodward, all white females, media and public interest was significantly more widespread than in the case of Manjit Basuta, an Asian woman. For the former three individuals to be tried and convicted by the courts of an 'other' land meant that a pure, white innocent notion of English femininity was very much under threat. As each of the cases went into their appeal stages, at 'home' the overwhelming public reactions essentially amounted to a defence of a unique and superior national identity. But, there was a distinct difference in the way that this defence was achieved in each case.

The trial of the two nurses, who were convicted of killing their colleague, Yvonne Gilford, became an opportunity to vilify Islamic law and Saudi judicial standards. The headlines were dominated by reports of the defendants making forced confessions and being subjected to physical and sexual abuse in prison. Not meeting the expectations of the 'superior' English judicial system was seen to render the Saudi courts incapable of conducting a fair trial. The 'innocence' of the two defendants was implicitly maintained in the British press and in the minds of large sections of the public on the basis of an inferior Saudi judicial process and outdated sentencing laws. Representations from British officials to the Saudi government helped secure a royal pardon and the two women were released within months after they had been sentenced.

By contrast, the public engaged in very limited scrutiny of the conduct of the trial of Louise Woodward in which she was accused of murdering an eight-month-old baby, Matthew Eappen. Rather, the media and public defence of Woodward in England revolved around an image of a young woman who had come from a 'normal' loving family. This young woman had performed well at school and her headteacher was so full of praise for her that he was willing to take the stand as a character witness. Within this construction, Woodward's desire to celebrate a successful end to her trial with eating chocolate perhaps represented the epitome of her innocence.

Significantly, the courtroom drama involving Woodward became an event for the media and her supporters to re-establish qualities of the true English character. For example, the local hostelry, the Rigger pub in the village where Woodward grew up, emerged as the base for the campaign to clear the young nanny's name. The media and Woodward's family and friends resolved to remain undeterred when the jury returned a guilty verdict and accelerated their efforts to rescue their damsel in distress. And, in the face of victory, there was the good old sing-a-long with a national flavour. When Judge Hiller Zobel reduced the original murder verdict to involuntary manslaughter and re-sentenced Woodward to time already spent in jail (279 days), the entire Rigger pub on live television broke out into the Euro '96 chorus, appropriately reworded 'She's coming home, she's coming home, she's coming, Louise is coming home', as if to provide a perhaps unconscious, but nevertheless intricate, link between a sublime, virtuous femininity and another bastion of Englishness – football.

   In contrast to the overwhelming public investment in a safe return 'home' for
Parry, MacLaughlan and Woodward, the case of Manjit Basuta failed to generate a
similar level of support. The little media attention the case did attract reflected
upon the lack of interest in Basuta's welfare amongst the public and press alike,
even though huge similarities were to be drawn with the case of Louise
Woodward.[19] Like Woodward, Basuta too was employed as a nanny in the United
States and accused of shaking to death a child in her care, thirteen-month-old
Oliver Smith. In her original trial Basuta, as in Woodward's case, was found guilty
of murder. Her family, like Woodward's, set up a campaign and appeal fund to
help secure her freedom. Their failure to attract the level of media and public hype
surrounding Louise Woodward has been uncannily reflected in the process by
which Basuta was eventually released from prison. Her retrial was secured three
years after her original conviction compared to a few months in Woodward's case,
and, though her appeal was successful in reducing the original murder verdict to
manslaughter, there was no immediate release from prison for Basuta. She had to
serve out another year in prison until she was eligible for parole. Her eventual
release, in August 2003, did not produce the kind of jubilant scenes with which
Woodward was welcomed back to England, but passed relatively unnoticed,
confirming the inconsequential status that Basuta's fate was accorded in the
public's imagination for maintaining an innocent notion of English femininity.
   My comparative analysis of the public reactions to the murder convictions of
Parry, MacLaughlan, Woodward and Basuta highlights the contradictory, and
sometimes subconscious, ways in which a pure white innocent notion of femininity has been kept intact. It shows how mutually exclusive boundaries of 'race' are
maintained and continue to define a superior English national identity amidst the
reality of an ever increasing racially diverse population. In the recent 'War on
Terror' these racial boundaries are being reinvented and invoked in such oppositional constructions as the 'surgical precision bombing of the allies' compared to
the 'brutal and barbaric tactics of the enemy', or the 'emphasis on the Geneva
Convention as a basis for opposing the unlawful treatment of allied prisoners of
war' compared to the 'emphasis on the danger posed by Taliban and al Qaeda
terrorists to justify the unlawful treatment of suspects held at Guantanamo Bay'.[20]
But if my discussion of the cases of Parry, MacLaughlan, Woodward and Basuta
underlines the pervasive nature of oppositional constructions of 'race' within
popular conceptions of Englishness, then the widespread public demonstrations
against Tony Blair's decision to go to war in Iraq in 2003 might be viewed as
signalling a notable degree of discomfort, amongst the British population, of
debating the current crisis in international relations in 'black and white' terms.

---

19 See, for example, 'Colour of Fair Trial' in The *Tribune* (India), 6 Oct. 1999. Also see www.news.
    bbc.co.uk/hi/english/world/americas/newsid_412000/412542.stm   and   www.sky.com/skynews/
    article/0,,30100–12701424,00.htm.
20 Guantanamo Bay is where the USA built the prison Camp Delta for the specific purpose of detain-
    ing soldiers captured during the war in Afghanistan.

This is not to say that the opposition to the war in Iraq is conclusive evidence that the 'masses' are ready to rctreat from the established superior configurations of Englishness. At the same time, the level of doubt being expressed against the policy of war as necessarily the best response to the events of '9/11' carries a somewhat implicit realisation that a national identity defined by rigid boundaries of 'race' may be detrimental to the 'survival' of the English themselves. But new, more inclusive notions of national identity cannot be forged overnight. In this regard, the migrant's strategy of 'survival', of discovering 'how newness enters the world' may prove invaluable.[21] It is in this context that I want to discuss the film *Bhaji on the Beach* and assess how it may be seen to penetrate an insular vision of England, injecting it with more diversity and fluidity. More specifically, I examine the ways in which *Bhaji* interrupts a racially pure and culturally distinct notion of English femininity, replacing it with a more complex and dialogic conception. In this conception the diverse experiences and cultural negotiations amongst South Asian women in England inform the English way of life as much as they are informed by it.

At 'home' in Blackpool

Bhaji's narrative is constructed around nine Asian women on a day trip to Blackpool for 'a female fun time'. The outing is organised by Simi (Shaheen Khan), co-ordinator of the Saheli Asian Women's project. The day-trippers include Ladhu (Nisha Nayar) and Madhu (Renu Kochar), two teenagers out not so much for the sea air but an alternative to the boys in Birmingham. Accompanying them are three aunties – Pushpa (Zohra Segal), Asha (Lalita Ahmed) and Bina (Surendra Kochar) – who pass judgement on the way the younger women on the trip choose to run their lives. Also along are Ginder (Kim Vithana) and Hashida (Sarita Khajuria) who spend the day negotiating their marital and sexual relationships respectively, and Rekha (Souad Faress), a visitor from Bombay.

The film begins with a careful introduction to the three main storylines which focus on Hashida's relationship with Oliver (Mo Sesay), Asha's frustrations of serving her family and not being able to capitalise on her college education, and finally the decision by Ginder to leave her violent husband and his possessive family. All three foci link the film to 'common sense' racist discourses which have effectively excluded South Asian women from an English identity through the idea that they are a very private and closed people whose movements are very strictly under the surveillance and authority of patriarchal family structures. Such a perception has been translated and maintained in dominant media representations through a heavy reliance on and reproduction of visual images of South Asian women that are firmly rooted in the home, the community or the family business. The narratives of these images are constructed around religious and

---

21 Bhabha, *The Location of Culture*, pp. 212–35.

cultural issues such as the practice of purdah, arranged marriages and extended families. Seldom are they cast or positioned in settings considered specifically 'English' such as the countryside or the village pub.

The setting for *Bhaji* is the seaside resort of Blackpool which proves an important choice for two reasons. Displacing the women from the confines of their households and families suggests that there is a life for South Asian women outside of home and community. In addition, by situating them in a distinctly 'English' setting, the characters acquire a sense of Englishness denied them by dominant discourses and representations of 'race'. The film further reinforces their 'Englishness' in that, although it is a social realist text, it has the feel of the *Carry On* comedies which, as Andrea Stuart notes, have a very 'constructed sense of Englishness'.[22] The suffusion of comedy and charm that results from this strategy projects a more optimistic feel about the lives of South Asian women than the ideologues of the 'new' racism would have us believe.

Bhaji, however, goes further than merely embedding South Asian women into what are essentially 'official' sites or symbols of Englishness. It also provides subtle glimpses of the dynamic character of English culture itself, how it is constantly evolving in dialogue with what are more commonly regarded as 'other' cultures. For example, the film uses the soundtrack of Cliff Richard's *Summer Holiday* (1963) as the theme tune but it is appropriately dubbed in Punjabi. Some of the characters display an ability to switch between English and Punjabi dialect with relative ease. There are also various forms of dress on display – from the sneakers, jeans and bomber jacket of Ladhu and Madhu to the sari and salwar kameez of Asha and Pushpa. Simi fashions a leather jacket on top of her salwar kameez. Perhaps the scene that most cunningly conveys this fusion of cultures is the shot of Pushpa and Bina sitting on the Blackpool promenade enjoying their bag of chips with a sprinkling of chilli powder.

Multi-racial complexions

Amidst the more astute intimations of how in the most mundane of everyday activities the definitions of Englishness are under constant negotiation and transformation, *Bhaji* also confronts a more deeply ingrained concern amongst nationalists and puritans of whatever racial background – the biological purity of races. In England the myth of the English as constituting a pure, white 'race' has primarily been sustained through a particular construction of female sexuality. As my earlier discussion of the cases of Parry, MacLaughlan, Woodward and Basuta illustrates, defending an innocuous female identity, imperious to and untarnished by the 'other', has been symbolically important for maintaining a close association between Englishness and whiteness. But, as Bhikhu Parekh points out, to suggest that racial groups are biologically unique and distinct from one another is

---

22 Andrea Stuart, 'Blackpool Illumination', *Sight and Sound* (Feb. 1994), pp. 26–7.

misleading, given that there has been so much racial intermixing.[23] In its portrayal of Hashida's relationship with Oliver, *Bhaji* makes some bold statements about the racial complexity of the English population.

Hashida is due to start medical school. She is introduced holding a positive pregnancy test in the bathroom whilst her parents proudly discuss her future downstairs. This discovery leads to a division between Hashida and Oliver stemming from their anxiety about the likely reaction from Hashida's 'aunties' and parents, from whom the relationship has been concealed. When their journey to Blackpool is broken up with a stop at a motorway service station, Hashida shares with Simi her disappointment in Oliver's reaction. Unknown to them, Asha, who is in one of the toilet cubicles, overhears their conversation.

Later, when the aunties are seated in their deck chairs on the beach 'putting the world to rights', Hashida's secret is revealed to the rest of the group. In an emotional outburst about the corrupting effects of Western culture on Asian youth, Asha points to Hashida as an example. The scene reaches a climax when the aunties unduly insult Hashida for being pregnant out of wedlock. Hashida responds in kind by shouting 'You're not my fucking sisters', before storming off, with Ladhu and Madhu in pursuit. Up until this point, the storyline depicts a stereotypical view of a young South Asian woman who, having had a taste of freedom that she has kept secret from her family and 'community', is in danger of being left to cope on her own.

As the Hashida/Oliver relationship unfolds, however, the narrative deviates from the way other mainstream texts have tended to treat such a theme. First of all it does not conform to the white person/'other' relationship sometimes depicted in dominant texts, which, as bell hooks has documented, is often fraught with problems and rarely materialises.[24] By contrast, Hashida and Oliver's relationship is a mixed race union that has a future, not by one party making all the compromises but through both independent and mutual negotiation and re-negotiation. After the initial split, both characters seek advice from people they confide in. Hashida speaks to Simi whilst Oliver discusses the situation with his friend. Both are advised to go their own ways. Later, encouraged by his father not to leave things half finished, Oliver leaves for Blackpool in search of Hashida. There, after further discussions about their future, they are reconciled. This reconciliation challenges 'common sense' assumptions that the coming together of individuals belonging to different ethnic and cultural groups is inevitably doomed.

Secondly, by making the mixed race relationship between a South Asian female and an African Caribbean male, the film draws attention to the fact that diasporic

---

23 Bhikhu Parekh, 'Reflections on the Language of Racism' in *The Black and White Media Show Book*, ed. J. Twitchin (London: Trentham Books, 1988).

24 bell hooks illustrates this in her critique of the films *The Crying Game* and *The Bodyguard*. See her essay, 'Seduction and Betrayal' in *Outlaw Culture: resisting representations* (London: Routledge, 1994), pp. 53–62.

populations are negotiating their identities and situation in England in dialogue with, not just the 'host' community, but also other migrant/diasporic groups. In this regard, the position of black people in England has all too often been documented and measured against the position of white people who colonise conventional ideas of Englishness. The sexual intermixing of non-white racial groups may at first appear inconsequential to the preoccupation of English nationalists concerned only for the purity of the 'white' race. Yet, the offspring of such mixed race relationships have grave implications for nationalist policies to rid England of its immigrant population. How would they repatriate Hashida and Oliver's child? Would they force him/her to spend six months in the Caribbean and six months in the subcontinent?

So far I have examined *Bhaji* from the perspective of an 'objectified notion of culture', 'where the meaning (is) in the object, not in the process of its production'.[25] In the following section, I shift focus from 'culture contained in its embodiment to its generativity'. In other words, I examine more closely how *Bhaji* interweaves 'specific relations between elements, symbols, behaviours, institutions, structures of meaning'.[26] By extending the debate in this way, it will be possible to identify how, in *Bhaji*, Englishness retains its notion of superiority.

Myths about the 'past'

Bhaji may expose the tenuous nature of any attempts to preserve a vision of England and Englishness as stable and untainted by the presence of black people, but there are times where the narrative pathologises South Asian family life. In this way, it reinforces 'common sense' perceptions of the dynamics characterising race relations in England. For example, although the different types of clothes worn by the women do not serve to distinguish the characters in terms of traits such as modesty, they do serve to demarcate the women in relation to generation and tradition. They signal varying degrees of affiliation to the institution of patriarchy and the practice of arranged marriages as well as the ability to escape these 'restrictive' customs. The older, 'traditionally' dressed women voice their discord on learning about Hashida's relationship with Oliver. They are also quick to accord the blame to Ginder for her separation from her husband and extended family. Asha, one of the three aunties, never publicly expresses her own unhappiness at not having capitalised on her college education due to familial responsibilities. And it is Hashida and Ginder who actively negotiate their situations to suit their needs whilst Asha only ever grieves privately. The marking of these three characters by age, clothing and their ability to negotiate their discord satisfactorily with

25 Jonathan Friedman, 'Global Crises, the Struggle for Cultural Identity and Intellectual Porkbarrelling: cosmopolitans versus locals, ethnics and nationals in an era of de-hegemonisation' in *Debating Cultural Hybridity*, ed. P. Werbner and T. Modood (London: Zed Books, 1997), p. 82.
26 Friedman, 'Global Crises', p. 82.

their personal relationships augments the idea that the young are more likely to reject the cultures and customs of their communities. And their ability to do so is enhanced by their adoption of 'English' values, which is primarily reinforced by the mutually exclusive predicaments characterising the respective futures of Asha and Ginder and which are specifically linked to their ability to defy expectations of 'honour' and 'duty' to the family.

The private expressions of regret by Asha at not being able to exploit her college education as a result of being bound to serving her children, husband and family business are depicted in the form of fantasy sequences. The opening scene is one such sequence. Asha is shown facing the statue of a Hindu god and is about to perform puja. The voice-over repeats the words, 'duty', 'honour', 'sacrifice' and there are individual flashes of Asha pictured with her son, daughter and husband. The sequence ends with her stumbling over larger than life-size items from her shop as the voice-over states 'Asha – know your place'. Thus, the film relates the unhappiness and frustration Asha feels back to family, tradition and religion. The final fantasy sequence is similar to the first, only this time, just in case the audience had any doubts about the message, Asha herself voices her unhappiness to the statue: 'I was a good singer at college', she says. 'I never had headaches and I wasn't born selling bloody newspapers! Duty, honour, sacrifice. What about me?'

In contrast to Asha's private remonstrations, Ginder actively negotiates instead of passively accepting her relationship with her violent husband Manjit (Jimmi Harkishin). However, her predicament accentuates 'common sense' ideas of South Asian men, the extended family and Asian customs which expect women to obey their husbands and become their property. In the film the aunties describe Ginder as the modern Asian woman, so liberal-thinking that she has had to stray away from family and tradition. Ginder herself is convinced that her husband's violence has resulted from their position within the extended family. In Blackpool she tells Simi that away from the family, life with her son and husband could be different. She thereby displaces the focus of blame from her husband onto the constraints placed upon them by the extended household structure.

Accompanied by his two brothers, Manjit tracks Ginder to Blackpool in pursuit of a reunion. The destiny of their relationship is concluded in the penulti-mate scene in which they fail to reconcile their differences. Manjit lashes out at Ginder and, aided by Balbir (Tanveer Ghani), the 'bounty hunter' of the two brothers, tries to snatch his son Amrik (Amer Chadha Patel). Asha helps snatch Amrik back and momentarily it appears as though the culmination of Ginder's predicament before their eyes might lead the aunties to break out of the shackles of duty and honour. However, the moment is very much a transient one, as confirmed by Pushpa's resignatory comment, 'What can you do?' as the women leave Blackpool passing Hashida and Oliver in embrace.

Placed alongside Asha and Ginder's marital discord, Hashida's relationship with Oliver reinforces 'common sense' conceptions that the subordinate position occupied by South Asian women directly results from the repressive systems prac-tised by their families. Hashida is involved with someone outside her own 'community' and hers is the only relationship of the three that concludes with a brighter future ahead. The idea that tradition and religion, completely devoid of rationality, wholly dominate 'conventional' Asian family structures is too simplistic a construction. For example, to intimate that in England there is no room for the extended family or a modification of that social formation is to overlook the support such families provide their members from a racist society and from their socio-economic situations. This is not to suggest that expectations about sexual and marital relations do not vary significantly between the generations. These are contentious issues being challenged and negotiated in modern England. Where *Bhaji*'s narrative becomes reductive is in its firm rooting of the thinking and cultural identities of the older women in an India they left behind some 'twenty years ago'. When the aunties blame the respective predicaments of Hashida and Ginder on their modern way of living and their rejection of morals from 'back home', Rekha interrupts, 'Home! What home? How long is it since you've been home? Look at you, your clothes, the way that you think … Come on "yar" you're twenty years out of date.'

Rekha's response draws attention to the fact that England is now the home of the aunties and intimates that the country from which they migrated has moved on. However, to suggest that the older women are a neat replica of a stagnant and outdated India ignores the changing dynamics and contexts in which the identities of this generation, identities that may have been necessary for their 'survival', evolved in both the subcontinent and England. But it also misrepresents the India that the older women left behind. As Peter van der Veer has argued, 'The idea that Indians lived their lives with restricted notions of time and space in autarkic villages until colonialism came to wake them up … is still very much among us'.[27] In *Bhaji* the character Rekha not only upholds this idea but also affirms a linear conception of cultural change in which 'Western' culture is positioned as a model for 'other' cultures to follow.

Linear conception of cultural change

Rekha arrives at the meeting point from where the women set off for Blackpool donning a bright pink suit, stiletto shoes and a cigarette holder. Her dress, mannerisms and comments give her a distinctly 'Western' appearance. As with the younger, British-born Asian characters, Rekha's identity is presented as being at a more advanced stage than the 'outdated' cultural outlooks the aunties are accused of clinging to. The fundamental weakness of such a narrative is that by linking Rekha's 'modern' and more 'progressive' Indian identity with firm 'Western' attributes, *Bhaji* concedes the 'superior' status of 'Western', and therefore also English,

27 Peter van der Veer, 'Introduction: the diasporic imagination' in *Nation and Migration: the politics of space in the South Asian diaspora*, ed. P. van der Veer (Philadelphia: University of Pennsylvania Press 1995), p. 4.

culture. By doing so, the negotiation of a liberated forward-looking notion of South Asian femininity becomes interlinked with an embracement of a specifically Western conception of modernity. This conception is closely aligned to that of social scientists who have 'grounded their theories of modernity in a secularisation thesis and thus find it hard to comprehend the persistence of religion and its increased importance in the public domain'.[28]

The mutually opposing identities of Rekha and the younger Asian women against those of the aunties evoke rigid binaries between tradition and modernity which tacitly suggest that the offspring of migrant populations have little recourse for religion in negotiating more assertive, independent and fulfilling lifestyles. This is an oversimplistic representation which neither reflects reality nor confronts the current crisis of relations between 'East' and 'West'. For instance, for large numbers of second-generation South Asian youth, modernity has not lessened the significance of religion.[29] Further, to suggest that religion has no place for the independent-minded, rational thinking and sexually liberated Asian woman not only ignores the dynamic contexts in which religious identities are negotiated, but it is also insensitive to what social and sexual freedom means to different people. For example, dominant Western discourses have interpreted the growing prominence of the hijab in both Muslim and non-Muslim societies as the proliferation of a religion that is inherently oppressive to women. But, as Leila Ahmed has described, for an increasing number of Muslim women the adoption of the hijab forms part of an active dialogue with their faith that has been a liberating and empowering experience.[30] The significance of these observations is not to ignore the fact that religion has been used as a subordinating force; but that it is instead the prominence of religion (through independent choice) in the lives of many South Asians born in Britain, who have had first-hand experience of Western ideals of modernity, which is indicative of 'other' narratives of modernity that may be equally valid for negotiating more progressive visions of the future.

Thus, beyond such sites as music, food, language and the biological purity of the English race, *Bhaji* presents a vision of a more progressive and modern notion of Englishness that remains itself too homogeneous and too simplistic. The destiny of all nine characters is predictably constructed around the idea that South Asian women can find fulfilment only outside the home and communal structures. To some extent this weakness is compounded by the 'burden of representation' on black film-makers, which Mercer describes as the 'inordinate pressure on each individual film to be *representative*, or to say as much as possible in one single

---

28 Phillip Lewis, 'Arenas of Ethnic Negotiation: cooperation and conflict in Bradford' in *The Politics of Multiculturalism in the New Europe: racism, identity and community*, ed. T. Modood and P. Werbner, (London: Zed Books, 1997), p. 143.

29 See Lewis, 'Arenas of Ethnic Negotiation'.

30 Leila Ahmed, *Women and Gender in Islam: roots of a modern debate* (New Haven: Yale University Press, 1992).

filmic statement'.[31] With three major storylines and nine main characters who range across three generations and three religions (Muslim, Sikh and Hindu), *Bhaji* clearly attempts to 'carry' rather than 'displace' the burden of representation. But it finds doing so an impossible task which restricts the narrative to skirting around, as opposed to exploring and articulating, the complexity of each character's circumstance and situation. As such the film depicts the institutions of patriarchy and racism as affecting very distinct aspects of the lives of South Asian women in England. The women confront racism outside the home whilst their domestic situations appear the direct result of the structure of their families and the attitudes of South Asian men. But it is the complex interweaving of the two that defines the position of South Asian women both within and outside of their household environments. As Mercer asserts, only when films 'speak from the specificity of one's circumstances and experiences' rather than '*for* the entire social category in which one's experience is constituted' do they begin to displace the 'burden of representation'.[32] Only then can they break out of the constraints of the master codes and, perhaps more importantly, break out of a linear conception of cultural change.

Conclusion

In the space of a day trip from the Midlands to the northern seaside resort of Blackpool, *Bhaji* destabilises many of the official symbols and perceptions of England – from the traditional fish and chips to the racial composition of the English population. As the characters play out their respective situations against the backdrop of Blackpool's golden mile, the film challenges many of the secure images of 'Olde England' and exposes their fallibility in the presence of the 'other'. But *Bhaji*'s most profound antithesis to a racially exclusive notion of Englishness is situated in Hashida's relationship with Oliver. The film positions Hashida's sexuality and social identity in opposition to that of the older women whose movements are strictly under the surveillance of tradition and religion. On the one hand, as I argued earlier, this transition of a South Asian femininity policed and controlled by tradition and religion to one which is negotiated by rational choices conforms to dominant stereotypes. Yet, a closer appraisal of this now formulaic narrative discloses the contradictory status of the fundamental characteristics on which a superior 'English' femininity has been constructed. Hashida embodies a gender identity in which the traits of submission and passivity are replaced with rationality and active negotiation. But Hashida is also involved with a partner of a different racial background; they are sexually active and she is pregnant out of wedlock. If Hashida's identity is more acceptable by 'English' standards and is to be read as

31 Mercer, *Welcome to the Jungle*, p. 91.
32 Mercer, *Welcome to the Jungle*, p. 92.

superior to conventional Indian female sexuality, then the hallmarks of 'purity' and 'innocence' become hard to reconcile with English femininity.

However, *Bhaji*'s vision of a more inclusive and progressive notion of Englishness remains very much predicated on a reductive understanding of modernity. This understanding is not only inextricably linked to the West, but all too readily and neatly divorces the 'past' (in the form of the older 'traditional' characters) from the 'present' (the younger modern characters). In that sense, *Bhaji* does not provide any routes for thinking through the interweaving of past and present which might also then make it possible to comprehend how the narrative of Western racism may be an outcome of Western modernity, making the latter an unviable option for the migrant's 'survival'.[33] In the end, *Bhaji* has its own 'ideal' of England. It conveys this ideal through the identities being negotiated by the younger female characters. It is, in essence, a reductive vision. Life's contradictions, which are construed as emanating from the rigid opposition between tradition and modernity, are gradually eroded as societies and their peoples adopt more 'rational' lives. Yet it is precisely this homogeneous, simplistic notion of modernity, in constant search for a knowable truth and observable phenomena, that has proved so damaging to the tensions that currently pervade both within and between nation states.

---

[33] For an insight into how racism may be interpreted as a product of Western modernity see Ali Rattansi, '"Western" Racisms, Ethnicities and Identities in a "Postmodern" Frame' in *Racism, Modernity and Identity on the Western Front*, ed. A. Rattansi and S. Westwood (London: Polity Press, 1994), pp. 15–86. The 'superior' status of western culture is reinforced in Gurinder Chadha's latest feature, *Bend it Like Beckham* (2002), in which the central Asian female character, Jesminder (Parminder Nagra), negotiates her 'freedom' from Asian family norms by becoming a successful footballer and foresees an even brighter future in the United States.

10 *The Black Album*: Hanif Kureishi's revisions of 'Englishness'

Bart Moore-Gilbert

As Thatcherism accelerated its programme of restructuring British society with the self-confidence born of a second successive election victory, the mid-1980s witnessed a gathering interest in the origins of the established paradigms of British national identity and self-image which the New Right was apparently so vigorously challenging.[1] One specialised manifestation of this interest was a flurry of critical studies of the role English Studies had historically played in formulating and disseminating such paradigms.[2] This research has established that the discipline played an important ideological role in the (re)affirmation of (English) national identity at a number of important historical moments, beginning with Matthew Arnold's *Culture and Anarchy* (1869), now recognised as the founding text of modern English Studies. Arnold was primarily concerned, in this text, with the threat to national unity and identity posed by increasingly bitter and competing class relations within Victorian Britain. As *On the Study of Celtic Literature* (1867) suggested, however, other factors were making his an era in which 'Englishism pure and simple … is losing that imperturbable faith in its untransformed self which [formerly] made it imposing.'[3] Arnold saw the study of (English) literature as the potential source of a new, consensual set of values

---

1 Many would argue that Thatcherism was dedicated to the revival of a superseded (Victorian) model of national identity, rather than the construction of a genuinely new one. For examples of critical studies of national identity in the mid-1980s, see, notably, Patrick White, *On Living in an Old Country: the national past in contemporary Britain* (London: Verso, 1985); Robert Colls and Philip Dodd, *Englishness: politics and culture 1880–1820* (Beckenham: Croom Helm, 1986); Robert Hewison, *The Heritage Industry: Britain in a climate of decline* (London: Methuen, 1987). This interest has continued unabated; see, for example, Raphael Samuel, *Theatres of Memory*, 2 vols (London: Verso, 1994, 1996); Linda Colley, *Britons: forging the nation* (London: Yale University Press, 1992); Jeremy Paxman, *The English: a portrait of a people* (London: Michael Joseph, 1998). More specifically literary-critical examples of such investigations include Ian Bell (ed.), *Peripheral Visions: images of nationhood in contemporary British fiction* (Cardiff: University of Wales Press, 1995); Simon Gikandi, *Maps of Englishness: writing identity in the culture of colonialism* (London: Columbia University Press, 1996); Stefan Collini, *English Pasts: essays in culture and history* (Oxford: Oxford University Press, 1998).
2 See, for example, Francis Mulhern, *The Moment of Scrutiny* (London: New Left Books, 1979); Chris Baldick, *The Social Mission of English Criticism 1848–1932* (Oxford: Clarendon, 1983); Brian Doyle, *English and Englishness* (London: Routledge, 1987); and Bernard Bergonzi, *Exploding English: criticism, theory, culture* (Oxford: Clarendon Press, 1990).

which could help the nation to reaffirm itself in the face of the 'foreign' threats posed variously by Fenianism (a spectacular danger to the integrity of the nation in the 1860s), rebellion in the empire (the 1865 Morant Bay uprising in Jamaica brought uncomfortable reminders of the Indian Mutiny eight years earlier) and the increasing political and economic challenge represented by nations like Germany and the United States.

The substance of Arnold's vision was reiterated on several occasions at times of crisis in national self-esteem over the next hundred years. Thus the Newbolt Report of 1921 turned to literary education as a panacea for the problems posed by a newly militant mass labour movement, inspired by the example of the Russian Revolution and further radicalised by the economic depression which accompanied victory in the First World War. The Report proselytised for the consolidation of English at the core of secondary school syllabuses in part because the subject was deemed to offer 'a unique opportunity of reviving local patriotism and so laying a popular basis for a new renaissance'.[4] Half a century on, as a Britain increasingly beset by economic and political decline prepared for integration into (or, as many considered to be the case, surrender to) the European Common Market, the most famous literary critic in England, F. R. Leavis, echoed this aspect of the Newbolt Report. Describing himself in *Nor Shall My Sword* (1972) as 'the scion of a line of little Englanders', Leavis argued that a reaffirmation of the conception of literary education bequeathed by his predecessors could counter 'the loss of a national sense of identity' which would inevitably accompany the transfer of power to Brussels.[5]

Given its genesis in an age of imperialism, it was perhaps inevitable that the debate about the connections between literary education and British identity should have been imbricated from the outset in discourses not just of nation, but of race. In *Colonial Desire*, Robert Young demonstrates how much Arnold's conception of culture is inflected by contemporary Victorian thinking about ethnicity, the drive to taxonomise which was fuelled primarily by the rapid growth of British hegemony over the non-Western world.[6] For example, Young shows that in *On the Study of Celtic Literature*, Arnold conceives of the literary critic as a kind

---

3 Matthew Arnold, *On the Study of Celtic Literature* (London: Smith, Elder, 1867), p. xvii. Dickens's *Great Expectations* (1860–1) seems to echo Arnold's unease about Englishness in a period for long represented as 'the age of equipoise'. Pip recalls the period of his youth in the following terms: 'We Britons had at that time particularly settled that it was treasonable to doubt our having and being the best of everything' (London: Everyman, 1966, p. 151). The implication seems to be that by the 1860s, the time that Pip is looking back from, Britain has lost that confidence.

4 [Henry Newbolt], *The Teaching of English in England* (London: HMSO, 1921), pp. 143–4.

5 F. R. Leavis, *Nor Shall My Sword: discourses on pluralism, compassion and social hope* (London: Chatto & Windus, 1972), p. 132.

6 In *Masks of Conquest: literary study and British rule in India* (New York: Columbia University Press, 1990), Gauri Viswanathan argues persuasively that English literary studies were, in fact, first institutionalised in India as part of the larger colonial strategy of producing Indian compliance in British rule.

of ethnologist. Just as the latter classifies physiological marks of racial difference, such as the 'square head' of the German, so the literary critic – according to Arnold – must be alert to the 'spiritual marks which determine the type, and make us speak of the Greek genius, the Teutonic genius, the Celtic genius, and so on'.[7] In his attempt to characterise the 'English genius', Young argues, Arnold introduced an identification of cultural tradition not just with nation, but with race, which strongly influenced later thinking about English Studies. For example, Leavis argued in the 1930s that the poet was 'the most conscious point of the race in his time' and that the 'critical minority' (epitomised by the English department) 'constituted the consciousness of the race'.[8]

If the archaeologies of English Studies inaugurated in the 1980s performed many signal services in tracing the historical interconnections between the emergence and consolidation of the discipline and ideologies of national identity, they generally proved reluctant to trace such legacies into the contemporary period – partly, perhaps, because there have been few manifestos of English Studies of any substance since *Nor Shall My Sword*. The deep-seated nature of the assumptions identified above about the interconnections between race, Englishness and literary studies can, however, be clearly tracked in two post-war academic fictions written a quarter of a century apart, Malcolm Bradbury's *Eating People is Wrong* (1959) and David Lodge's *Nice Work* (1988). These novels were authored by two of the most distinguished Professors of English Studies of recent times, both of whom enjoyed a wide following outside academia. What is particularly significant in the context of a discussion of Kureishi's *The Black Album* (1995) is that each text considers the potential of English Studies to mitigate a sense of national self-doubt and unease which is to an important degree bound up with the challenge of finding a new, post-imperial, role for Britain in the modern world.

Eating People is Wrong is set in the later 1950s, after Indian independence (1947) and the Suez crisis (1956) had fatally undermined Britain's continuing pretensions to the status of a global power, and appeared at the end of the decade which witnessed the first large-scale migration to Britain of peoples from the former empire and countries on the verge of being decolonised. Both developments, which quickly began to provide a significant challenge to established conceptions of national identity and belonging, are registered to some extent in the novel, although it is primarily concerned, at the political level, with problems of class. For example, the racial violence suffered by the Nigerian student Eborebelosa seems, to some extent, to be reflecting on the Notting Hill and Nottingham race riots of 1958. Yet what is remarkable about the text is the way that such issues fail in any serious way to disturb received models of Englishness, let alone to challenge the inherited conceptualisation of English Studies as the

---

7 Cited in Robert J. C. Young, *Colonial Desire: hybridity in theory, culture and race* (London: Routledge, 1995), p. 81.
8 F. R. Leavis, *For Continuity* (Cambridge: Minority Press, 1933), pp. 12, 15.

embodiment of (invisibly racialised) values which, in the context of decolonisation and the changing demography of Britain in the 1950s, were now becoming
potentially socially divisive and exclusive. Those characters in the novel who come
from non-British cultures (including other Europeans!) are consistently represented as civilisationally and/or morally inferior. Thus Eborebelosa (who is linked
to a nationalist group which is symptomatically associated by the narrative voice
with terrorism rather than a principled struggle against colonial oppression) is
characterised above all by his sexual incontinence and 'childishness'. These are, of
course, qualities which were stereotypically attributed to subject peoples in colonial discourse, a regime of representation which – as critics as diverse as Ngugi,
Said and Bhabha have argued – was underpinned by a drive to reinforce the superior self-image and self-esteem of the dominant culture.

The quasi-colonialist nature of Bradbury's discourse is most apparent at the
embarrassing departmental staff–student party (a pastiche of the Collector's
'bridge' party in *A Passage to India* (1924)), where the foreign students and representatives of the 'host' culture are supposed to mingle in the hope of promoting
mutual understanding. Discomfited by her failed attempt at communication with
Eborebelosa, Emma Fielding (her name obviously invokes the protagonist of
Forster's novel), who is the mouthpiece of Bradbury's 'liberal' values in the novel,
opines thus: 'After all, there was one thing that every Englishman knew from his
very soul, and that was that, for all experiences and all manners, in England lay the
norm … and an occasion like the present one was not likely to prove that things
had altered.'[9] Seen in its historical context, there is an inescapable sense that *Eating
People is Wrong* is, on one level, an attempt to compensate its British readers for the
loss of their empire to 'backward' anti-colonial nationalists like Eborebelosa, by
reaffirming the superiority of England's cultural tradition, in which literature, of
course, occupies a privileged position. In the course of the departmental trip to see
a Shakespeare play at Stratford-upon-Avon, which includes a stop-over at a stereotypical English country house, an established conception of the role of English
Studies in incubating a sense of national identity and belonging is reinscribed. The
visit is focalised once more through Emma Fielding who conceptualises
'Englishness' in terms of a well-established matrix of race, tradition, social hierar-
chy and rural experience: 'The parkland and the grazing cattle were a fundamental
part of one's Englishness. It was the high civilisation of a liberal and refined race
that was commemorated in this parkland and this house and this tamed countryside' (p. 264).

Nice Work is set at a more recent moment in post-war history when severe pressure is being exerted on the conceptions of national identity which are reaffirmed at
the end of Bradbury's text. As with Bradbury's novel, the part played by (the legacy
of) Britain's role as an imperial power in this crisis is an important theme. At the

---

9 Malcolm Bradbury, *Eating People is Wrong* (1959; London: Arena, 1986), p. 43. Further references
   to this edition will be given in parentheses in the text.

outset of the novel, the Falklands war has begun, as the Thatcher government makes a desperate attempt to reverse what the New Right perceived to be Britain's irreversible decline as a power in the world, by reasserting its claims to far-flung overseas territories acquired by conquest centuries ago. Of the various internal divisions which threaten the nation, class plays a much less important role than in the earlier discourses of English Studies from Arnold to Bradbury (in *Eating People is Wrong*, Eborebelosa is a less central figure than the working-class student Louis Bates). Much the most pressing danger is the possibility of interracial conflict of the kind which had in fact erupted across many major urban centres in Britain during the early 1980s. On the one hand, the novel recognises the kind of social and economic disadvantages faced by 'New Commonwealth' migrants, which make the ghetto of Angleside a potential tinder-box. On the other, it sympathetically acknowledges the anxiety of the 'host' culture about what even so mild an old man as Wilcox's father considers to be an 'invasion' of alien cultures.

Towards the end of the novel, the enthusiastic and idealistic new English literature lecturer Robyn Penrose has a vision of the university bringing together the races (as well as classes and genders), on an equal basis, to their mutual benefit. To this extent she seems to reaffirm the Arnoldian vision of the potential of (literary) education to heal social division and conflict. Yet, as Robyn herself finally recognises, the reality of the university as a social institution in the early 1980s is that it reproduces rather than mitigates the burdens borne by 'New Commonwealth' migrants. After her moment of vision, Robyn notices her (white) students relaxing in the pleasant grounds of Rummidge University, oblivious of the black gardener who tends the flower-beds around them. Remembering her utopian fantasy, Robyn 'smiles to herself. There is a long way to go.'[10] To this extent, Lodge's text certainly acknowledges the challenges posed by the 'translation' of formerly colonised subjects into metropolitan citizens, not just to conceptions of national identity which were dominant twenty-five years earlier, but to received ideas about the social mission of English Studies.

However, the limitations of Lodge's attempt to rearticulate the traditional vision of the social mission of English Studies in the changed demographic context of 1980s Britain are evident in the very terms within which the novel conceives of the non-white migrants. For instance, during her vision, the undoubtedly well-meaning and 'liberal' Robyn represents them by using stereotypes of the kind found in popular television shows, such as *The Black and White Minstrel Show*; she conjures up 'a lost army, headed by Danny Ram and the two Sikhs from the cupola and the giant black from the knock-out, their eyes rolling white in their swarthy, soot-blackened faces' (p. 347). Moreover, Robyn's interventions on behalf of Danny Ram have inescapable overtones of the often misguided benevolence towards the subaltern displayed by the female missionary in the colonial period. Such limitations are not

---

10 David Lodge, *Nice Work* (Harmondsworth: Penguin, 1988), p. 384. Further references to this edition will be given in parentheses in the text.

just defects of Robyn's vision, however. It is Lodge's own narrative choice to present these migrants either as victims (like Danny Ram) or as threatening (like the drug-dealer in Angleside).[11] In the descriptions of hapless tropical migrants in the Angleside winter, moreover, it is clear that the novel's narrative persona has problems in accepting them as 'properly' British. Perhaps inevitably, then, neither Robyn nor *Nice Work* itself is able to imagine in any convincing way how English Studies can help bridge the racial divide of modern Britain.

Like *Eating People is Wrong*, or *Nice Work*, Kureishi's *The Black Album* is a 'condition of England' novel in the mode of social realism (Priestley and Orwell are generic predecessors cited in the text), which locates its enquiry into the state of the nation, and issues of national identity and belonging, within the context of a higher education institution which functions as a microcosm for the social and cultural challenges that the nation faces. Kureishi, too, is centrally concerned with the social function of literary studies in the context of what he sees as ever-increasing social atomisation and division. Set in the late 1980s, shortly after Prime Minister Margaret Thatcher turned her back on 'one nation politics' and pronounced notoriously that 'there is no such thing as society', Shahid's college represents a disastrous collapse of the community life which the university, and more particularly the English department, can still claim, however tenuously, to represent in the fiction of Bradbury and Lodge. Deedee's popularity derives in part from her willingness to mix with students and thus to challenge a social regime which makes it 'unusual to see a student and staff member sitting together'.[12] Even the student body is fragmented. Thus Riaz's group appeals to Shahid, 'who had barely received or been able to give an amicable smile since he'd started at college' (p. 2), largely because it represents the one obvious alternative to the isolation which he experiences as endemic to modern (student) life. (By contrast, Brownlow remembers the 1960s as a time when students were a 'united force' (p. 179).)

What Kureishi sees as the more fractured – and fractious – nature of Britain in the late 1980s is one important reason for the often sharp differences of tone between *The Black Album* and *Eating People is Wrong* or even *Nice Work*, which is set during the first Thatcher government, before the New Right had consolidated itself sufficiently to begin systematically dismantling the Welfare State and undermining the consensual values which the latter claimed to embody. An early symptom of intent, however, was the 'reform' of the university sector, which began during Thatcher's initial term in office, a development with which Lodge's text is clearly deeply preoccupied. The emphasis in Kureishi's text is on the student's experience of the effects of these 'reforms.' Bradbury certainly makes some

---

11 Lodge's split vision of the migrants illustrates one of Homi Bhabha's arguments about the conflictual regime of colonial stereotype. See Homi Bhabha, 'The Other Question: stereotype, discrimination and the discourse of colonialism' in *The Location of Culture* (London: Routledge, 1994), pp. 66–84.

12 Hanif Kureishi, *The Black Album* (London: Faber, 1995), p. 2. Further references to this edition will be given in parentheses in the text.

attempt to incorporate the student's point of view, especially through Emma Fielding (although, as a postgraduate student in the 1950s, she is clearly in a privileged position compared with Shahid – and she reaffirms, rather than challenges, the social norms of the English department);[13] and Wilcox regards Rummidge in the later parts of *Nice Work* from the perspective of a prospective part-time student. However, Kureishi gives much greater weight than his predecessors to 'the view from below'. *The Black Album* is especially sensitive to the poverty which has become an increasingly common feature of student existence since the 1980s. Shahid's grotty digs, his mean diet, the difficulties of getting books, these are all aspects of student reality which are absent from the novels of Lodge and Bradbury.

But the most significant factor in *The Black Album*'s revision of Bradbury's and Lodge's treatment of the relationship between the discourses of English Studies and those of national identity is the fact that the domestic British racial 'other' plays a much more significant role in Kureishi's text than in the fiction of his predecessors. The latter is focalised through the perspective of those who belong to the dominant ethnic group, irrespective of the comparative disadvantages which, in the case of Robyn Penrose or Louis Bates, their gender or class identities may nonetheless still entail. In *Eating People is Wrong*, this domestic British racial 'other' is absent (Eborebelosa is a visiting student, destined to return to Africa after completing his studies); and in *Nice Work* he is in reality, if not in Robyn's hopeful vision, admitted only as a low-paid menial (the gardener who services the grounds of Rummidge University). In *The Black Album*, by contrast, members of British ethnic minorities have penetrated the bastions of British higher education (or at least certain sectors of it) in significant numbers and are now participating in the discipline which Bradbury and Lodge, like Arnold, Newbolt and Leavis before them, identify as the example *par excellence* of a social institution which encourages national unity and belonging.

Perhaps the most immediately obvious contrast between Kureishi and his predecessors in this respect involves the differences in the settings of the three novels. The educational institution which Kureishi's protagonist attends is not an 'old' university of the kind represented by the solidly provincial and still relatively self-confident red-brick institutions which feature in *Eating People is Wrong* or *Nice Work*. Described as a 'local college' (p. 2), it resembles an inner-city former polytechnic or further education college in the last days of the old binary divide in higher education, compared with which even Rummidge seems well resourced. For example, Deedee's office is crammed and claustrophobic, being 'only three times the size of a telephone booth' (p. 21). For students, the facilities are even poorer: 'The library was also in the basement and it was one long room, cramped and hot, like a submarine. The desks had been churned up by knives and many of the books had been stolen' (p. 25). The chill winds of Thatcherite 'reform' gathering in *Nice Work* have become a

---

13 For example, it seems significant that in her musings at the staff–student party in *Eating People is Wrong*, Emma adopts the normative perspective of the English*man*.

gale in *The Black Album*. Privatisation looms and with it a collapse of staff morale engendered by the prospect of compulsory redundancies, a threat which requires Deedee's absence from class at many union meetings. Indeed, Brownlow's intervention at the book-burning organised by Riaz's cohort might be explained, in part, as an act of recklessness born of the knowledge that he is on the point of being forcibly retired.

The depressing material environment of Shahid's college takes on particular significance in the light of the observation that it 'was sixty per cent black and Asian' (p. 20). The inescapable implication of Kureishi's novel, when read in conjunction with those of Bradbury and Lodge, is that access to higher education in contemporary Britain is still overdetermined to a great degree by larger patterns of social exclusion and disadvantage. It strongly reinforces the impression given by *Nice Work* that, while the obstacles to participation within the elite sectors of higher education which were habitually encountered by women and the traditional working classes (obstacles which are still well entrenched, if not insuperable, in *Eating People is Wrong*) have been to a large degree removed, significant barriers against such participation remain for Britain's racial minorities, which are relegated instead to far less prestigious institutions. One of the greatest ironies offered by *The Black Album*, indeed, is the sense that it is precisely the existence of these larger patterns of social exclusion and disadvantage, notably a relative lack of access to employment opportunities, that accounts for the presence of many of the ethnic minority students whom Deedee teaches (and which explains what she perceives as their characteristic lack of motivation): 'They're not being educated, just kept off the dole. I've never known such a lack of inner belief' (p. 25).

The racial composition of Shahid's college reflects, of course, the ethnically mixed nature of the area of London in which it is located. In contrast to the small-town idyll of *Eating People is Wrong* and to the Rummidge campus, set at a safe distance from ghetto areas like Angleside, Shahid's college is surrounded by inner-city London. But whereas the emphasis in Kureishi's first novel, *The Buddha of Suburbia* (1990), is on London as a potential space, within certain clear limitations, in which can take place the productive mingling of different ethnic groups and cultural communities to produce what Karim Amir describes as a 'new breed' of Englishman, *The Black Album* is much more pessimistic.[14] For Shahid, at least, there is far less evidence of the kind of mixing which Karim experiences:

He had noticed, during the days that he'd walked round the area, that the races were divided. The black kids stuck with each other, the Pakistanis went to one another's houses, the Bengalis knew each other from way back, and the whites too. Even if there was no hostility between groups – and there was plenty ... there was little mixing. And would things change? Why should they? A few individuals would make the effort, but wasn't the world breaking up into political and religious tribes? The divisions were taken for granted, each to his own. (p. 111)

---

14 Hanif Kureishi, *The Buddha of Suburbia* (London: Faber, 1990), p. 3.

This increasing polarisation and hostility in society at large is mirrored in the gangs which roam Shahid's college, which is the site of endemic conflict on a scale sufficient to require the presence of a squad of full-time security personnel.

Moreover, the 'host' culture in the part of London which surrounds Shahid's college, at least, is a good deal more aggressively resistant to migrants than is the case in the leafy South London outer suburbs or relatively affluent areas like Barons Court which provide the principal settings for *The Buddha*. Far more explicitly than either *Eating People is Wrong* or *Nice Work*, *The Black Album* stresses the endemic racism of British society, even in the cosmopolitan heart of the capital. For Shahid, so simple a chore as using the laundrette at night involves the risk of attack. The obstacles faced by migrant minorities are systematic, as is suggested not just by the educational and economic discrimination alluded to above, but by the stories of police harassment which surface at Riaz's surgery, or the campaign of terror waged against the Bengali family on behalf of which Shahid and his friends intervene. *The Black Album* suggests that racism infects every sector of society. Even in the bohemian cafes and clubs (one has the unfortunately apposite name The White Room), there is a *de facto* 'colour bar' which is as difficult to circumvent as the barriers described in migrant fictions set three decades earlier, such as Sam Selvon's *The Lonely Londoners* (1956): 'People came and went, but [Shahid] was the only person there with a dark skin. That would be the fact in most places he went with Deedee' (p. 101).

In this context, the barriers to achieving the social mission traditionally associated with literary education seem all the more formidable. For many of the students, Deedee accepts, 'the great tradition' is an object of deep suspicion: 'Many of them regarded the white elite culture as self-deceiving and hypocritical. For some this was an excuse for laziness. With others it was genuine: they didn't want to find the culture that put them down profound' (p. 112). Even Shahid, who is from the outset more enthusiastic than his peers about the canon, has some sympathy for the doubters, remembering as he does the way he was taught in his younger days: 'Literature hadn't been like this at school, where books were stuck down their throats like medicinal biscuits, until they spat them out' (p. 62). This suspicion about the regulatory function of literary studies in a secondary education system which, the novel implies, itself acts primarily as a means of social control, influences Shahid's conception of higher education, too: 'Could this place be like those youth clubs that merely kept bad kids out of trouble?' (p. 22).

Deedee makes considerable efforts to mitigate such suspicions by adjusting the traditional syllabus of English Studies to make it reflect more the experience of the various kinds of historically marginalised constituencies that she is addressing as a lecturer (she herself has used a literary education to emancipate herself from the social disadvantages of her early life). Thus she is keen on extending the syllabus to incorporate more women's writing and popular genre fiction. To make explicit the ethnocentric assumptions of the established canon and to emphasise the historical links between metropolitan culture and the histories of imperialism, moreover, she offers a 'course on colonialism and literature' which leaves Shahid, for one, 'in a

fog of inchoate anger and illumination' (p. 25). These initiatives are complemented by her consistent efforts to introduce aspects of popular music, especially
'black' popular music, into her teaching. The fact that Shahid's first assignment for
her is on Prince suggests Deedee's acceptance that such figures, and the medium in
which they work, are of something like equivalent importance to the established
high cultural canon, which Hat lampoons as 'the whole white doo-dah' (p. 181).

Yet *The Black Album* ends by being much more positive about the value of
canonical Western literature than might be inferred from either Deedee's initiatives or Hat's attitudes. Indeed, it reiterates the argument of *The Buddha*, where
Jamila's scathing and wholesale critique of the Western canon, which is inspired by
the rejectionist logic of certain varieties of minoritarian cultural nationalism, is
itself in the end clearly rejected by Karim. This affirmative attitude to the canon
may be explained in part by the fact that, even more explicitly than the novels of
Bradbury and Lodge, *The Black Album* registers the challenge to 'high culture'
posed in a modern nation space which is being increasingly reconfigured by
consumerism, democratisation and globalisation – and ever more dominated by
'mass' cultural forms such as pop music and the visual media. The declining rele-
vance and prestige of 'great' literature is registered in the fact that even Deedee has
to steel herself to get through texts like *Little Dorrit*; this fact forces on her some
uncomfortable reflections:

Serious reading required dedication. Who, now, believed it did them good? And how many
people knew a book as they knew *Blonde on Blonde*, *Annie Hall* or Prince, even? Could literature connect a generation in the same way? Some exceptional students would read hard
books; most wouldn't, and they weren't fools. (p. 111)

Shahid, of course, dissents from this pessimistic analysis, a response which can be
largely attributed to the fact that he is a would-be 'serious' writer with an appren-
tice's burning conviction of the superiority of his medium: 'Sometimes I see certain people and I want to grab them and say, read this story by Maupassant or
Faulkner, this mustn't be ignored, a man made it, it's better than television' (p.
17). Such views undoubtedly correspond closely to Kureishi's own position. For
example, despite his own considerable success in both television and film,
including an Oscar nomination for the script of *My Beautiful Laundrette* in 1986,
Kureishi has argued that 'the cinema cannot replace the novel or autobiography as
the precise and serious medium of the age while it is still too intent on charming
its audience'.[15]

However, Kureishi provides an interesting twist to this discussion of what is a
conventional topic in the post-war academic novel by revisiting and reorienting
what is, equally, a common theme in postcolonial literature, the difficulties of
retaining one's culture of origin in the process of migration to the West. In *The*

---

15 Hanif Kureishi, 'Some Time with Stephen' in *Sammy and Rosie Get Laid: the script and the diary*
    (London: Faber, 1988), p. 95.

Black Album, anxieties about cultural heritage and identity are as much characteristic of the 'host' culture as they are of the migrants'. Outside the conurbations,
what Deedee calls 'the whole Orwellian idea of England' (p. 89) still has some
purchase. By contrast, the area in which Shahid's college is located is certainly no
longer English in the sense that this construct would be understood by the characters in *Eating People is Wrong*; the digs which Shahid inhabits are a model of the
Babel surrounding it. In inner-city London, at least, a living, specifically English
culture has, in the main, disappeared. According to Shahid, his schoolfriends
'knew nothing of their own culture' (p. 22) and he is disgusted by the cultural
deracination of the white supremacists on the estates where the Muslim students
perform their vigilante role: 'How could they bear their own ignorance, living
without culture, their lives reduced to watching soap operas three-quarters of the
day? They were powerless and lost' (p. 113).

In this respect, there appears to be an important change of emphasis vis-à-vis
The Buddha. The latter suggests that there is still at least one 'popular' form which
can be identified as a dynamic, evolving cultural resource, capable of generating
and mediating a distinctively British identity – popular music. The decline of
British pop from its achievements in the 1960s and 1970s is implied at several
moments in *The Black Album*, notably in Deedee's choice of musical accompani-
ments for her classes, such as Prince, Madonna and George Clinton. The focus on
such figures seems to symbolise the increasing dissipation of British cultural identity in a postmodern age increasingly dominated culturally – as well as politically
and economically – by the United States. In this context, British racism is represented, more than anything else, as a form of envy of the cultural tradition enjoyed
by at least some migrant minority communities. Whereas characters like Riaz
appear to have comparatively little difficulty in retaining a strong cultural identity,
in the run-down housing estates surrounding the college, at least, racism and
xenophobia provide a last shrunken focus of identity for the indigenous inhabitants, whose traditional culture has been swamped by globalised mass media pap,
epitomised in the decade on which Kureishi focuses by American television soaps
like *Dallas* and *Dynasty*.

Given his seemingly traditionalist affirmation of the enduring importance of
(canonical) literature and his distaste for 'mass' cultural forms – certain kinds of
film and pop music aside – it is little surprise that on more than one occasion,
Shahid has doubts about Deedee's attempt to tilt English Studies in the direction
of 'cultural studies': 'She and the other post-modern types encouraged their
students to study anything that took their interest, from Madonna's hair to a
history of the leather jacket. Was it really learning or only diversion dressed up in
the latest words? Were students in better colleges studying stuff to give them the
advantage in life?' (p. 22) Later in the text, Shahid reconsiders this issue from a
somewhat different angle, in a formulation which connects it directly with
Kureishi's broader enquiry into the social potential of the traditional 'high'
cultural canon in the context of modern multiracial Britain: 'He didn't always
appreciate being played Madonna or George Clinton in class, or offered a lecture

on the history of funk as if it were somehow more "him" than *Fathers and Sons.* Any art could become "his", if its value was demonstrated' (p. 112). Shahid's position may, on first reading, seem somewhat surprising. From one perspective, indeed, his response might be taken as an affirmation of a form of humanist universalism which would not be out of place in the staff-rooms frequented by figures like Professors Treece and Swallow, in the novels of Bradbury and Lodge.[16] Yet Shahid is undoubtedly right to wonder whether Deedee's strategy does not itself embody – albeit unconsciously – a subtle new form of exclusion, rather than empowerment, of the racial minorities on whose behalf she seems so interested.

Shahid's uneasy response reflects the deeply troubled tone of the novel's larger enquiry into the paradoxes of metropolitan liberalism's efforts to promote anti-racist initiatives which might foster a greater sense of unity and commonality in national life. At one point, Deedee identifies herself quite explicitly as a 'liberal' (p. 173) and is thus comparable in terms of her ideological leanings to fictional predecessors such as Professor Treece or Robyn Penrose. Of these two figures, she is closer to Robyn Penrose, of whom she is a more radicalised version, both in respect of her pedagogical politics and the conduct of her private life. As with Robyn Penrose, there is the unmistakable whiff of the missionary about Deedee. The manifestations of her social conscience extend far beyond an interest in adapting the traditional literary syllabus or a maternal concern for students of the kind which in the first instance, at least, seems to animate her interest in the painfully lonely Shahid. For instance, amongst the three college students who are lodgers in her home are two Asian British women whom, the novel implies, Deedee sees herself as having 'liberated' from an oppressive and 'obscurantist' home environment. Yet as Chad complains, Deedee's intervention as both feminist and liberal is by no means unproblematic: 'Would I dare hide a member of Osgood's family in my house and fill her with propaganda? If I did, what accusations? Terrorist! Fanatic! Lunatic! We can never win. The imperialist idea hasn't died' (p. 191).[17]

The deep ambiguities surrounding Deedee's benevolence in this instance derive in part from the fact that, as a landlady, Deedee is herself profiting from the predicament she is attempting to alleviate. In fact, from the outset of the novel, questions are raised about the integrity of her attitudes towards the racial Other

---

16 Gauri Viswanathan points out that the same 'liberal humanist' universalism underpinned colonial thinking about educational programmes for the Indian subject in the first half of the nineteenth century. Officials like T. B. Macaulay and Charles Trevelyan insisted on 'the universality of a single set of [principally English literary] works ... in an effort to assimilate individuals [of different races] to a single identity'. See Viswanathan, *Masks of Conquest*, p. 167.

17 Kureishi's text corroborates the anxieties expressed by Gayatri Spivak about the misplaced 'benevolence' of Western radicals, including feminists, on behalf of the 'subaltern.' See G. C. Spivak, 'Can the Subaltern Speak?' (1988), reprinted in Patrick Williams and Laura Chrisman (eds), *Colonial Discourse and Post-Colonial Theory: a reader* (Hemel Hempstead: Harvester Wheatsheaf, 1993), pp. 66–111.

and these questions are all the more forceful given the fact that she is certainly not, at any conscious level, acting in bad faith. There are uncomfortable echoes of the paternalistic district officer (or his wife) of imperial fiction in the conduct of at least one of Deedee's classes: 'They passed the hut in which she was teaching "her" girls, a class of black women fashion students. One of them was, somewhat embarrassedly, standing on a chair. The others were giggling and clapping. Deedee was also laughing and pointing at the woman's shoes' (p. 184). The location (a 'hut'), the 'spectacle' which the black student is making of herself, presumably at her teacher's behest, Deedee's response to this 'performance', the emphatic use of the possessive adjective – all contribute to making this scene a parodic reinscription of a common trope in colonial discourse, the dominant gaze of the coloniser at the 'manners and customs' of the subject peoples.

Prior to her intervention at the book-burning, it is Deedee's relationship with Shahid, however, which raises the most questions. Kureishi performs a bold stroke in revising a widespread theme in post-war academic fiction, the desire of male lecturers for female students. From Amis's *Lucky Jim* (1954), through *Eating People is Wrong*, Bradbury's *The History Man* (1975), to Howard Jacobson's *Coming from Behind* (1983) and Lodge's *Small World* (1984), this is a trope of the genre. *The Black Album* is perhaps the first novel of its kind to admit the possibility that women lecturers in English, characteristically represented by male writers as neurotic, isolated and unlovable, especially if they have feminist inclinations, can be both attractive and capable of desire, which might even extend to their male students.

Deedee's attitude to her lover nonetheless reinscribes certain elements of Orientalism. Classically, according to Edward Said, colonial discourse constructed the Orient as female and conceived of it as a space where sexual experiences not commonly available in Europe can be enjoyed. Moreover, in the writing of figures as diverse as Flaubert and Burton, the Oriental female is presented as a passive, silent and willing partner in the Western male's appropriation of her.[18] Kureishi reverses the gender economy which Said sees as characteristic of Orientalism and Shahid cannot in general be said to be either passive or silent; he has abandoned a girlfriend after a late abortion and at moments glories in his 'possession' of Deedee. While the liaison also conforms in some respects to the conventions of an *éducation sentimentale* (Flaubert's text is part of Deedee's recommended syllabus for Shahid), from the moment that Deedee takes the initiative in instigating the liaison, there is undoubtedly some sense that she is abusing her position of power, as she herself seems to acknowledge in being so anxious that the relationship should not be discovered. The unequal power relations are particularly evident early in their affair, when Shahid often feels coerced: 'But he didn't like being slotted into her plans, as if he were being hired for a job, the specifications of which she had prepared already' (p. 102). Sadiq's comment that 'she is having it away with two Rastamen' (p. 190) may be simply a slur to alienate Shahid from her, but there is no evidence to contradict the supposition

---

18 For example, Edward Said, *Orientalism* (1978; Harmondsworth: Peregrine, 1991), pp. 208 ff.

that Shahid's colour and 'exotic' cultural background are crucial factors in Deedee's choice of him as a sexual partner. As Tahira complains: 'Our people have always been sexual objects for the whites' (p. 190).

Above all, Deedee sees it as her mission to 'save' Shahid from the fate that his attraction to Riaz's community represents in her eyes. As time goes on, Deedee increasingly makes her partner's unequivocal rejection of Riaz a condition for the continuation of their relationship, an insistence which at one point leads to a temporary separation between the pair. Yet Deedee's antagonism to Riaz cannot be explained away simply as a lover's jealousy of her partner's competing loyalties and interests. In the ultimatum which Deedee makes, Kureishi also raises questions about the limitations of her version of liberal anti-racism. The demand for Shahid's loyalty requires his rejection of cultural affiliations which for much of the novel he regards as potentially crucial parts of his identity, a gesture which implicitly reaffirms the value system of the centre as the norm which the migrant should aspire to adopt. Moreover, Deedee's attempt to disrupt Riaz's protest against the offending text (one assumes that it is *The Satanic Verses* (1988), though it is never identified as such) – it is she who calls in the police – contradicts the strong line she has taken against censorship in her classes on Plato and Orwell. As Sadiq complains: 'Our voices suppressed by Osgood types with the colonial mentality. To her we coolies not cool' (p. 181). Liberalism, it seems, may be no less absolutist – and no less unwilling to resort to force and censorship in support of its objectives – than the 'fundamentalism' it opposes.

The coercive tendencies behind Deedee's apparently progressive views are replicated in the positions taken up by Brownlow, the husband from whom she is alienated, who represents a quite different version of metropolitan anti-racism. Instead of promoting assimilation, his approach is organised ostensibly by the principle of respect for cultural difference. As is the case with Deedee, the text identifies positive elements in Brownlow's attitudes. In his solidarity with Riaz's desire to defend his own culture, Brownlow ends by risking his career and he acts throughout with a kind of 'mad honesty' (p. 203) which Shahid finds beguiling. On closer inspection, however, Brownlow's cultural relativism is no more satisfactory, or less self-interested, than Deedee's unwitting endorsement of an 'assimilationist' model of relations between dominant and minority cultures. In the first instance, this is because Brownlow's investment in the cause of minorities seems as personally compromised as Deedee's. The descent of this representative of the 'upper-middle-classes' (p. 26) on the vigilante group during their defence of the Bangladeshi family smacks of the kind of 'political tourism' which has been prefigured in his fact-finding visit to Soweto. His attitude of 'unmistakable lewdness' (p. 78) towards Tahira aligns him with the male Orientalist gaze anatomised by Said. His misrecognition of Shahid at the end of the text (p. 178) implies that to Brownlow, stereotypically, all members of the ethnic minorities, 'look the same'. Finally, as Brownlow admits, in itself the book-burning appals him. Such qualms inevitably make his grim determination to show solidarity with Riaz somewhat disingenuous. And, as Shahid points out, Brownlow's support for the book-burning contradicts his opposition to censorship (which was a big factor in his activism in the 1960s), as does Deedee's intervention on the other side.

But the problems in Brownlow's attitudes are not just of interest in revealing his personal shortcomings. Their contradictory nature is represented as intrinsic to the kind of Left politics that he represents. On the one hand, Brownlow adopts various perspectives which place migrant cultures in a subordinate position to the supposedly normative history of the West. Thus he sees racism in the last analysis as an expression of economic disadvantage amongst both those who manifest and experience it, implicitly reducing the experiences of ethnic minorities to a subordinate term in the larger dialectic of class struggle at the heart of traditional Left thought. Moreover, Brownlow's advocacy of a master-narrative of 'Reason' – which Riaz astutely contextualises as the 'reason' of 'a minority who live in northern Europe' (p. 82) – leads him at times to represent his ally as 'the slave of superstition' (p. 80). Such positions radically conflict with Brownlow's ostensible commitment to respect for cultural difference. Moreover, the latter principle in fact leads him at times to view the minorities in a way which replicates the common colonial conviction of the ontological difference of the subject peoples – which had its most pernicious expression in apartheid. Brownlow's conception of cultural difference, then, slides all too easily into the coercive demand for 'authenticity' or cultural 'purity' on the part of minorities of the kind evident in Strapper's disgust at Shahid's attempt to situate himself in a 'hybrid' position, 'in-between' cultures:

'I thought you loved the Asian people.'
    'Not when they get too fucking Westernized. You all wanna be like us now. It's the wrong turnin'.' (p. 162)

In the end, Shahid rejects both Riaz and Brownlow to side with Deedee – and plays a crucial part in protecting her from the wrath of Riaz's followers. But the reconciliation between the lovers at the end of the novel is provisional, the clear implication being that their relationship must be renegotiated on a day-to-day basis. Conversely, if Shahid has committed himself definitively against aspects of the 'fundamentalism' represented by Riaz, who pronounces 'the word "liberal" as if it were the name of a murderer' (p. 153), he has by no means committed himself against everything that Riaz stands for. In contrast to Deedee, Shahid respects Islam as a faith and understands the solidarity which both the traditional extended family and Riaz's group represent for embattled minorities. He also endorses, albeit in a troubled way, the use of force by minorities to defend themselves against physical attack. Above all, Shahid recognises that the question of intercultural conflict in the metropolitan West cannot be resolved within a legal and cultural framework which is exclusively concerned with the rights of the individual. The novel's often sympathetic representation of Riaz's group (and one of the most important insights of the text is that Islam is a hybrid and not a homogeneous social formation, as is assumed by many of its Western critics) testifies to Kureishi's awareness that a dialogue between the centre and minorities must begin with the recognition that for these minorities it is often the rights of the group rather than of the individuals which comprise that group which must take priority. If Shahid dissents in the end from Riaz's conviction of a given community's right to determine the social function of art and the social responsibilities of an artist who is deemed (rightly or wrongly) to belong to that community, his position does not represent the wholesale affirmation of the ideology of liberal humanist individualism of which Deedee is the mouthpiece.

The Black Album is a much less sunny novel than *Eating People is Wrong, Nice Work* or indeed *The Buddha of Suburbia,* and its attempts at humour are, by comparison with any of these texts, strained. At the end of Kureishi's earlier novel Karim Amir is triumphant, having carved out for himself a 'third space' in an 'in-between' area between centre and margin, which draws productively on a variety of cultural traditions and formations to provide revised, 'hybridised' models of both personal and national identity.[19] By comparison, the space that the semi-fugitive Shahid finally clears for himself seems much more compressed, vulnerable and provisional and is much more closely and uncomfortably aligned with the dominant culture – principally because the borders between cultures (and between centre and margin) appear much more rigid and closely policed than is the case in *The Buddha. The Black Album*'s stress on the difficulty of 'translating' what often seem to be incommensurable social codes, values and roles between 'host' and migrant cultures is a subject too bleak for the essentially optimistic and comic register of earlier academic novels by writers like Bradbury and Lodge. Their texts seek to resolve the social problems and divisions they anatomise in a new consensus built around an affirmation of the 'liberal' values and attitudes supposedly embodied in the English department. This consensus is only possible, however, so long as the implication of those values in a traditionally racialised conception of national culture, identity and belonging is not fully confronted. As Brownlow argues of the racial antagonisms and cultural rivalries which surround him: 'Liberalism cannot survive these forces' (p. 180). In such a divided social context, Kureishi's novel suggests, the ideologies of 'Englishness' underlying the traditional conception of the 'humane education' (p. 179) to which Brownlow and Deedee are each, in the end, as committed as fictional predecessors like Professor Treece and Robyn Penrose, requires radical revision. Only then will it be able to take proper account of the histories, experiences and differences of the ethnic 'other' in both modern Britain and the universities which represent the nation in microcosm.

---

19 These terms are Homi Bhabha's and are used to describe the taking up of a cultural/political position which resists both sublation into the dominant culture and the temptation of a retreat to 'roots', which are conceived in much cultural nationalist discourse in essentialist terms. See, for example, 'Interview with Homi Bhabha' in Jonathan Rutherford (ed.), *Identity: community, culture, difference* (London: Lawrence and Wishart, 1990), pp. 207–21; and Bhabha, *The Location of Culture, passim.* See my *Hanif Kureishi* (Manchester: Manchester University Press, 2001) for a fuller discussion of this aspect of *The Buddha.*

11 Beyond revisions: Rushdie, newness and the end of authenticity

Martin Corner

Icons of authenticity

I grew up in the 1940s, during and after the Second World War. That was a high point of national self-awareness. My childhood was surrounded by images of Englishness, iconic images that had a power and authority tangible even to a child. The Houses of Parliament against a clear blue sky; the royal family on the deck of HMS *Vanguard*, off to visit South Africa; Churchill standing in the ruins of the bombed House of Commons. My stamp album was half devoted to British territories, from Aden to Zanzibar. On all the stamps, the gently authoritative, diffidently paternal head of the King appeared; the same image for a fifth of the earth's land surface. At Christmas we listened as he stumblingly greeted his 700 million subjects.

Some of my elders knew better, of course; realised that the economic base of the country, compromised by the First World War, had been shattered by the Second. Knew that a country so shaken could not continue to assert its authority over a quarter of mankind. But for a child, and for most adults who in the moment of triumph did not wish to dwell on future difficulties, the images, the icons, still had force. And the force that they had was a deep authenticity. Pugin's Gothic façade, rising into the sky above an apparently unpolluted Thames, *spoke* a deep identity, was redolent with a presence of Englishness that had only to be set alongside the images of other nations for its uniqueness quietly to declare itself. At least, that was how one child felt.

Of course icons and authenticities change. If I had grown up around 1900, my images would have been different: Victoria riding through the streets at her Jubilee, the ranks of imperial soldiery, the Byzantine wonders of the Imperial Institute in Kensington. I would have believed that it was un-English to queue, that only the regimented Germans did that. But what I have experienced in my lifetime has not been a change of icons of Englishness: it has been their disappearance. There are no longer common points of reference which convey an authenticity of Englishness, which authenticate English identity. Perhaps the 1960s understood that. The factitious raking together of images out of Union Jacks, London buses and the Beatles was a realisation that authenticity was at an end.

Englishness and the problem of the new

Salman Rushdie's *The Satanic Verses* (1988), with much else, is a complex exploration of the problem of Englishness in the late twentieth century, and in particular of the relation of Englishness to its iconic self-expression. A phrase like 'revisions of Englishness' implies that, having laid aside old forms of Englishness, we shall come up with new forms, with some new icons of authenticity. But it is a central theme of Rushdie's novel that 'new authenticity' is oxymoronic; that any examination of what England is must reach the conclusion that the new and the authentic are necessarily in conflict, and that if there is to be a new, revised Englishness it can emerge only through the abandonment of the ideal of authenticity and the search for its iconic embodiment. The problem that England faces, as Rushdie understands it in this novel, is not the reinvention of some authentic national identity but the recovery of a capacity for the new which the inherited apparatus of the iconic had disabled.

Rushdie is, of course, not the first to see that the obstacle is the English attachment to the past, the deep cultural conservatism that suspects newness in all its forms. His 'proper London' (which stands for England for most of the novel) is deformed by a past that it cannot leave behind:

London had grown unstable once again, revealing its true, capricious, tormented nature, its anguish of a city that had lost its sense of itself and wallowed, accordingly, in the impotence of its selfish, angry present of masks and parodies, stifled and twisted by the insupportable, unrejected burden of its past, staring into the bleakness of its impoverished future.[1]

This thraldom to the past is equally powerful in the private lives of his characters, particularly those who are most strikingly English, such as Rosa Diamond and Pamela Chamcha (*née* Lovelace). Rosa, the ninety-year-old who takes in Saladin and Gibreel when they land on her Sussex beach, is surrounded by the debris of a former Englishness: 'the random clutter of an English life, cricket stumps, a yellowed lampshade, chipped vases, a folding table, trunks' (p. 156). She is deeply nostalgic for the 1930s in the Anglo-Argentine community of Buenos Aires. Pamela, a descendant of a sixteenth-century Witchfinder General, loathes her inherited voice that speaks 'tweeds, headscarves, summer pudding, hockey-sticks, thatched houses, saddle-soap, family pews' whenever she opens her mouth (p. 180). Even Saladin's adopted Englishness has the same retrospective quality; as Pamela points out: 'Him and his Royal Family, you wouldn't believe. Cricket, the Houses of Parliament, the Queen. The place never stopped being a picture postcard to him' (p. 175). The appeal of the past in its fixity and reliability is constitutive of what many English people are and wish to be, and the public and iconic life of the English confirms that. So much we have heard before.

---

1 Salman Rushdie, *The Satanic Verses* (1988; Dover, Delaware: Consortium, 1992), p. 320. All further references to this edition will be given in parentheses in the text.

Yet even in this attachment to the past, Rushdie finds clues that are pointers to the nature of the contemporary problem, as his treatment of British imperialism shows. Normally the empire is read simply as an aspect of the past that constrains and distorts the present, a reservoir of outworn iconic images; and certainly for Rushdie the imperial identity is a burden that the English have great trouble discarding. But though the imperial project is of the past, he sees hidden within it a revolt against the very pastness and fixity that have dominated England. Through the figure of Rosa Diamond, he suggests that the impetus toward empire was, on an individual level, very often a revolt against the constriction and narrowness of the home culture, its confinement within the past, the familiar, the predictable. Empire contained within it a revolt, a wish to break free. When she arrives in Argentina with her far more conventional Anglo-Argentine husband, Rosa instantly recognises the immensity of the *pampas* as a place of possible newness:

> She arrived in that immensity, beneath that infinite blue vault of sky, because Henry popped the question … But when she arrived she asked herself a bigger question: of what was she capable in all that space? What did she have the courage for, how could she *expand*? To be good or bad, she told herself; but to be *new*. (p. 145)

For Rosa that newness takes the form of an affair with one of the gauchos of her husband's *estancia*, an affair that ends in murderous operatic jealousy, so un-English that she and her husband are forced home. Newness and expansion have their limits. Yet Rosa has seen something more than the studied conventionality of the Hurlingham and the Buenos Aires Harrods. For her empire was not just a sacralisation of the fixities of English culture, a narrative of history that grounded English identity; it was also a thirst for the unpredictable and the new. That Rushdie places this impulse in Argentina, where the English did not rule, rather than (as one might have expected) in India, has its own significance. Without the administrative impulse and the wish to paint the map red, other imperial motives could come to the fore. Somewhere within the imperial project, Rushdie understands, there was, and simultaneously, a reaching for and a denial of the new.

Englishness and the authentic

But the empire of risk and newness is hardly the one that is remembered. What the early twenty-first century recalls is the Edwardian–Elgarian–elegiac empire of Raj and durbars that behaved as though it had existed for ever, that continues to exercise its force through the icons of nostalgia. Much of this is, of course, a selective fiction; but in its continuing power the fear of the new is apparent; and it is this fear, Rushdie suggests, that explains the English attachment to authenticity. For the authentic authenticates by its priority; it precedes what it validates. A culture that constantly searches for validation will, in its turning to icons of authenticity, also turn from newness.

In *The Satanic Verses* Rushdie sets out many of the picture-postcard icons of English authenticity: Victoria Station, the Bank of England, Earls Court, cultural icons such as the RAF and the MG. But his primary vehicle for authenticity is voice. Whether they love it or loathe it, for many of his characters authentic Englishness is a way of speaking. We know that Rosa Diamond is the genuine article just as she knows it herself, because her speech is built up from clichés that define a certain Englishness: 'the well-worn phrases, *unfinished business, grandstand view*, made her feel solid, unchanging, sempiternal ... ' (p. 130). Pamela's appeal to Saladin, as she suspects, is her unquestionably authentic Home Counties voice: 'it was as loud as a dinner-jacketed drunk throwing bread rolls in a Club' (p. 180). Most significantly of all, Saladin's conquest of an authentic Englishness is through voice; his brilliance as a mimic enables him to speak as the English speak, to obliterate every last trace of Indianness.

Yet his success in acquiring this badge of authenticity is in itself, of course, an inauthenticity, as his Bombay friends tell him when he goes back to tour in *The Millionairess*. His mastery of 'Proper London' English only plunges Saladin into all the conflicts of mimicry and ventriloquism, of the need to speak with the voice of the other whilst knowing that the voice he utters is not his own. This is already his problem in the first pages of the novel. As he falls from the wreck of flight AI420, Saladin, the genius of voice-overs, has a disgusted sense of that 'pathetic personality, that half-reconstructed affair of mimicry and voices' which is himself and his life. But as he plunges toward the earth he feels himself gripped by something that 'could work his mouth, his fingers, whatever it chose', as though he were a ventriloquist's dummy, and out of his mouth comes a voice not his own, a command to Gibreel falling by his side: 'Fly! Sing!' (p. 9). The two of them sing and fly; and Gibreel finds himself taken over by an unknown voice as he sings a song he does not know to a tune he has never heard.

For the first time in the novel, though by no means for the last, Rushdie brings together the complementary categories of mimicry and ventriloquism; categories which equally, though in different ways, place authenticity in question. Mimicry is both the achievement and the betrayal of authenticity; it is both the acquisition and the loss of identity. But if mimicry is a problem, ventriloquism is worse. At least the mimic initiates the process and so retains that degree of identity; the dummy through which the ventriloquist's voice speaks is purely passive, only qualifies for the role by virtue of having no identity of its own, is entirely subsumed in the voice of another. For Rushdie, this strange, interdependent economy (each mimic looks to place himself in the power of another's voice, each ventriloquist looks for another through which to speak) describes a great deal in English culture. In the voices of the English both ventriloquism and mimicry are to be heard; to be English is to mimic the approved voices, to allow those voices to speak through you without resisting them. The novel is full of such voices, of class, profession, politics, advertising: voices which are nobody's but to which everyone feels obliged to submit. It is precisely because Englishness habitually trades in mimicry and ventriloquism that someone like Saladin, with a talent for both, can establish himself so successfully in England.

Mimicry and ventriloquism become, in English culture, the same act. For the mimic is, finally, the ventriloquised; to copy the voice of the other is, in the end, to be taken over by the other's voice, to become simply the lay-figure through which that voice is heard. In this alienating complicity every trace of authenticity, whatever that might have been worth, is lost. Rushdie can approve of none of this, and he uses Chamcha to demonstrate the bankruptcy of this peculiarly English complicity. Rejected and forced to hide as his body mimics the goat-devil that the English perceive him to be, Saladin suffers the mimic's breakdown and despair:

For what was he … being punished? … Had he not pursued his own idea of *the good*, sought to become that which he most admired, dedicated himself with a will bordering on obsession to the conquest of Englishness? Had he not worked hard, avoided trouble, striven to become new? Assiduity, fastidiousness, moderation, restraint, self-reliance, probity, family life: what did these add up to if not a moral code? (pp. 256–7)

All of this effort has been encoded in his voice, and now even his voice is failing him. But Rushdie's objection is not to inauthenticity; he is not suggesting that Saladin should have held to some true, original voice that would properly have defined who he was. None of the main characters in the novel possess a voice that they can inhabit with a secure sense of its being their own. Inauthenticities abound; Pamela, loathing her voice 'stinking of Yorkshire pudding and hearts of oak', is set against Allie Cone, the Polish-Jewish second-generation migrant who has become the ice-queen of English female athleticism. And Gibreel Farishta, Saladin's counterpart throughout the novel, is no more authentic than Saladin. Gibreel's brilliant career has been built on his ability to flip casually from one filmic identity to another; he never knows whether his voice is his own or the archangel's.

The problem for Rushdie is not inauthenticity but authenticity, the false allure of what appears to be thoroughly itself, self-grounded, self-justified. At this point it might seem that Rushdie's thinking is moving with the postmodernist attack on origins, centres, authenticity itself, and he does follow that route so far. But he has more to say than that. His distinctive argument comes from placing the question of authenticity within the larger question of the new. Icons of authenticity are, for him, always a rejection of newness; and as a consequence, newness can be won only by renouncing not just the existing icons of what it is to be English, but any icons at all. The central question for him is not the adequacy or acceptability of older or newer embodiments of authenticity but the conditions of newness itself: how, through change and metamorphosis, the old can give birth to the new.

Voices of metamorphosis: Saladin

The Satanic Verses is pervasively metamorphic; it is fascinated and intoxicated by change, by the transformation of one identity into another. The endless permutation of changes is both the fascination and the difficulty of the novel; no sooner has the reader attached some significance to a figure or action than it transforms itself into something else. But this instability, a problem from the reader's point of view, is of course the point. Rushdie is undermining the fixities and identities that normally serve as reference points for the reading of a text.

But not all metamorphoses are the same, and not all of them admit the new. The central contrast of the novel, between the two main characters Saladin and Gibreel, is a contrast in modes of metamorphosis. Each of them is an actor and each of them changes form, Saladin into the satyr and Gibreel into the haloed archangel; but the meaning of the changes is not the same, and it is not a simple matter of contrasting good and evil. Rushdie understands two modes of change: toward that which already exists, and toward that which does not yet exist. Only the second admits newness. The first is a mode of closure, because it limits itself within the already existing. Only the second is a mode of openness, because only the second risks what does not yet exist.

Saladin Chamcha's career is an example of the first. His self-transformation is more complete than that of any other character in the novel. He begins by making himself more English than the English. He goes on to proliferate his metamorphoses endlessly through his genius as a mimic: 'on the radio he could convince an audience that he was Russian, Chinese, Sicilian, the President of the United States' (p. 60). But at every point, what he imitates is already there: a character, a way of speaking. Though each voice is 'new' in relation to what went before, each voice is also a confinement in a form of authenticity, a closing around the iconic. And because authenticity is always involved with the past, what is really being taken on here is not newness at all, but a variety of pastnesses.

Some of these he chooses, but one – almost fatally – chooses him. Having invested his life in the 'Proper London' Englishness, which has become his obsession, he finds another English identity forced upon him: the ancient, prejudiced, hated identity of the alien, the dirty priapic Oriental, Saladin the enemy of the cross. His 'love' of England turns him into the racist's icon of the non-English: the demonic, hypersexual satyr. It is as though his perverse love of the former has left him with no defence against the latter; or, more tragically, as though the former were his attempt to expunge the implication of the latter. The perversion of love is at the centre of all this. For Saladin's love of England grows out of his hatred of himself. This is why his liberation, in the later stages of the novel, is brought about through love and hate. First he must turn his hatred outward, away from himself. He is released from the goat form by his hatred for Gibreel, 'Mr Perfecto, portrayer of gods, who always landed on his feet, was always forgiven his sins' (p. 294) and who, when the police arrived at Rosa Diamond's house, watched in silence as Saladin was dragged away. He expresses this hate in his destruction of the Club Hot Wax:

When Mishal, Hanif and Pinkwalla ventured into the club-room several hours later, they observed a scene of frightful devastation, tables sent flying, chairs broken in half ... and at the centre of the carnage, sleeping like a baby, no mythological creature at all, no iconic Thing of horns and hellsbreath, but Mr Saladin Chamcha himself, apparently restored to his old shape, mother-naked but of entirely human aspect and proportions, *humanized* – is there any option but to conclude? – by the fearsome concentration of his hate. (p. 294)

Later, and more viciously, his hate phone-calls destroy Gibreel's relationship with Allie Cone. But evil though these acts are, they represent the beginnings of a liberation from deformity. Fuller recovery comes when he returns to India to visit his dying father. His hatred of his father has been part of his hatred of himself; now, as the old man lies dying, he experiences something genuinely new. 'To fall in love with one's father after the long angry decades was a serene and beautiful feeling; a renewing, life-giving thing, Saladin wanted to say, but did not, because it sounded vampirish; as if by sucking this new life out of his father he was making room in [his] body for death' (p. 523). The Saladin who has lived by sucking the identity out of all the mimic roles that he has chosen to play now, in his love, discovers a living identity of his own.

But it is important not to mistake this for a return to or love of some authentic Indianness; this is not some penitential act that pays for Saladin's obsession with England. Changez Chamchawala has rejected his son not for his Englishness (he, after all, sent Saladin to an English public school), but because he has chosen to be an actor rather than carry on the family business. Changez's speech is as inauthentic a mixture of Indian and English idiom as could easily be found. He is not some truth of India; as Saladin's lover Zeeny says, India *is* inauthenticity: 'borrow ... whatever clothes seemed to fit, Aryan, Mughal, British ... Actually, we're all bad Indians' (p. 52). The house Changez lives in is a bizarre amalgam of East and West, of classical, British and Indian styles, which one of his three wives decides will be pulled down for high rise redevelopment.

None of this suggests a nostalgia for authenticity. What saves Saladin is not a return to himself but a readiness, for the first time, to go from himself toward something that he does not, at least in anticipation, already possess. Englishness was there for him to pick up, like the wallet with the sterling notes that he found as a child outside the house in Bombay. He knew what it was he wanted and what he would get if he succeeded. Now he meets something that he does not expect, something that is not just lying to be picked up: love for his father. And this brings about a metamorphosis of the second kind, toward the unknown and unpredictable, away from the pastness of authenticity toward the openness of the future.

With the shadow of authenticity withdrawn Salahuddin resumes his own name and, in consort with his father, starts to speak with a voice that is not mimicry:

'I want you to know', he said to his son, 'that I have no problem about this thing at all. A man must die of something, and it is not as though I were dying young. I have no illusions; I know I am not going anywhere after this. It's the end. That's okay. The only thing I'm afraid of is pain, because when there is pain a man loses his dignity. I don't want that to happen.' Salahuddin was awestruck. *First one falls in love with one's father all over again, and then one learns to look up to him, too.* 'The doctors say you're a case in a million', he replied truthfully. 'It looks as though you have been spared the pain.' (p. 529)

What happens at the end is a true metamorphosis toward the new, not the false transformation of mimicry. Imitation, mimicry, can never admit newness because they are always directed to something that already was, just as love of the iconic expressions of a culture will always be an infatuation with the past. Salahuddin has ceased to be a mimic; and he has learnt, through his father's death, to love the unexpected and the new.

Voices of metamorphosis: Gibreel

Both Gibreel Farishta and Saladin Chamcha are actors; but Gibreel is never a mimic. Nor do the icons of Englishness mean anything to him; his tendency is, in general, to dislike things English. This makes him available for newness in a way that Saladin only achieves at the very end of the novel. Although he is a metamorphic figure like Saladin, the mode and the direction of his metamorphoses are quite different.

If Saladin's metamorphosis is toward that which already exists, Gibreel's is toward that which does not yet exist. Saladin's mimicry has only two points: himself and the object, which he imitates. The first is to be lost in the second; nothing new emerges. Gibreel's has three: himself, some other's desire, and the unpredictable outcome of their conjunction which is newness. His metamorphoses are both the facilitation of that outcome and the outcome itself.

This is made clear in the earlier parts of the novel, those that describe Gibreel's brilliant film career. Rushdie stresses how deeply inauthentic all this is; Gibreel takes pretty well any role offered to him, and is so little committed to his performances that he can keep several running at the same time. His roles are not even human; he begins as the elephant god, moves on to Hanuman the monkey god, and then becomes the infinitely repeatable screen lover able to support eleven films at the same time. Like Saladin, he aims at models; but not to take on an authentic self. In fact the opposite is his aim. In the rush of roles he loses track of himself: '*I'm not myself*, he thought … But what does that mean, anyway, he added bitterly. After all, "les acteurs ne sont pas des gens", as the great ham Frederick had explained in *Les Enfants du Paradis*. Masks beneath masks until suddenly the bare bloodless skull' (p. 34).

Authenticity is not what matters here. What is important, Rushdie suggests, is that Gibreel has a rare genius for responding to the desires of others and for giving those desires imaginative form. It hardly matters that the resulting form is worthless by the criteria of artistic authenticity. What is important is that he is able to make himself the channel for what others long for, even if those longings are themselves transient and trivial. He is prepared to undergo the metamorphoses that these longings require. This openness, this availability is at least the precursor of love; it is not fortuitous that Gibreel is known as the great screen lover. The love is there in the availability of his art. And it is for the same reason that Rekha Merchant pursues him so mercilessly; having offered himself as the vehicle for everyone else's love, he denies this to her.

But the price of this availability is high. His film career almost destroys his body, and his later archangelic career almost destroys his mind. Gibreel as archangel takes us to the heart of this version of metamorphosis, the meeting of self with the desire of another to produce some unforeseen outcome of newness.

The quasi-sexual drama that is enacted between Gibreel and Mahound is Rushdie's exploration of the metamorphic element in all art, the sense in which all art involves an unpredictable self-transformation in the conjunction of medium and desire. And for the artist in words, this transformation must take the form of a metamorphosis of voice.

For Rushdie, art begins with voices, in attention to voices. The moment at which Saleem, in *Midnight's Children* (1981), knows himself an artist is the moment when, hidden in the washing chest and involuntarily spying on his mother, a catastrophic sneeze releases the voices of the thousand children into his head. These voices are the new India, and he knows that he must be the vehicle for them. Just as the Prophet must mediate the voice of Gibreel, the Angel of the Recitation, so Saleem must convey these voices, the thousand desires of the moment of independence. Rushdie makes the analogy explicit: 'Muhammad (on whose name be peace, let me add; I don't want to offend anyone) heard a voice saying "Recite!" and thought he was going mad: I heard, at first, a headful of gabbling tongues, like an untuned radio, and with lips sealed by maternal command, I was unable to ask for comfort.'[2]

Like the storyteller in *Haroun and the Sea of Stories* (1990), Saleem is called upon to be a vehicle, a medium for what others desire. In both *Midnight's Children* and *The Satanic Verses* this mediumship is placed close to madness; Gibreel's archangelic episodes can also be viewed as schizophrenia. But only in this way can the self-destructive circuit of Saladin's involvement with the already fixed icons of a past authenticity be avoided. The true metamorphosis of the artist arises from an openness to desire, not a closure upon the given, the iconic. In this way newness is born. It is this requirement that Gibreel Farishta fulfils on the screen, and Gibreel the archangel on the mountain of the recitation.

The satanic verses

The figure who meets Mahound on Mount Cone both is and is not Gibreel Farishta, the ham Bollywood actor suddenly projected into an unmanageable theological role. His inadequacy almost overwhelms him; but only because he is faced by a desire more powerful than he has ever known and because the outcome of mediating that desire is absolutely beyond his comprehension. Otherwise he is doing exactly what he did on the screen, and for Rushdie this is meant with deep seriousness. For him this is not some playing around with the sacred; the closest that we have to the sacred is the human ability to give desire imagined form. Only in this way does newness enter the world.

To see how this happens it is necessary to follow this section of the novel in some detail. It is accepted within orthodox Muslim tradition that, though the Koran is in its Arabic text the verbatim deliverance of God, through the Archangel

---

2 Salman Rushdie, *Midnight's Children* (1981; London: Picador, 1982), p. 163.

Gibreel, some parts of the text were amended, generally by God himself, and usually because of a change in the circumstances of the world to which they were addressed. Some passages in the Koran appear to acknowledge such modifications. In the case of the 'satanic verses', the tradition states that Muhammad received what he took to be a revelation relating to the acceptability of idols, saying that three popular female divinities, worshipped at the Kaaba in Mecca and vital to the city's economy, were worthy of the worship of Muslims and could intercede with God on their behalf. According to the account given in *Bell's Introduction to the Qur'an*, the first revelation said:

> Have you considered al-Lat and al-'Uzza,
> and Manat, the third, the other?
> These are the intermediaries exalted,
> intercession is to be hoped for.
> Such as they do not forget.[3]

But though he recited the verses to his followers, Muhammad came to distrust them, because they seemed to be in contradiction of the strict monotheism of Islam; and returning to the place of recitation and to Gibreel, he received another revelation:

> Have you considered al-Lat and al-Uzza,
> and Manat, the third, the other?
> Are you to have sons and He daughters?
> That would be a strange division.
> These are names that you have dreamed of,
> You and your fathers. God places no authority in them.[4]

Not only did Muhammad receive new words which revealed the falsity of those received earlier, but it was also shown to him that the speaker of the former words was not Gibreel but Shaitan, Satan. The first words were 'satanic verses'.

Rushdie follows this tradition closely, except for one decisive detail. As in the tradition, his Mahound receives both revelations and recognises the falsity of the first, and is convinced that the first words came from Satan. But in Rushdie's version Gibreel tells us that both revelations came from the same source. Gibreel and Shaitan are not distinguishable, not even to Gibreel, and Mahound's distinction between the two messengers is a false one.

Told in the traditional way, the story is one of authenticity; the question is, which is the true word from God and which the devilish imposture. The outcome, the accepted Koranic text, is a verbal icon of unquestionable authenticity. But Rushdie retells the story not as one of authenticity but as one of desire, and of the

---

3 W. Montgomery Watt (ed.), *Bell's Introduction to the Qur'an* (Edinburgh: Edinburgh University Press, 1970), p. 55.
4 *Qur'an*, Sura 53:19ff.

artist's openness to the desire of others. Its outcome is not some verbal construction of undoubted iconic authority but the recognition that such an outcome is impossible.

The process begins with Mahound's overwhelming need to ask the archangel for a deliverance on the matter of the idols; at this stage he hopes that the answer will confirm the position of the three goddesses, so that his new faith will be acceptable to the ruler of the city and his tiny band of followers will grow. The starting point is an intensity of desire; the end point, the words that will result, is not known even to Gibreel. He feels like a second-rate actor who has not studied his script:

Today, as well as the overwhelming intensity of Mahound, Gibreel feels his [Mahound's] despair, his doubts. Also, that he is in great need, but Gibreel still doesn't know his lines ... he listens to the listening-which-is-also-an-asking: Mahound *asks*: They were shown miracles but they didn't believe ... What can I do? What shall I recite? (p. 110)

Gibreel is overwhelmed by the questions that are running through Mahound's mind, by the Prophet's wish to justify the rapid expansion of the faith: 'Mahound's anguish is awful. He *asks*: is it possible that they *are* angels? Lat, Manat, Uzza ... can I call them angelic? Gibreel, have you got sisters?' (p. 111). Finally he senses words arising within him:

It happens: revelation. Like this: Mahound, still in his notsleep, becomes rigid, veins bulge in his neck, he clutches at his centre. No, no, nothing like an epileptic fit ... The dragging again the dragging and now the miracle starts in his my our guts, he is straining with all his might at something, forcing something, and Gibreel begins to feel that strength that force, here it is *at my own jaw* working it, opening shutting; and the power, starting within Mahound, reaching up to *my vocal cords* and the voice comes.
      Not my voice I'd never know such words I'm no classy speaker never was never will be but this isn't my voice it's a Voice. (p. 112)

Gibreel has mediated to Mahound what Mahound's desire could not produce: words, but words that Mahound, for all his desire to hear them, could never have spoken himself, and words which Gibreel did not know.

Of course the words are, from the orthodox perspective, false and inauthentic; but when Mahound returns to the mountain of recitation and confronts Gibreel again, the process is no different, except that this time Rushdie's suggestions are sexual rather than defecatory. As Gibreel experiences it:

once again his wanting, his need, goes to work, not on my jaws and voice this time, but on my whole body ... his gravitational field is unbelievable, as powerful as a goddam megastar ... and then Gibreel and the Prophet are wrestling, both naked, rolling over and over, in the cave of the fine white sand that rises around them like a veil. *As if he's learning me, searching me, as if I'm the one undergoing the test.* (p. 122)

From this comes the second revelation, the accepted one. But the difference lies not with Gibreel or even with God; from Gibreel's side, one revelation is as authentic as the other. The difference is in the nature of Mahound's desire. In his first questioning of Gibreel, Mahound already knew the answer that he wanted. He wanted permission to ease the way for the new faith by admitting the invocation of the idols. His desire was that Gibreel would pick up this already existing answer, much as Saladin picked up the wallet full of notes. The treasure was already there; it remained only to take it. But to his second question, Mahound knew no answer. Whatever came would be new; but the price was the willingness to turn away from the existing icons of the idols. The difference between the two revelations was not authenticity. Mahound's problem, like that of England, was his willingness to admit the new.

Mediating the desire of a nation

The thread through this argument, and the thread that connects it to the question of Englishness, is the relationship between the authentic, the iconic and the new. Rushdie's novel is a complex analysis of these elements, which are themselves at the heart of any new understanding of Englishness; and Rushdie shows himself aware of this connection. In the discussion of Koranic revelation, Englishness may seem to have been left a long way behind. But it is only from an understanding of these central sections of the novel that it is possible to see what Rushdie has to say about Englishness and its central problem: its relationship to the new. In his treatment of the 'satanic verses', as in his treatment of Englishness, authenticity is not Rushdie's point; the point is newness, openness to the new. Newness relates to metamorphosis; but a metamorphosis which is directed towards the iconically already existing, which simply mimics existing authenticities, is confinement and closure, not openness. The metamorphosis that allows for the entry of the new is the one that mediates the desires of others into imagined form, without knowing in advance what that form may be or looking to it for iconic authenticity.

The London, the England, which Rushdie presents is pervasively metamorphic: there is no lack of change. But he insists, as was the case between Saladin and Gibreel, that not all change is the same, that not all change admits the new. Some versions of the transformation of England are shown to be factitious and destructive. The explicitly Thatcherite figure of Hal Valance, entrepreneur of culture as a commodity, has the ambition to sell England to the world: 'I … love this fucking country. That's why I'm going to sell it to the whole goddam world, Japan, America, fucking Argentina. I'm going to sell the arse off it' (p. 268). He looks around for those icons of authenticity that will sell; if he mediates anything, it is the factitious non-desires that are summoned up by the market out of thin air. Such desires can never give rise to the new; and Rushdie suggests that England is swamped in these false novelties. Television is full of them. As Saladin, during his enforced seclusion, hunts through the channels, he sees 'that the box was full of freaks: there were mutants – "Mutts" – on *Dr Who*, bizarre creatures who appeared to have been crossbred with different types of industrial machinery: forage harvesters, grabbers, donkeys, jackhammers, saws, and whose cruel priest-chieftains were called *Mutilasians*' (p. 405). This arbitrary, random metamorphosing of cultural elements as a device of the market is enough to make the country appear different; but it is not an entry of the new.

Against this falseness, Rushdie sets certain voices that represent, not just a change of cultural scenery, but genuine newness. Most particularly he presents the voices of migrants in this way: the irreverence of the young British Asian girls Mishal and Anahita Sufyan, with their readiness to go beyond the fixities of British and Asian culture exemplifies this. Another example is the accused, and later killed, activist Dr Uhuru Simba. He is himself inauthentic, as his enemies point out; his name is a clumsy pan-African invention ('freedom lion') veiling the identity of someone born in Brixton. But it is significant that Rushdie gives this inauthentic character some of the most important words of the novel. Simba recognises change in himself and understands it not in terms of authenticity but as willingness to embrace the new. Authenticity is lost in migration; but to accept that is to open the way for the new thing that will happen:

'Make no mistake', he said in that court, 'we are here to change things. I concede at once that we shall ourselves be changed; African, Caribbean, Indian, Pakistani, Bangladeshi, Cypriot, Chinese, we are other than what we would have been if we had not crossed the oceans, if our mothers and fathers had not crossed the skies in search of work and dignity and a better life for their children. We have been made again: but I say that we shall also be the ones to remake this society, to shape it from the bottom to the top. We shall be the hewers of the dead wood and the gardeners of the new. It is our turn now.' (p. 414)

The new Englishness will not be the old icons appropriated by the new arrivals, as Saladin appropriated the speech of 'Proper London'; but neither will it be some new set of icons, some manufactured authenticity of multicultural stereotypes. Only those who have known what it is to change, who have accepted the unpredictable metamorphosis that comes through opening themselves to the desire of others, can be agents of newness. Migrants encounter not just new places and peoples but new desires; and so the migrant is, for Rushdie, the model of the future of England, not because migrants bring with them new icons, new authenticities, but because they more than anyone have lived the experience of doing without these things. Rushdie's case is that England has to find a way to embrace a true metamorphosis, to follow Gibreel Farishta in the expensive, risky project of opening to the new, with all the unpredictability of that; but it must be a newness driven by real desires of real people, not conjured out of the false desire-simulacra, the never-to-be-fulfilled wishes of the media and the market.

The final section of the novel, in which Salahuddin's father dies, makes the point powerfully that desire and wish-fulfilment are not the same. Desire works in the real world, the world of cancer and loss. Nations inhabit the real world of history, which cannot be wished away. But humanity's only weapon against the determinism of the historical process is the power of creative imagination, the ability to transcend the fixities of the past in favour of the unknowable and riskily new. In *The Satanic Verses* Rushdie shows us many who are willing to do this, to abandon the normative forms of identity, to cut loose from authenticity. Perhaps, he is suggesting, a nation can find the courage to break from its icons, to begin to function as the medium for the innumerable desires that compose it, to mediate those desires into a newness of life. Only in that way can Englishness escape its confinement in the past.

Whatever Englishness may be in the future, it will be different; not just in features and characteristics, not just in the images that support it, but *in its nature*. It will be so not just because the world has changed around it; not because we now have the European Union and we no longer have the empire. It will change because, as Rushdie has shown better than any, the old authenticities were always inauthentic. The withdrawal and loss of the icons that dominated an imperial childhood should be understood not as loss but as liberation, because they always carried with them an encapsulation in the past, an incapacity for the new. Against all our stock assumptions, they spoke not of a wider but of a narrower world. The Englishness of the future will not just 'revise' its stock of iconic reference points, dispose of the worn-out in favour of the new, run some multicultural symbols up the flagpole in place of the monocultural symbols of the past. The true revision of Englishness is away from this way of proceeding altogether; it must now be a revision of revision, towards a position in which the nation can begin to mediate the newness of its own desires.

Postscript: Englishness in transition: Swift, Faulkner and an outsider's staunch belief

David Rogers

> If nations are still the substance of the world, if England too at last needs to see itself as a nation, it can by example still show the world that nationalism need not only mean narrowness and intolerance. English nationalism, that enigmatic and elusive thing, so long conspicuous by its absence, might, newborn, show what a truly civic nationalism can look like. (KRISHAN KUMAR)[1]

> Every man is an island. But clearly, some men are part of island chains. Below the surface of the ocean they are actually connected. (ABOUT A BOY)[2]

'Americans', writes David Gervais, 'have always been amongst the staunchest believers in England and "Englishness"'.[3] Ralph Waldo Emerson, arguably the first spokesperson of modern American consciousness, devoted a whole book to what he saw as *English Traits*.[4] William James spent much of his career exploring 'Englishness' and its contrasts to the emerging ideology of American manners and individualism. And, most recently, Bill Bryson has seemingly entertained the entire nation with his observations of the country and its national characteristics in *Notes from a Small Island*, my favourite of which is his suggestion that given the English temperament communism might well have succeeded had it started here rather than Russia.[5]

But why this belief, and why so 'staunch'? One reason must be the historical link between the two countries. For a people generally obsessed with tracing their 'roots' there seems to be in the United States a particular fascination for what remains the original family connection. 'Englishness' represents what most first non-native Americans were. Many Americans also seem to want to believe in England because it is both us and not us; a 'them' that's not completely a 'them', an 'other' against which we can define ourselves while knowing that English 'otherness' confirms rather than

---

1 Krishan Kumar, *The Making of English National Identity* (Cambridge: Cambridge University Press, 2003). Quoted by Bernard Crick, 'The Friendly Face of Nationalism', *Guardian* (26 Apr. 2003).
2 *About a Boy*, director Nicholas Holt, 2002.
3 David Gervais, *Literary Englands: versions of Englishness in modern writing* (Cambridge: Cambridge University Press, 1993), p. 22.
4 Ralph Waldo Emerson, *English Traits* (London: George Routledge & Sons, 1856). All further references to this edition will be given in parentheses in the text.
5 Bill Bryson, *Notes from a Small Island* (New York: Random House, 1997).

questions the basis for our self-definition. England unconsciously signifies for Americans an older, more conventional, safer world, and in a language that they can understand (it's hard to overestimate just how large a part 'fear' has contributed to the American character; America 'started' as a very big blank and threatening space after all). In this sense, 'Englishness' signifies all that being American, at least in mythic terms, is not: bound to convention and tradition; stuffy and reserved; comfortable, superior and wedded to 'common sense' rather than willing to take the risk of enterprise and reinvention that marks – at least for me (and Thom Gunn) – the more pleasant side of the mythological American Dream.[6]

Emerson puts these perceived qualities into their Victorian context. There is a genuine affection in Emerson's writings about England, although in typical Emersonian fashion his characterisations are often contradictory (his belief in 'self-reliance' and spontaneity meant Emerson never feared contradiction). England, he writes, is 'the best of actual nations'(p. 283). The 'composite' nature of their national character 'betrays a mixed origin'(p. 53). The English are a 'people of myriad personalities' who owe their 'many-headedness' to the 'advantageous position of the middle class' (p. 286). They are 'tender-hearted', resolved 'to see fair play' (p. 82), but behind this attitude of tender-hearted fairness they are 'aggressive' (p. 143) and 'arrogant' (p. 141). The 'secret of their power', he argues, lies in 'their mutual good understanding'. Not only were there 'good minds … born among them', he says, 'but all the people have good minds' (p. 98).

Emerson qualifies this compliment, however, just as we might expect from the first American transcendentalist and the 'father' of American pragmatism. These good English minds, he says, overvalue 'utility' (p. 84) and 'fact' (p. 80). They are neither 'imaginative' (p. 242) nor 'expansive' (p. 244) enough 'in their habit of thought' (p. 288). They 'hate innovation' and 'will not be baffled by or catch at clouds'. The English, he writes, 'must have a symbol palpable and resisting'. They 'have lost sight of the fact that poetry exists to speak the spiritual law' (p. 243). Overly literal by implication, the English are correspondingly 'materialist, economical, and mercantile' (p. 222). Their 'taste' is 'conservative' (p. 167) and there is a 'drag of inertia which resists reform in every shape' (p. 288). Their conservative temperament and social practice, however, their commitment to the status quo (and contemporary American activities suggests most dominant powers turn conservative), provides them with a second source of political might. English strength, claims Emerson, 'resides' in the country's commitment to tradition, its 'dislike of change' (p. 109). It rests on the stability of a way of life grounded, as Edmund Burke argued for eighteenth-century England, in the local, the provincial; in the domestic and the ideal of home: the 'motive and end of their

6 Reflecting on America or at least San Francisco, Thom Gunn writes in 'A Map of the City', 'By the recurrent lights I see / Endless potentiality, / The crowded, broken, and unfinished / I would not have the risk diminished' (*Norton Anthology of English Literature*, vol. 7, gen ed. M. H. Abrams (New York and London: Norton, 2000), p. 2577).

trade and empire is to guard the independence and privacy of their homes'. 'Domesticity', Emerson writes in his inimitable, metaphorical style, 'is the taproot which enables the nation to branch wide and high' (p. 107). Yet such branching fails to make the English visionary in the widest sense: the English, observes Emerson, cannot 'readily see beyond England' (p. 283).

Having conceptualised the idea for this collection and seen it through publication with John McLeod, I suppose I must count myself among Gervais' staunch believers. The English, however, I have discovered, believe in 'Englishness', 'rather' less staunchly, 'one' might say, 'as it were'. And I understand why. Being English comes with a lot of imperial baggage. 'Englishness', as Gervais rightly observes, has often appealed mainly to Little Englanders who feel the country's past values are under threat. It stirs up passionate and historically valid tensions among the other countries of Britain and the country's various regions, especially between London and the South-east. Even in this age of devolution, when, as Kumar notes, the nation state represents such a norm within the world that to assume that England can or should avoid discussions of national identity seems not only mistaken but possibly a missed opportunity, appeals to 'Englishness' continue to appear inherently base to many thoughtful English people, a sign of continued inflated self-worth that smacks of unlearned lessons from the past. The poet Kim Wright would seem to sum up these attitudes when in 'Everyone Hates the English' he writes, 'Anyone ever born English / Should shut up, or fuck off, or die.'[7]

And these reservations have merit. Gervais is surely wise to remind us that 'Englishness' is a 'treacherous cultural tool'. So too is James Wood when he warns against too readily trying to read 'the nation' into texts. Antony Rowland explains clearly the preference of many contemporary English poets for concentrating on the representation of regional identities rather than following the example of Ted Hughes to reconnect with a traditional English mythology, or to establish a new one. Like the implications for 'Englishness' in the 'borrowings' between Hughes and Larkin, any notion of a collective 'Englishness' is, as Rowland rightly observes, a 'red herring' for poets such as Carol Ann Duffy and Tony Harrison.

Yet Wood is surely also right to argue that it is a mistake to allow traditional 'Englishness' – 'white', 'upper middle class', 'Southern', 'male' and conveyed by birth alone – to remain immobilised and silent and, because of that immobilised silence, to remain dominant. As John McLeod says in his introduction, the England of *that* 'Englishness' has undoubtedly changed since the end of the Second World War and changed dramatically. To revise it may, given Emerson's assessments, seem an oxymoronic act. But not to acknowledge the fact of change and therefore not to debate new, more fitting (and more complicated) ways of 'being English', of what 'Englishness' does or can signify at the start of the new millennium, seems to me more complicitous than base, more apathetic than politically correct.

---

7 Kim Wright, *Hoping It Might Be So: poems 1974-2000* (Oxford: Leviathan, 2001).

That, and that alone, is for me the key assumption behind this collection. The essays were commissioned without any theoretical remit. We encouraged contributors to be autobiographical where and to the extent that it suited them and to write in a personal style, if they wanted, for at the very least one strategy for revising 'Englishness' must be additive, or substitutive. The acts of revision they analyse may not always have succeeded, but all of them imply the need for revision as they expose the workings of the ideology of pre-war 'Englishness'. All of the essays identify ways for adding new voices and creating new spaces for identity that may potentially make English national belonging more inclusive, more representative.

McLeod sets the tone for such a strategy in his introduction. Taking his metaphor from Julian Barnes' short story 'Interference', he establishes the fact and causes of change in England over the past fifty-nine years, the slippage of 'old hierarchies' in the country. He contrasts the observations of Beryl Bainbridge as she retraces the route of J. B. Priestley in *English Journey* with those of Angela Carter in her essay 'Bath, Heritage City' to illustrate his point. For Carter the inappropriateness of 'imperious Englishness', with its 'rigid authoritarianism' presuming a 'passive submission' and a 'marshmallow sentimentality', opens up a chance, according to McLeod, for a celebratory, optimistic, forward-looking view of the country. It is to facilitate this opening up that the collection, as he writes, 'constitutes its own "interference"'; that it opposes the 'Englishness' of silent, shared assumptions with a cacophony of different ethnic and cultural voices rising from the new groups of Englanders who have arrived since the Second World War.

Elizabeth Maslen documents an early example of a similar type of interference in her analysis of the revisionary efforts of Alan Sillitoe and Sam Selvon. Sillitoe and Selvon, she argues, radicalised conventions of 'Englishness' by elevating the use of non-standard dialects from the margins of dialogue to the mainstream of narrative voice. Recognising how the 'values' of Englishness in the 1950s had been defined by the middle class, Sillitoe and Selvon, Maslen writes, both resisted the 'miasma of Englishness' by their choice of subject matter and perhaps more radically, more fundamentally, by the 'medium of language'.

Wood proposes a strategy of 'literalisation' for exposing the unspoken assumptions of conventional 'Englishness'. Such a strategy, he argues, can act as a means of 'mobilising Englishness' from its status as 'an attribute' into 'an activity'. Too many English novelists, according to Wood, rely on a kind of 'literary appeal to anteriority' that paradoxically keeps the idea of 'Englishness' 'mysterious' and 'indefinable': 'Englishness' remains 'unspeakable because what it speaks' is, by implication, 'so well known'. For Wood, this gesturing too easily for effect towards an 'Englishness' that the writer assumes he does not have to name for his audience to know has led to the lack of epic writing in contemporary English fiction. In an effort to redress this lack, Wood aligns the revisionary strategy of Alan Hollinghurst with those of Lawrence and Woolf, who, he argues, 'does nothing less than dissolve Englishness' in *Mrs Dalloway*. By provocatively adding 'boy's cocks' to his list of otherwise traditional elements of English pastoral, Hollinghurst undermines the genre and at the same time 'forces Englishness out of its inaudibility' and into a new 'voice'.

Vesna Goldsworthy implicitly supports Wood's contention that acts such as Hollinghurst's lay bare an unexamined but assumed 'Englishness' when she 'outs' the unspoken preference of the English for the in-betweenness of suburban life. As Goldsworthy notes, while contemporary debates about 'Englishness' usually centre about the respective merits of the values of city and country, most English people reject both locations. They choose instead to live in the suburbs, their secret desire for the likes of 'the Surbiton of *The Good Life*' evidence of the English love that 'dare not speak its name'.

Goldsworthy situates her comments in the context of her own Yugoslavian background, and other contributors speak directly to their personal experiences of trying to overcome the dominance of an overly simple, homogenised and monotoned 'Englishness' and to create their own spaces. Vic Seidler poignantly argues that this assimilating voice of 'Englishness' is a product of the Enlightenment vision of the rational self for whom cultural identities were secondary, 'private' and 'personal'. As such this voice cast a cloak of 'invisibility' over those with more complicated feelings of identity that combine a range of ethnic and cultural customs and allegiances. Seidler calls for the type of revisioning that allows for such complications; that recognises 'a multicultural society' and offers 'space' to explore 'diverse identities' and create 'new hybrid' ones.

The lifelong struggle Seidler himself experienced before he could create his own space and acknowledge his Jewishness as part of his personal 'Englishness' testifies to the difficulty of such revisioning. So too does the experience of Alan Sinfield within the academic community's acceptance of a gay revision of literary studies. While narrating his own ability to find identity as a gay English academic, Sinfield remains exasperated with the refusal by some in the academy to accept the right of gays to construct their own history of English studies. Punning on the the idea of a standard, defining accent for 'Englishness', he notes the potential 'afforded' for 'some kind of purchase on English queerness' by 'doing English'. Class may have initially stopped literature from providing a 'workable concept of gayness', but by the 1970s the 'new way' of being gay – being 'up-front, organised, egalitarian, defiant' – had raised hopes for some type of resolution between 'dissident sexuality' and English literature. Despite the creation of successful and popular courses in Queer Studies, however, resistance, in the form of the silence typical of mainstream 'Englishness', continues.

Both Bart Moore-Gilbert and Bilkis Malek disclose similar problems in the face of what we might call an ever assimilating 'Englishness' in their respective readings of Kureishi's *Black Album* and *Bhaji on the Beach*. For Moore-Gilbert, Kureishi stresses the 'endemic racism of British society' in his attempt to revise the 'condition of England' novel situated, in the tradition of social realism of Bradbury and Lodge, within the metaphorical context of English Studies with its connections between 'Englishness', ethnicity and literary texts. The novel illustrates the difficulties of 'retaining one's culture of origin in the process of migration to the West'. Ultimately, however, it remains 'more positive' about the 'value of canonical Western literature' than Moore-Gilbert, by inference, would prefer.

Malek sets her analysis into the context of theories of 'common sense' and argues similarly that *Bhaji* ultimately fails to provide a 'more inclusive and fluid construct that no longer resists difference or change or holds them in constant tension'. Narrated from the perspective of South Asian women, the film succeeds in providing a voice for their subjectivities. It offers a 'fresh angle' on many elements crucial to the constructions of 'a superior, racially exclusive English identity' sustained, as she writes 'through a particular construction of female sexuality' as 'pure' and 'white'. But, in spite of its 'progressive' attempts to interject signs of South Asian identity into this English sexuality, its construction of female subjectivity 'remains very much predicated on a reductive notion of modernity'. In the end, *Bhaji* 'has its own "ideal" of England'.

Ingrid Gunby reveals another difficulty in revising qualities of the abiding 'Englishness' in her reading of Adam Thorpe's *Still*. The novel, she writes, posits 'late-twentieth-century Englishness' insightfully as a 'melancholic misreading of its own history'. Thorpe, she argues, tries to 'imagine an alternative reading of England in the post-war period'. Yet he fails. His attempt to counter the period's lapse into nostalgia ends with his succumbing to the allure of nostalgia himself. The novel offers no 'complex' alternative. Its 'execution falls somewhat short of his conception', and the work of 'reimagining millennial Englishness through a more comprehensive understanding of its history' remains, for Gunby, unfinished.

The idea of notions of 'Englishness' remaining unfinished seems, however, precisely the point for Gervais and Martin Corner in their respective readings of Geoffrey Hill and Salman Rushdie. For Gervais, revision means situating Hill in a tradition of European writing coterminous with any English one. Hill, whose method of yoking opposites violently together reminds us of Shakespeare and the metaphysical poets, demonstrates what the collection as a whole might well take as its premise: that 'Englishness' is a 'process' rather than a time-honoured essence; nationalisms may generally evoke an idea of 'essence', as Wood notes, but revisions of 'Englishness' should not.

Corner endorses a similar view in his reading of Rushdie's rejection of both the icons of 'Englishness' and the premise of the 'authentic' that lies behind any form of iconography. Rushdie, Corner shows, uses the motifs of ventriloquism and mimicry central to the maintenance of expressions of a conventional 'Englishness' to question the validity of any revisionary strategy based solely on acts of addition or substitution. Replacing current, outdated icons with newer ones leaves fundamental qualities and assumptions of 'Englishness' intact. Rushdie therefore advocates a new aim: to 'mediate the desires of others into imagined form, without knowing in advance what that form may be or looking to it for iconic authenticity'. 'Englishness', it would seem, to be new cannot simply *be* in transition. To be new it must 'reside', to quote Emerson, in the transitional itself.

Faulkner and Swift

A lot can be read in the reading tastes of a nation. One of my favourite American writers is the Mississippi novelist William Faulkner. Until recently, with the popularity of writers such as Toni Morrison, Faulkner attracted more critical attention in the United States than practically any other writer with the exception of Shakespeare, the only influence Faulkner ever publicly acknowledged. For this reason, I was more than a little surprised when I moved to England to discover that the English had (and still have) practically no interest in the creator of Yoknapatawpha County, winner of the Nobel Prize in 1950. Bookshops stocked rows of the novels of John Steinbeck (a good writer but hardly that pertinent to an understanding of the States today), but they seldom carried more than the occasional copy by Faulkner and then usually either *The Sound and the Fury* (1929), his most famous novel, or *Sanctuary* (1931), his most infamous.

The reason may be as simple as the fact that the French, by contrast, practically idolise Faulkner and produce some of the most penetrating readings of him. So too the Japanese, and South Americans. Or it may be, as the late Antony Easthope might have argued, because Faulkner is a modernist and the English, in Easthope's view, reject modernism.[8] And he may be right. I suspect, however, the reason is Faulkner's a Southerner, as I am, and the image of the American South – at least the one to which Faulkner often liked to play – is not one many English people readily embrace. The South's an 'other' that remains firmly in the 'other's' camp.

Yet this indifference, we might say cultural ignorance, of Faulkner, still strikes me as odd, and also a shame, given what most critics would agree, I think, has been a relatively unambitious period of English fiction with regard to revisions of 'Englishness'. For the revision of the early-twentieth-century South was a prime aim of Faulkner, and the cultural assumptions of his region were not dissimilar to those of post-war England. Like England since the late forties, the American South of the 1920s and 1930s defined itself against a specific, traumatic, society-changing war, in its case the Civil War rather than the Second World War (England, remember, supported the South). It too had lost its sense of greatness and longed nostalgically for an earlier time when things seemed simpler, grander and more secure, more easily categorised and defined. And like pre-war England's, the idealised society for which the post-war South pined was hierarchical, deferential and highly mannered; it was based on strict differences of class, race and gender, and its dominant ethnic group assumed a general sense of social and moral superiority. Faulkner's South continued to imagine itself as rural, anti-capitalist and anti-modern, more refined than the rest of the country (for England, read 'rest of the world'). Its collective sense of self befitted an island mentality.

And like England's Little Englanders, the homogenised 'white' South instinctively turned in upon itself. It became defensive, insular and backward-looking,

---

8 Antony Easthope, *Englishness and National Culture* (London: Routledge, 1999).

mournful for a time it 'remembered' as simpler and more tranquil. It sought to preserve the ideal of itself as an ethnically 'pure', agrarian society of high principles in the face of modernity and the 'other' in the shape of freed African American slaves. Its leading intellectuals of the time even made a virtue of the region's conservative tenets expressed most explicitly in *I'll Take My Stand*, a collection of essays, the title of which comes from a song the next line of which is, of course, 'to live and die in Dixie'.

But the similarities between my place of birth and my adopted homeland go 'deeper' to a shared philosophical 'taproot'. Both rest on a belief in Platonic idealism, symbolised, respectively, through the figures of the Southern maiden and the English 'rose'. Emerson identifies this tradition for the English in *English Traits*. 'The influence of Plato', he writes, 'tinges the British genius.' We see this Platonic influence, Emerson observes, in the writings of the 'many disciples of Plato' including Frances Bacon, who, for Emerson, 'marks the influx of idealism into England', Sir Philip Sidney, George Herbert, John Donne, Herbert Spencer, John Milton, George Berkeley and Jeremy Taylor. They also include Shakespeare, that literary icon above all other literary icons in the bastion of conventional 'Englishness'. All, according to Emerson, colour English thinking and literary traditions. '[A]ll', he writes, 'have a kind of filial retrospect to Plato and the Greeks' (p. 229).

Emerson regretted what he saw as the loss of 'the faculty of Plato and Aristotle' in the English of his time because of the influence of Locke, but his association of idealism with class and with it a metaphysics of hierarchical relations, indicates its continued, if less overt, role in English conservatism. The English are 'climbers on the staircase of unity'. When 'the [English] mind takes a step', it does so in order 'to put itself at one with a larger class, discerned beyond the lesser class with which it has been conversant' (p. 226). Early critics considered Faulkner a conservative idealist, an apologist for the ideology as well as the customs of the old South. They mistakenly identified him with the heroic failures in his novels such as Donald Mahon in *Soldier's Pay* (1926), Bayard Sartoris in *Flags in the Dust* (1929/1973), Darl Bundren in *As I Lay Dying* (1930), Quentin Compson in *The Sound and the Fury* and Gavin Stevens in the Snopes trilogy, *The Hamlet* (1940), *The Town* (1957) and *The Mansion* (1959). (Sartre once famously and wrongly characterised Faulkner as a man riding in a fast car always with his head turned behind him, looking back.)

Faulkner typically represents these figures as 'aspirants' of some sort, usually as fliers, and associates them with the colour of 'horizon blue' and all it implies, and they strive in their respective novels to maintain the ideals of the tradition of the old South. Their physical, mental and emotional 'flight', Faulkner shows, amounts in the end, however, to a desire to escape. Faulkner's flyers want to transcend the rigours and uncertainty of the modern world. They want to find a 'sanctuary', as Faulkner suggests overtly in the title of his bitterest novel and the one that revolves most conspicuously around the defamation of the central icon of the South's ideal of itself and the 'purity' of its pursuits.

The title of that novel, however, turns out to be ironic, and across his canon Faulkner rhetorically rejects the attitude of these figures. His idealists repeatedly fall victim to the ruthless uncertainty of the modern twentieth-century world, and Faulkner formally replaces them at the centre of his narrative with figures I have called elsewhere his 'marginal' men.[9] These 'men' progressively develop a pragmatic, 'tough-minded' attitude toward a modern, post-Darwinian world signified by figures such as Faulkner's 'unwed mothers'. This world is promiscuous, non-hierarchical, and no longer underpinned by the authority of the father or the Father. It is, we might say, 'naturally perverse', the values that eighteenth-century idealism had seen as 'natural' now 'turned upside-down'.[10]

But it is the style of Faulkner's revision as much as his commitment to revision alone that provides a potential insight, English novelists, I think, have generally missed. As a rewriter of Southern history, the creator of a fictional 'world elsewhere' that reveals the influence of Thomas Hardy (whose unwed mother Tess (1891) provides the model for figures such as Lena Grove in *Light in August* (1932) and Dewey Dell Bundren in *As I Lay Dying* and Laverne in *Pylon* (1935), so central to Faulkner's texts), Faulkner is a realist. But he is only a realist of sorts. To read his characters as if they were representations of the real rather than rhetorical figures is a mistake; so too to treat his settings and any detail of his novels as merely denotative. To ignore the connotations of his formal experiments is to remain blind to the fundamental quality of what amounts to his 'art of deconstruction'.[11] Faulkner radically undermines the conventional attitudes of the South as if from within.

We might refer to Faulkner's form of realism as 'rhetorical realism'. Through his rhetoric, Faulkner creates the possibility of cultural revision by constructing a space in which characters must reconcile themselves – and in so doing connote the need for such a reconciliation generally – to the idea of change, to the notion that life and selfhood are synonymous with change. To resist that fact or deny it, to attempt to retain individual or collective ideals of identity in the face of it is self-defeating, counter-productive. Accepting it, on the other hand, means being able to live, in effect, in a state of suspension, to exist in a state of perpetual 'becoming' rather than try to 'fix' a position of 'being'. To live in such a condition requires the ability to tolerate existence without essence, life as an in-between state. It means 'belonging' without coveting icons to symbolise that belonging; it is to live emotionally in transit; to be able to tolerate a nationalism suspended between and among genders and ethnicities, without the need for the security of a permanently defined 'home'.

---

9 David Rogers, 'A Masculinity of Faded Blue: V. K. Ratliff and Faulkner's creation of transpositional space', *Faulkner Journal*, 15:1–2 (fall 1999/spring 2000), pp. 125–50.

10 I use the term 'perverse' here literally though as Michel Foucault and Jonathan Dollimore have shown, 'perversity' signifies subversive sexual and structural potential.

11 David Rogers, 'Maternalizing the Epicene: Faulkner's paradox of form and gender', in *Faulkner and Gender: Faulkner and Yoknapatawpha 1994*, ed. D. M. Kartiganer and A. J. Abadie (Jackson: University of Mississippi Press, 1996), pp. 97–119.

Faulkner signifies this state of mind most completely in the figure of V. K. Ratliff, his alter ego who travels the length and breadth of Yoknapatawpha County in a converted car ostensibly selling his sewing machines. Devoid of any emotional or psychological belonging tied inherently to a stationary home or its iconic symbols (he gives the house he lives in to his sister), Ratliff begins *The Hamlet* as a conventional Faulknerian idealist on the margins of the formal and figurative binary between the idealist and his gendered object of desire that structures all of Faulkner's novels. His subsequent incorporation into the trope of perpetual travel situates him within the series of Faulknerian 'wanderers', foreshadowing, as it does, however, the similar trope that Simon Gikandi identifies for English migrant literature (this trope allows migrant writers, Gikandi argues, to counter a traditional Englishness characterised by 'loss of self-esteem, nostalgia, and plurality of cultural traditions and beliefs').[12]

By the end of the Snopes trilogy Ratliff has emerged as the composite of all Faulkner's wanderers, moving formally into the 'transpositional' space Faulkner creates across his entire canon.[13] His 'brown' sunburned skin leaves him floating between the two 'races' of the South. He is also ambiguously gendered, his constant identification 'on the wagon' in Faulkner's rhetoric tying him to the figures of 'woman' epitomised by Lena Grove who embody the natural perversity of the novels. As a rhetoric figure Ratliff formally occupies a space that connotes the freedom and loss of ego necessary in Faulkner to accommodate that natural perversity and the state of perpetual change and lack of essence it implies. Identified finally by the 'faded blue' denim shirts that he makes, washes and irons himself (Lena too is a figure of faded blue), Ratliff simultaneously marks and overturns the South of the 'horizon'-seeking idealists in the novels. He does not simply connote transition. He *becomes* it, in both senses of the word.

The influence of Hardy on Faulkner implies the presence of a tradition of 'rhetorical realism' within English fiction of the nineteenth century, and we can trace back a shared Anglo-American tradition through Bram Stoker's *Dracula* (1899) and Hardy to Samuel Richardson's *Clarissa* (1747) that rests on the same premises of language, identity and the transitory nature of the material world that we find in Faulkner. That tradition includes Edgar Allan Poe's 'Imp of the Perverse' (1845), Dickens's *Dombey and Son* (1848), Nathaniel Hawthorne's *The Scarlet Letter* (1850) and Elizabeth Gaskell's *Ruth* (1853). Signifying the way revolutions in America and France and in scientific thinking had reversed normalised assumptions about the social and the material, this tradition documents a parallel line of thinking opposed to the Western enlightenment so problematic to the construction of complex, ethnically mixed national identities. It articulates up to and through Faulkner the 'feminine' notions of the irrational, the emotional and the corporeal that Enlightenment thinking denied.

---

12 Simon Gikandi, *Maps of Englishness: writing identity in the culture of colonialism* (New York: Columbia University Press, 1996), pp. 8, 33.
13 See my reference to Alice Jardine, *Gynesis: configurations of women and modernity* (Ithaca: Cornell University Press, 1985), in 'A Masculinity of Faded Blue'.

English novelists since the Second World War seem largely to have ignored this tradition in favour of a tradition we might by contrast call 'literal realism', just as they have ignored the lesson of revision Faulkner provides. Emerson seems to predict such a choice when he laments the rising influence of Locke over Bacon in English literature and philosophy. Much more recently Blake Morrison implies this same preference when he notes that the English fondness for making lists as a way of characterising their nationality ought itself to be understood as a sign of English character.[14] In any case, a bias towards 'literal realism' implies something of a collective nostalgia for English writers for a time when signs were stable and not arbitrary, where their meanings fitted an external world 'out there', when language could be considered without question as denotative.

We see evidence of the limits of literal realism in Ian McEwan's most recent novel *Atonement* (2002). *Atonement* is a brilliant book. McEwan is a brilliant stylist and creator of scenes, and he sets up a number of potentially Laurentian revisions of the Englishness at the heart of his narrative. But he resists them all in favour of an examination of the power of the writer's imagination for good and bad and a realistic representation of the conditions Robbie endures fighting in France in the Second World War. The form of the novel splits rather than coheres. McEwan chooses to give his narrative voice to his upper-middle-class writer Briony rather than to Robbie, the working-class boy put back in his place for his pretensions of equality. He rejects the chance to allow his setting to resonate with the revisionary discourse about national identity his Laurentian plot provides. He does not exploit the potential of the novel's most potent symbol: the vase that Robbie and Cecilia break in the pivotal scene that signals their mutual love and sexual attraction. Instead he gives licence to Briony's destructive imagination. His broken vase remains a broken vase and nothing more.

The English novelist who, more than any other, clearly understands the potential of Faulkner's formal and figurative strategy and illustrates its potential for radical revision is Graham Swift. It took English readers and critics an inordinate time to realise the debt Swift owed to Faulkner in *Last Orders* (1996), and, much like Faulkner, Swift has been (and continues to be) criticised for the apparently conservative way in which he has addresses the issue of Englishness. The main cause for criticism is that Swift, in the manner of Faulkner, concentrates mainly on 'white' Englanders rather than ethnic minorities. His strategy for revising Englishness does not consist of adding to the list of ethnic groups and voices considered 'English'. His 'expansion' of Englishness, like Faulkner's, happens as if from inside out, as if revising 'Englishness' requires not only addition or substitution but also a fundamental undoing.

We see this strategy in *Out of This World* (1988), the title of which connotes for the English a Faulkner-like desire for sanctuary.[15] As in *Last Orders*, Swift 'borrows'

---

14 Blake Morrison, 'England at Sea', *Independent on Sunday* (27 Aug. 2000), Sunday Review, p. 19.
15 Graham Swift, *Out of This World* (London: Penguin, 1988). All further references to this edition will be given in parentheses in the text.

his formal strategy from Faulkner. In the style of *As I Lay Dying* and *The Sound and the Fury*, the narrative is told by a number of narrators, in Swift's case four, one of whom is, as in *As I Lay Dying*, dead. All signify figuratively, their names and situations, their occupations and family relations radiating beyond the denotative to transform what is a slim novel into an epic account of what proves an inescapable allure of idealism within conventional notions of Englishness. 'Englishness', the novel argues, is predicated on a philosophical desire to escape, to seek a secure sanctuary in the face of an increasingly complicated, undemarcated world. Idealism contributes fundamentally to this English tendency, as Emerson notes, to cut off from the rest of the world, to allow its island location to create an island mentality, to be insular and hence 'out of this world'.

Unlike McEwan, however, Swift uses the details of his novels to make his central family and their setting a metaphor for establishment England. Grandfather Beech, the family's patriarch, is a 'true Brit' (p. 86), 'a true Englishman of the old school' (p. 91). Born in 1900, he has lived across 'the full, galloping gamut of the twentieth century' and won the Victorian Cross (p. 90). The family home, an eighteenth-century Queen Anne house named Hyfield House in Surrey built by 'Nicholas Hyfield, Gent', echoes Emerson's realisation of the secure 'domesticity' central to the country's imperial mercantilism (p. 65). The house is, in the words of the granddaugher Sophie Beech Carmichael, '[t]he genuine, historical English thing' (p. 65). Sophie, who says 'We all want Greece in our hearts ... Blue air and marble Apollos' (p. 132), imagines it as always having 'clear eighteenth century blue sky' (p. 66). Yet, as with Faulkner, their 'home' is not simply a 'home'. For the Beech family residence also houses the family's arms-manufacturing business, begun in 1875 and now the country's largest supplier of arms. The world thus knows Hyfield House as 'the head-quarters'. Harry refers to it as 'the arsenal' (p. 62). The reader realises that, as for Harry's dead wife, Anna (who is Greek), the English are 'peace-loving people ... who know the value of military strength' (p. 178).

For the modern world beyond the sanctuary in Faulkner, Swift posits the world of postmodernism with its gross uncertainties and, perhaps most pertinently for the start of the new millennium, its border-denying terrorism. The world beyond the apparently safe and enclosed world of the Beech family home is, Harry says, 'new and barbarous'. Like the world of Faulkner's would-be escapists, the world of the novel is 'perverted', having suffered, according to Harry, an 'imperceptible inversion'. National boundaries have gone the way of island moats, nations and their inhabitants 'no longer keeping to [their] former demarcations, former protocol' (p. 92). The world has become 'all one territory and everywhere, everywhere can be a target'. There are not, Harry says, 'any safe, separate places any more' (p. 111). Everywhere there are '[b]ombs going off in airports, embassies, shopping centres', and even, with the IRA bombing that kills the grandfather and his chauffeur on St George's Day in the drive of Hyfield House, in 'homes' (p. 92).

The condition of this perverted world goes to the nature of identity itself: 'what', Harry wonders, 'does it mean to *act* naturally?' (p. 189). In an attempt to find an answer to this question, people, Harry thinks, seek new technological means of extracting themselves from the world. The 'cinema', he says, has become a substitute for the 'vision of Greece and Rome' (p. 188). The world wants 'to be claimed and possessed by the camera. To translate itself, as if afraid it might otherwise vanish, into the new myth of its own authentic-synthetic photographic memory' (p. 189). The photograph provides its own form of sanctuary; it allows for a 'reprieve, an act of suspension' from the world, 'a charm': 'If you see something terrible or wonderful, that you can't take in or focus your feelings for – a battlefield, the Taj Mahal, the woman with whom you are falling in love – take a picture of it, hold the camera to it. Look again when it's safe. I have always loved flying' (p. 122).

Harry's association of safety and flight discloses his instinctive desire for escape. As a lover of flight, Harry fits the mould of Faulkner's idealists. Swift, however, gives Harry the potential to join the ranks of marginal men. An orphan and father of the motherless Sophie (in Faulknerian fashion the novel is loaded with absent mothers), Harry discovers as a teenager that the cultural practices of establishment England themselves force him into existence in a transitional space, a 'transit region', an 'in-between state':

It never occurred to me [...] that a whole system of English education was based on the removal of the young to, at least, the next county. I should have found the outward journeys, the back-to-school journeys, the more wretched. But I could never have said which was worse, going to school or going home, because I dreaded both places. The two dreads would sometimes cancel themselves out into a sort of numb suspension, so that I would say to myself: You belong nowhere. Or rather. *This* is the only place you belong – this transit region, this in-between space. (p. 121)

It initially seems as if Harry will choose to accommodate this space. He rejects his legacy of the family business in favour of a job as a Magnum-like photographer who takes ultra-realistic photos from the air of the victims of the contemporary warfare his family facilitates. A photographer, he says, 'is neither there nor not there, neither in nor out of the thing' (p. 49), and with his choice Harry confronts the violence perpetrated to maintain the security of the family 'home'. He lives potentially very much 'in' the world, it seems, rather than 'out' of it.

Yet Harry, unlike Ratliff, fails to cast off the cultural drag of English idealism. He secures his apparently transitory existence with his own quainter version of the English symbol of safety and insularity, a cottage in Wiltshire 'which', as Sophie remarks, 'might be a picture from one of his [her travel company salesman Joe's] brochures come to life' (p. 58). Indeed, his house, as Sophie realises, represents the 'same dream' that the United States offers to the English, 'only in reverse: golden memories of the Old World. Thatched cottages and stately homes, patchwork scenery; sweet, green vision' (p. 192). Harry also chooses to marry. Jenny, his young bride-to-be first means 'the world' to him, as if to imply their marriage will connote an undoing of English insularity, the desire for safety and security. Yet Jenny proves instead his English rose. She is, he realises, 'out of this world' (p. 36), and the decision Sophie makes to fly home with her two sons after years of estrangement from her father, saying 'Let's just be together, here, above the world', simply re-inforces the lack of nerve Harry expresses when he closes the novel. Harry, we see, has lost all belief in the possibilities of inhabiting such a transit space:

I used to believe once that ours was the age in which we would say farewell to myths and legends, when they would fall off us like useless plumage and we would see ourselves clearly only as what we are. I thought the camera was the key to this process. But I think the world cannot bear to be only what it is. The world always wants another world, a shadow, an echo, a model of itself. (p. 187)

The irony the reader understands in Harry's retreat is not shared by Harry himself. Such is not the case, however, with *Last Orders*.[16] Infused with Faulknerian tensions between motion and stasis and becoming and being, the novel pays even more direct tribute to *As I Lay Dying* (the length of time it took English critics to recognise this borrowing indicates just how little they have known about Faulkner). Faulkner's novel depicts the epic journey of a family of poor Southern whites as they honour the last wish of their mother and wife by transporting her body by buckboard into the nearest town to be buried. Death – or more exactly – corporeality and the perversity it implies for the individual in a post-Darwinian world 'lies' at the centre of the novel. The anxiety caused by such implications manifests itself most fully in the idealist of the family, Darl Bundren, whose emotional fragility situates him in the line of Faulkner's would-be flyers. Like Quentin Compson in *The Sound and the Fury*, Darl eventually goes insane; the description of his insanity by his brother Cash connects the (very English) metaphor of 'balance' with idealism and aligns the perverse with the fact that things, illustrated most convincingly by the body, are always already at a 'slant', that they 'ain't on balance' (p. 114).

The motif of burial, or, in Swift's case, ritually disposing of the ashes of Jack Dodds off Margate pier as he requests, structures *Last Orders* too, Swift's arguing that English idealism stifles revision, as Emerson recognises, in part through its justification of the class system. Class inequalities remain the most stubborn of old English characteristics, and Swift emphasises the need to address this point, most simply, through a figurative rejection of the idea of duty. Most of the men in the novel are known – and know themselves – by their occupation. They *are* what they *do* for a living, and, epitomised by Vic Tucker, a mortician, what they do is tanta-mount to the inability to renew themselves. Their need to do their duty ('like there was an order sent down from High Command', as Lenny says) (p. 132), which follows from their respective commitments to their jobs, mitigates against change and self-realisation, just as it has historically for the English working class. Duty in the novel is, as Gunby realises, 'immobilising'.[17]

---

16 Graham Swift, *Last Orders* (London: Picador, 1996). All further references to this edition will be given in parentheses in the text.
17 Ingrid Gunby, *Postwar Englishness in the Fiction of Pat Barker, Graham Swift and Adam Thorpe* (University of Leeds: unpublished PhD dissertation, 2002), p. 234.

Two characters, however, resist the immobility associated with doing one's duty, and each is associated figuratively with a sense of motion and of change. Vince, Jack's adopted son, overcomes the pressure to become a butcher. Rather than take his place as part of Dodd and Son, he chooses instead to run his own car dealership, building up his business from a single car ('What do you want to be?', Mandy asks Vince. 'Motors', he says (p. 159). He also extrapolates from his discovery that his stepfather 'aint Jack Dodds, no more than I'm Vince Dodds' in very Faulknerian – Cash-like – terms: 'Because nobody aint nobody. Because nobody aint more than just a body, than just their own body, which aint nobody' (p. 199).

Ray, who also realises that 'Jack's nothing' (p. 201), works, by contrast, in an insurance office, having been encouraged by his father not to follow in his footsteps as a scrap metal merchant. To emphasise his connotation of motion, Ray, orphaned after the war, continually jokes about the pub where the men drink: 'They call it the Coach and Horses', he says almost as a refrain, 'but it ain't never gone nowhere?' (p. 6). Ray, however, plays a more significant rhetorical role in the novel. He narrates more chapters than any other figure. He is also inherently associated with the geography of the country; as the narrative voice of the chapters entitled by the places through which the group travels on their way to Margate, Ray in effect 'speaks' for them. He and the land – he and England – are one.

Ray, thus, formally and figuratively revises the 'Englishness' Emerson characterises. He is not known for his occupation or for what it implies, security against the uncertainties of living. Instead he's known for his instincts, instincts (feminine in their association) that determine his nature. Ray is 'Lucky', a 'lovely man' as well as a 'lucky' one (p. 284): he is 'a little ray of sunshine', 'a little ray of hope' (p. 284). And, in the end, it is his lucky nature that clears Jack's final debt and frees Jack's wife Amy from her own fifty-year duty of care for their retarded daughter.

As the owner of a camper van, site of his sexual affair with Jack's wife, that aligns him connotatively with Vince, Ray recalls Ratliff. (It's he who realises at Canterbury that 'somewhere along the line we just became travellers' (p. 194).) His most direct formal alignment, however, emerges again with Ratliff's antecedent Cash. A meticulous carpenter, Cash substantiates his description of an imbalanced world when he sets out the thirteen principles behind building his mother's coffin 'on the bevel' (p. 66). Ray, in his equivalent chapter 'Ray's Rules', explains the premises for gambling successfully on the horses. Rules imply the idea of duty. Yet Ray undermines that implication when, in Faulknerian style, he expresses six of his eight rules in the negative: 'It's not the wins, it's the value', he says, for example; 'It's not the betting, it's the knowing when not to'; 'Never bet shorter than three to one'. Having marked the notion of duty, Ray's last rule, expressed in the positive, then overturns the premises behind it – 'You can blow all the rules if you're Lucky' (p. 202).

The deconstruction implicit in Ray's 'blowing the rules' becomes formally complete with the novel's final paragraph. As Gunby observes, Margate signifies the 'shedding' of the past, the groups' 'becoming new people' as if taking, in class terms, their 'last orders'.[18] Speaking as 'Margate' in the final chapter, Ray closes the novel in a way that not only defies safety but suspends the idea of closure itself:

The sky and the sea and the wind all mixed up together but I reckon it wouldn't make no difference if they weren't because of the blur in my eyes … the ash that I carried in my hands, which was the Jack who once walked around, is carried away by the wind, is whirled away by the wind till the ash becomes wind and the wind becomes Jack what we're made of. (pp. 294–5)

Here is an expression of the expansive spirituality that Emerson misses in the English and their literature. Ray rephrases the Faulknerian notion of the transitory nature of existence, the substantial yet profoundly corporeal without foundation in the abstract model provided by Platonic idealism. Spoken as the group stand facing out to sea, his vision combines with the formal strategy of the novel to connote, as Gunby writes, 'the *figurative* instability of national boundaries' (my emphasis). The rhetoric of the novel posits a nationalism 'beyond an insular Englishness', a connection with a 'wide world', fluid and in constant motion, perpetual transition and renewal.[19]

According to Homi K. Bhabha, the narration of a nation demands this sense of beyondness, a national sense of self that is 'international in consciousness'.[20] For this outsider, Swift, borrowing from Faulkner, implies such an international consciousness in his revision of 'Englishness', and it takes no great leap to imagine a subsequent English insularity compatible both with English scepticism and the exemplary nationalism Kumar advocates. Emerson may have seen the English as each 'an island himself, safe, tranquil, incommunicable' (p. 104). But with its determined regionalism, its increasingly multicultural population and its justified legacy of tolerance, a new 'Island England' seems appropriate now as a metaphor for spaceship Earth, 'Englishness' resonant as a signifier for a 'civic' vision encompassing the local and the global. This is conservative England transformed into conservationist England, the country's post-war sense of smallness inverted, finally, into something suitably big. Now that's an 'Englishness' that I could believe in, and staunchly.

---

18 Gunby, *Postwar Englishness in the Fiction of Pat Barker, Graham Swift and Adam Thorpe*, p. 246.
19 Gunby, *Postwar Englishness in the Fiction of Pat Barker, Graham Swift and Adam Thorpe*, pp. 230, 127.
20 Homi K.Bhabha, 'Narrating the Nation', in *Nations and Identities: classic readings* ed. Vincent P. Pecora, (Malden, Mass: Blackwell Publishers, Ltd., 2001), p.363.

Index

Note: 'n' after a page reference indicates a note number on that page.

Abigail's Party 104
About a Boy 169
Ackroyd, Peter 61
  English Music 61
Afro-Carribean 24, 26
Albee, Edward 33–4
  Zoo Story, The 33
America 42, 58, 61–2, 69, 108, 178
  see also United States
American
  culture 3
  Dream 170
  pragmatism 170
  South 76, 175–7
  transcentalism 170
Amis, Kingsley 42, 69, 87, 150
  Lucky Jim 150
Anderson, Benedict 96, 96n
Anglo-Argentine 155–6
Anglocentric 65
Anglo-Jewry 23
Anglo-Saxon heritage 50
Anglo-sceptic 65
anti-pastoral 107
anti-Semitic discourses 25
anti-Semitism 21, 26
Arisoto, Ludovico 65, 68
Armistice Day 30–1
Armitage, Simon 4, 82, 83
  All Points North 83
Arnold, Matthew 35, 38, 59, 65, 68–9, 72, 138–40, 142, 144
  Culture and Anarchy 138
  Essays in Criticism 65n
  Function of Criticism, The 68n
  On the Study of Celtic Literature 138–9n
  'Thyrisis' 59
Arrowsmith, Pat 33
Asian/African Carribean cultures 125

Asian-British women 149
assimilation 17, 125, 151, 173
assimilationist English culture 24
Auden, W.H. 34–5, 43–4, 81–2
  'Spain' 43
Austen, Jane 7
authenticity 9, 152–63, 165–7, 174

Bacon, Frances 176, 179
Bailey, Paul 36
  An Immaculate Mistake 36
Bainbridge, Beryl 4, 5, 5n, 6, 7, 172
  English Journey 4, 5n
Bakhtin, Mikhael 9, 9n
Baldick, Chris 35, 138n
Baldwin, James, 34
  Giovanni's Room 34
Ballard, J.G. 104
B&Q 103
Banks, Ian 4
Banville, John 107n, 111n
Barnes, Julian 1, 2, 6, 60–1 172
  Cross Channel 1, 1n, 2, 6, 60–1
Barthes, Roland 69, 116, 116n
  Camera Lucida 116, 116n
Basuta, Manjit 123, 126, 128, 130
Bath 6, 7
Baucom, Ian 6, 108, 108n, 110, 110n, 121
Baudelaire, Charles 56, 67
BBC 1, 4, 71
Beatles, The 154
Beckett, Samuel 117, 117n
  Knapp's Last Tape 117
  'Still' 117
Beethoven, Ludwig 1
Bell, Quentin 113
Bell's Introduction to the Qur'an 163n
  see also Koran, The

belonging 3, 9, 22n, 31, 48, 124, 140–3, 153,
    172, 177
Benjamin, Walter 28, 29n, 118
Bentham, Jeremy 32
Bergonzi, Bernard 114, 114n
Berkeley, George 176
Berlin 4
Best, George 92
Betjeman, John 69, 88, 105
Bhaba, Homi 50, 118n, 122, 129n, 141,
    153n, 184
Bhaji on the Beach 123–5, 129–37, 173–4
Big Ben 75
Birmingham 31, 129
black British film-makers 122, 135
black British population 125
Blackpool 130, 136
Blair, Cherie 103
Blair, Tony 103, 122, 128
Blake, William 56, 56n, 61, 74, 78, 81, 93,
    100
    'Jerusalem' 61
    'London' 56
Boccaccio, Giovanni 68
body, the 24–6
Bonhoeffer, Dietrich 68, 77
Bonnefoy, Yves 69
Booth, James 84, 89
    New Larkins for Old 84, 89
Bradbury, Malcolm 140–9, 153, 173
    Eating People is Wrong 140–9, 153
    The History Man 150
Brideshead Revisited 60
Bristol 5, 6
Britain 3, 31–2, 40, 44–5, 97, 117, 121–5,
    139–43, 145, 148, 171
Britannia 4
British 50–1, 143
    cultural identity 148
    Isles 3, 6, 11, 32, 41
    press 127
    society 124
British Nationality Act 121
Britishness 3, 4, 23, 40–1, 81n, 95–8
Brixton 102, 124
Brooke, Rupert 66–7, 71, 75
    'The Soldier' 67
Brooks, Peter 110, 110n, 116n

Brown, Merle 71, 71n
Brussels 139
Bryant, Christopher 81, 81n
Bryson, Bill 169
    Notes from a Small Island 169
Bunting, Basil 89
Bunyan, John 77
Burke, Edmund 170
Burroughs, William 34
    Naked Lunch, The 34
Bush, George 122
Byatt, A.S. 59, 61
    Babel Tower 59, 61

Calderon, Pedro de la Barca 65
Capadocia 81, 93
Caribbean English 46
Carter, Angela 3, 6–9, 9n, 172
    *Shaking a Leg: collected journalism and
        writings* 4–9, 172
Catholic faith/Catholics 10, 15, 32, 40, 70
Causley, Charles 87–8
Chambers, Ian 3, 3n
change(s) 1, 3, 6, 8–9, 58, 67, 70, 114–15,
    134, 154, 158–9, 165–6, 170–1,
    177–8
Charlton, Bobby 89, 91
Chaucer, Geoffrey 42, 68
Cheyette, Bryan 25, 25n
Chopin, Frederick 1
Christian/Christianity 15–6, 24, 26–7, 70,
    77–8, 84
Churchill, Winston 154
Civil Rights movement 31, 32
Civil War
    (American) 175
    Spanish 43
Clare, John 35
class 8, 9, 35–7, 43–7, 82, 85, 86n, 114–17,
    142–4, 150, 157, 173 176, 182–3
Clough, Arthur 59
CND 31–3, 37
Common Market 7, 71, 139
'common sense' 170
Commonwealth 11
condition of England novel 35, 143, 173
Conservatives, the 102
Constable, John 75, 77, 100

Continental Europe 2, 16, 19
    see also Europe
Cope, Wendy 87, 87n
Corboz, André 101
Corneille, Pierre 70
Corner, Martin, 174
Cornwall 31
cosmopolitan England 81, 81n
Countryside Agency, the 99
Coventry 83–4, 93
Cowper, William 103–4
Cox, Brian (B.C.) 92
Crich, Gerald 80
cricket 68, 95–6
Croatian/Croats 97–9
cultural
    heterogeneity of the English 4
    identities 134
    relativism 151
    studies 37
culture 20, 34, 45–9, 71, 77, 141, 147–8
Cunningham, Gail 103, 104n

Dante, Gabriel Rosetti 57, 65
Davie, Donald 66
Day, Gary 38
Dearden, Basil 37
    Victim, The 37
Debating Cultural Hybridity 132
decay/decline 5, 7, 68, 114
Defoe, Daniel 58, 98n
    Tour of the Whole Island of Great Britain
        58
Delaney, Shelagh 37, 47
    A Taste of Honey 37, 47
De Quincey, Thomas 57
devolution 3, 81n, 83, 96–7, 171
Diary of a Nobody 106
Dickens, Charles 56–8, 116, 139n, 147, 178
    American Notes 58
    David Copperfield 58
    Dombey and Son 178
    Great Expectations 56–7, 111, 116
    Little Dorrit 147
Didsbury, Peter 86
difference/differences 21, 26, 31, 40
domestic/domesticity 4, 121, 170–1, 180
Donne, John 176

double consciousness 24
Dublin 28
Duffy, Carol Ann 82–4, 171
    Other Country, The 83
Dunn, Douglas 88
duty 18, 133, 182–3

Eappen, Matthew 127
Easthope, Antony 82–3, 75
    Englishness and National Culture 82n,
        83, 109n, 175n
East Yorkshire 89, 90
    see also Yorkshire
Eliot, George 65
Eliot, T.S. 34, 56, 56n, 69–71, 75–9, 91,
        112n
    Little Giddings 71
    Waste Land, The 34, 56
Emerson, Ralph Waldo 79, 169–71, 174,
        176, 184
    English Traits 169–70
empire 3, 30, 32, 36, 41, 43, 49, 67, 71, 81n
        109, 113, 139, 156
England 1–6, 9–10, 17–24, 29, 31–5, 43, 49,
        57–60, 62–3, 66–81, 84, 90, 93–7,
        100–3, 108, 111–16, 118, 121, 123,
        125, 127–9, 132, 134, 141, 165–6,
        172, 175, 183
English
    'heritage' 9
    judicial system 127
    landscape 72–3
    mercantilism 170, 180
    national identity 128
    National Party 8
    Renaissance 15
    Studies 138, 140–2, 144, 146, 148, 173
Enlightenment, the 17, 20–1, 24, 26, 178
epic 55, 60, 63
escapism 2, 82
essence 45, 55, 102, 137, 174, 177–8
essentialism 38, 55, 75, 81, 89
    see also quintessence; quintessential
        'Englishness'
ethnicity 9, 96, 173
ethnic minorities 44, 99
Europe 2, 3, 11, 16, 19, 27, 65–7, 69–72,
        74–5 77, 79, 99, 101, 106

European
  Community 72
  integration 83
  Jewry 23
  Union 167
'Europeanness' 65
Euro-sceptic 66
expatriate/expatriation 78–9, 107
explicitness 59–63
  see also literalism

'fair play' 170
Falklands War, the 142
family 18, 21, 28, 55, 63, 102, 129, 169,
    181–2
  -as-nation 55
Fanon, Franz 25, 50
  Black Skin, White Masks 25, 50
Faulkner, William 76, 169, 175–8,
    181–4
  As I Lay Dying 176–7, 180, 185
  Flags in the Dust 176
  Hamlet, The 176
  Light in August 177
  Mansion, The 176
  Pylon 177
  Sanctuary 175
  Soldiers' Pay 176
  Sound and the Fury, The 175–6, 182
femininity 123, 126, 128–9, 136
  English 127–9, 136
  South Asian femininity 123, 135–6
  white English 123
Fenton, James 72
Fielding, Henry 89
First World War 17, 59–60, 68, 106–7,
    110–11, 114–18, 139, 154
fixities/fixity 155–6, 159, 177
Flaubert, Gustave 150
Ford, Ford Madox 61
  Good Soldier, The 61
Forster, E.M. 33–5, 71, 141, 141n
  Howards End 33–4
  Passage to India 33, 141n
France 100, 178
Franchise Affair, The 82
French, the 68, 71, 74
Freud, Sigmund 109, 109n, 112, 112n

Gainsborough, Thomas 100
Gaskell, Elizabeth 178
  Ruth 178
Gay Liberation Front 37
Gay Men's Press 37
gayness/gays 4, 26, 34, 36–9, 40, 63–4,
    173
  gay people of colour 38
  gay work 38
Gellner, Ernest 97
  Nations and Nationalisms 97
gender 9, 34, 44
Geneva Convention, the 128
Georgian England 112
German Jewish 50
Germans 154
Germany 17–18, 100, 107, 139
  see also Nazi Germany; Weimar
    Germany
Gervais, David 42, 55, 83, 91, 108n, 109n,
    169, 169n, 171, 174
  Literary Englands: versions of
    'Englishness' in modern writing
    42
Gide, Andre 34
  Immortalist, The 34
Gifford, Yvonne 127
Gikandi, Simon 41, 82, 138n, 178
Gillray, James 78
Gilman, Sandra 25, 25n
globalisation 121, 147
Goethe, Johann Wolfgan von 69, 75
Golding, William 59
  Pyramid, The 59
Goldsworthy, Vesna, 173
Good Life, The 104, 173
Gramsci, Antonio 124, 124n
  Prison Notebooks, The 124, 124n
Gray, Thomas 100
Great Britain, England
  see United Kingdom
Great War see First World War
Greece/Greek 68, 180–1
Greene, Graham 42
Guerney, Ivor 77
Gunby, Ingrid 113n, 174, 182–4, 182n,
    184n
Gunn, Thom 88, 170, 170n

Hall, Stuart 121, 121n, 126, 126n
Hampstead 104, 105
Hardy, Thomas 65, 70, 112, 177–8
    see also Wessex
Hare, David 105
Harrison, Tony 4, 73, 82, 171
Hart, Kitty 23
    Return to Auschwitz 23
Hawthorne, Nathaniel 57, 178
    Scarlet Letter, The 178
Heaney, Seamus 68, 89–90, 90n
    Mercian Hymns 69
Hennessey, Peter 44
    Never Again 44
Herbert, George 176
heterosexuality/heterosexuals 3, 38, 104
Hidgell, John, 89
    Card, The 89
Hill, Geoffrey 69–80, 90, 109, 174
    Cannan 69, 73–5, 78–9, 88
    Enemy's Country, The 73, 76
    Mystery of the Charity of Charles Péguy
        69 70, 73
    Tenebrae 71, 78
Hines, Donald 48
    Journey to an Illusion: the West Indian in
        Britain 48
histories/history 19, 21, 28, 73–4, 78–9, 108,
        117, 156, 166
Hitler, Adolf 31, 50, 71
Hoggart, Richard 46–7, 47n
Hollingshurst, Alan 55, 57, 62–4, 172–3
    Folding Star, The 57, 62
Holocaust 16, 20, 32, 70, 74, 76
home 3, 10, 21, 48, 58–9, 71, 96–7, 101–2,
        114, 127–9, 134, 170, 176–8,
        180–1
Homer 65
homosexual
    liaisons 37
    practice 33
homosexuality 37–8, 64
    see also gayness/gays
hooks, bell 131, 131n
Hopkins, Gerard Manley 78
Hours, The 104–5
    see also Woolf, Virginia
House of Commons, the 154

Housman, A.E. 72–3, 100
    A Shropshire Lad 73
Hughes, Ted 71–2, 81, 83–94, 86n, 111n
    'Dog Days on the Black Sea' 92–4
    Hawk in the Rain, The 91–2
    Lupercal 91–2
    New Selected Poems 1957–1994 91
    'Pike' 72
    'Rain-Charm for the Duchy 84–9, 91
Hugo, Victor 70, 72
hybrid 26, 152, 173
hybridity 98, 152

iconic 155–9, 160–2, 164–7, 174
iconography 88
icons 82, 154, 163, 166–7, 176
ideal, 69, 137
    rural 99
idealism 174, 176–8, 180–2
ideals
    of country life 99
    of modernity 135
identity 7, 9–10, 15–16, 28–9, 69, 81–3, 95,
        97, 121–3, 129, 154, 157–8, 160, 166,
        172–3, 177
    politics of 83
immigrant communities 28
immigrants/immigration 97, 99, 121
Imperial Institute, the 154
imperialism 139, 146, 149, 156, 171
inaudibility 62, 64
India 49, 58, 134, 156, 162
Indian identity/Indianness 134, 157
Ingelbien, Raphaël 70n, 83n, 90, 109n, 113n
insular 79, 114, 175
insularity 4, 51, 68, 88, 92, 176, 180–1
interference 2, 3, 9–11, 172
invisibility/invisible 17–18, 98, 141, 173
Iraq 128–9
Ireland 10, 32
Irish/Irishman 28–9, 97
Isherwood, Christopher 34
island 48, 71, 169, 180–1
    'dream' 114
    mentality 175
    nation 40
ius sanguinis 96
ius soli 96

Jacobson, Howard 150
    Coming from Behind 150
James, Henry 56, 56n, 57n, 79
    What Maisie Knew 56
James, William 169
Jerusalem 20, 81
Jewishness 15–16, 19–21, 23–4, 27–8, 173
Jews 1, 15–21, 24–6, 29, 40, 97
Jhabvala, Ruth Prawer 49
    Esmond in India 49
Joyce, James 34, 69, 79, 105
    Dubliners 34, 69
    Ulysses 105
Judaism 20, 24

Karpf, Anne 22, 22n
Keats, John 35
Kipling, Rudyard 61, 71
Koran, The 162–3, 165
    see also *Bell's Introduction to the Qur'an*
Kristeva, Julia 98, 98n
Kumar, Krishan 81n, 169, 169n, 171, 184
Kundera, Milan 1, 4
Kureshi, Harif 4, 43, 50–1, 138–53, 147n,
        173
    Black Album, The 138, 140, 143–8, 150,
        153, 173
    Buddha of Suburbia, The 43
    My Beautiful Launderette 123, 147

Labour movement 31
Laforgue, Eliot, 67
Lancashire 83
Larkin, Philip 56, 59–60, 66–71, 81–94,
        99–101, 101n, 113–14
    'Aubade' 87
    Collected Poems, The 68n, 84n, 85
    'MCMXIV' 114
    'Mr. Bleaney' 56
    'To the Sea' 93–4
    'Water' 85
    'Whitsun Weddings' 60, 85–6, 89–93
Lawrence, D.H. 34–6, 45–6, 55–7, 62–3, 69,
        78–80, 172
    Rainbow, The 34
    St. Mawr 57, 62
    Women in Love 34, 79
Lawrence, Errol 124

Leavis, F. R. 35, 35n, 42, 139, 140, 144
    For Continuity 140
    Nor Shall My Sword 139–40
Leavis, Queenie 41–2, 41n, 50
lesbian/lesbians 4, 26, 38
Lesbian and Gay Studies 39
Lessing, Doris 42, 46–8, 49n
    In Pursuit of the English 46
Levinas, Emmanuel 20, 20n, 26–7
liberalism 33, 149, 151, 153
Light, Alison 111, 114, 114n
literalism 62–3, 172
    see also explicitness
Littlewood, Joan 31
    Oh! What a Lovely War 31
Little England 69, 81, 81n, 139, 171,
        175
Locke, John 176, 179
Lodge, David 140–50, 153, 173
    Nice Work 140–50, 153, 173
    Small World 150
London 10, 22, 33, 36, 56, 63, 78, 89, 95,
        97–101, 103, 105–6, 114, 145–8,
        154–5, 165–6, 171
Loseff, Lew 47
    In the Beneficence of Censorship 47
loss 7, 107, 110, 166
Lucas, John 55
    England and Englishness 55
Lunn, Ken 126, 126n
    'Reconsidering Britishness' 126
Lyotard, Francois 26, 26n

Major, John 102
Malek, Bilkis 126n, 173–4
Manchester 5, 10, 92
    United 92
'manliness'/'manly' 16, 34
    see also masculinities/masculinity
Mann, Thomas 34
    Death in Venice 34
Martin, Kenneth 37
    Aubade 37
Marvell, Andrew 78
masculinities/masculinity 16, 24–5, 27
    see also 'manliness'/'manly'
Maslen, Elizabeth 172
Mayakovsky, Vladimir 67

M25 98
McEwan, Ian 1, 4, 56, 179–80
    Atonement 179
    Innocent, The 56
MacLaughlan, Lucille 123, 126, 128, 130
McLeod, John 171–2
McLuhan, Marshall 79
melancholic/melancholy 107–10, 113,
        116–18, 174
memory 34, 110–11, 117
    and narrative 112
    'screen' 112
Mercer, Kobena 135–6, 136n
Merchant Ivory Productions 11
metamorphosis 159–62, 165–6
miasma 40, 43, 49
Middle Britain 102
Middle England 102
Middlesex 101
Midlands 83
migrant 166
    cultures 153
    fictions 146
    women 125
migrants 140, 142, 146, 166, 173
migration 147
Milton, John 65, 67, 68, 74n, 75, 78, 176
    Aeropagitica 67
mimicry 157, 160, 161, 174
Mitford, Nancy 44
mobilisation 55, 62, 64
modernism/modernist 70, 100, 105, 175
modernity 15, 17, 19–21, 23–4, 26–7, 114,
        117, 135–7
monarchy, the 67–8
Montale, Eugenio 67
Moore-Gilbert, Bart 173–4
Morgan, Kenneth O. 44
    People's Peace, The 44
Morris, William 125
Morrison, Blake 179, 179n
Motion, Andrew 87
mourning 59, 82 109–10, 116
Muldoon, Paul 82
multicultural
    community 24
    English population 3
    society 26

multi-ethnic 3
myth 83
    of racial purity and imperial
        superiority 41

Naipaul, V.S. 42, 46, 48, 48n, 110
    Enigma of Arrival, The 110
    Mystic Masseur, The 48
nation 1, 6, 43–4, 47, 55, 58, 63, 72, 124,
        139, 142, 153, 175
national 63, 79
    boundaries 180
    identity 3, 82, 127–9, 140–4, 153, 155,
        171, 177–8
    remembrance 60
nationalism 31, 59, 67, 70, 81n, 113n, 132,
        169, 172, 177
nationality 55, 57, 59, 67–8, 71, 74, 79, 95–9
National Lottery 76
nationhood 16, 51, 55, 67
nations 63, 79, 121, 166
NATO 30–1
Nazi 18, 21–2
Nazi Germany 20, 74
    see also Germany; Weimar Germany
new, the 155–6, 159–60, 165–6, 174
Newbolt, Sir Henry 71, 144
Newbolt Report, the 139, 144, 144n
new India, the 162
newness 154–62, 165–7
New Poetry, The (*anthology*) 85
New Right, the 138, 143
Ngugi, wa Thiong'o 141
Nietszche, Frederick 1, 24
North Africa 42
North America 11, 101
Northern Ireland 3, 32, 96–7, 99
nostalgia/nostalgic 2, 5, 7, 69–71, 78, 103,
        109, 118, 155, 160, 174, 178
Nottingham 45, 145
Notting Hill carnival 8–9, 140

'Olde Englande' 31, 121, 123, 136
Orwell, George 56, 102, 143, 151
Oswald, Alice 73
    Thing in the Gap-Stone Stile, The 73
other, the 26, 41, 122–5, 153, 169, 175–6
others 70, 96

outsider(s) 24, 122, 169, 184
Owen, Wilfred 31, 33, 70, 107n

Palmers Green 31, 37
Parekh, Bhikhu 130
Parliament 58, 75, 78, 154
Parmer, Pratibha 123n, 125, 126n
Passion of Remembrance 123
past, the 18–19, 23, 67, 70–1, 76, 109, 114
pastoral 2, 63, 89, 100, 114, 172
patriotism 67
Péguy, Charles 70–1, 77
people of colour 26
perverse/perversity 177–8, 177n, 180,
    182
Phillips, Caryl 1, 1n, 6
place 55, 58, 71, 89, 156
Plato 151, 176
Platonic England 67
Poe, Edgar Allen 178
    'Imp of the Perverse, The' 178
Poland/Poles 17, 21
postmodernism 24–5, 60, 158, 180
poststructuralism 77, 83
Pound, Ezra 69
Powell, Anthony 42, 61, 108
    Dance to the Music of Time 61
    Military Philosophers 61
Powell, Enoch 41, 121–2, 124
    and 'rivers of blood' speech 124
Priestley, J.B. 4, 143, 172
    English Journey 4–5, 5n, 172
privatisation 145
Protestants 15
Proust, Marcel 69
provincialism/provinciality 69, 90–1,
    170
Pynchon, Thomas 56
    Crying of Lot 49, The 57

Queen Elizabeth 30, 32
queer experience 34
queer literary English writing 36
Queer Studies 173
Quinn, Alice 89, 91
quintessence 66
quintessential Englishness 79
    see also essentialism

race 3, 9 16, 31, 43, 47, 96, 121, 123–4, 126,
    128–31, 140–1
racial minorities 145, 149
racial superiority 46
racism 8, 24, 26, 125, 136–7, 146, 148, 152,
    173
    'common sense' 124–6, 129–33, 174
    'new' 124–5
Reading, Peter 72
realism 143
    literal 179
    rhetorical 177
    social 173
    tragic 77
Reformation 15
religion 134–6
remembrance 60–1
rhetoric/rhetorical 62, 70, 114, 121, 177–8
Richard the Lionheart 81
Richards, Cliff 130
    Summer Holiday 130
Richardson, Samuel 178
    Clarissa 178
Rickman, Alan 99
Rise and Fall of Reginald Perrin, The 104
Rogers, David 11, 177n
romantics 65, 101, 104
Rosensweig, Michael, Rabbi 27
Rowland, Antony 171
royal family, the 85
Rushdie, Salmon 151, 154–9, 161–6, 174
    Haroun and the Sea of Stories 162
    Midnight's Children 162
    Satanic Verses, The 151, 155–67,
        174
Russell, Bertrand 32
Russia 17, 42, 47, 74, 169
    see also USSR

Said, Edward 41, 141, 150–1, 150n
    Culture and Imperialism 41
Salinger, J.D. 33
    Catcher in the Rye, The 33
Samuel, Raphael 40–1, 40n, 138n
sanctuary 176, 179–81
Sartre, Jean-Paul 19–21, 69, 176
    Anti-Semite and Jew 19–20
Sassoon, Siegfried 33

Scotland 3, 10, 32, 83, 97, 99
Scottish 96–7
Scruton, Roger 66
Second World War 17, 31, 32, 40–3, 61,
        83n, 112, 114, 116–18, 154, 171–2,
        175, 179
Seidler, Vic 15n, 22n, 25n, 173
Selvon, Sam 42, 45–8, 146, 172
        Lonely Londoners, The 45–8
Serbianness/Serbs 96–7
sexuality 2, 9–10, 24–5, 36, 38, 136
Shakespeare, William 15, 30–1, 33, 61, 74
        81, 100, 100n, 141, 174–5
        Henry V 74
        Merchant of Venice, The 16
Shapiro, James 15–16, 15n–16n
        Shakespeare and the Jews 15–16
Sheffield 82, 89, 92
Shelly, Percy 35, 65, 65n, 72
        Defence of Poetry, The 65
        'Ode to the West Wind' 65
        'Triumph of Life, The' 65
Shoah, the 19, 23, 26–7
Sidney, Sir Philip 176
Sillitoe, Alan 45–7, 172
        Saturday Night, Sunday Morning 45–7
Sinfield, Alan 30, 32n, 34n, 43, 113n, 173
slavery 5, 26
Smollett, Tobias 89
South Africa 32, 154
Southampton 4
South Asian
        men 136
        women 123, 125–6, 129, 130–1, 133,
            135, 174
Southern Rhodesia 46
Southey, Robert 7
space 24, 26, 28, 173, 181–2
Spencer, Herbert 176
sphere
        private 21
        public 21, 25
Spivak, Gayatri Shakravorty 83, 149n
        Post-Colonial Critic, The 83
Steinbeck, John 175
St George 81, 84, 93–4
        greedy flag of 4
        -like figure 86

Stoker, Bram 178
        Dracula 178
Stratford-upon-Avon 30–1, 35, 141
Stuart, Andrea 130, 130n
subaltern voices 25
suburban/suburbanness 100–6, 173
suburbanisation 99
suburbanites 101
suburbs/suburbia 56, 95–106, 146, 173
Sudjic, Deyan 99
Suez Crisis, the 140
Surbiton 104, 173
Surrey 101
Swift, Graham 90, 169, 175, 179–84
        Last Orders 179–84
        Out of this World 179–84
Swinburne, Algenon 67
Syal, Meera 4
Sydney 101

Tasso, Toquato 65
Taylor, Jeremy 176
Tebbit, Norman 96
Tennyson, Alfred Lord 32
        In Memoriam 32
terrorism 121, 141, 180
Thatcher government 121, 142
Thatcherism 76, 138
Thatcherite England 4
Thatcher, Margaret 41, 102, 143
Thawaite, Anthony 86–7, 87n–8n
Thomas, Edward 58–60, 64, 66, 70
        Heart of England, The 58–60, 64
Thorpe, Adam 107–13, 117–18, 174
        Pieces of Light 110
        Still 107, 111, 115, 117–18, 174
        Ulverton 107, 110
Tizzard, Sir Henry 44
Tomlinson, Charles 72
        Jubilation 72
tradition 8–9, 17, 24, 26–8, 31, 77, 94, 114,
        133–4, 136–7, 141, 146, 163, 173–4,
        178
        African 28
        ethnical 20
        Jewish 20
transgender people 38
transition(s) 74, 169, 174, 177–8, 181

transnationality 11
transsexuals 38
Traske, John 16
Trilling, Lionel 34
Turkey 81

Union Jack, the 3, 154
United Kingdom 4, 32, 96, 121–2, 140–1,
    153, 171
United Kingdom Independence Party 11
United States 3, 16, 25, 32, 122, 137n, 138,
    142, 148, 169, 181
    see also America
universal 20, 79
unspeakability/unspeakable 59, 61
unutterability/unutterable 60–2
urban/urbanities/urbanity 100–1, 103
USA see United States
USSR 3
    see also Russia

van der Veer, Peter 134
ventriloquism 157, 174
Victorian 68–9, 138–9, 170
Viswanathan, Gauri 149
    Masks of Conquest 149
voice(s) 3, 27, 62, 64, 84, 107, 123, 157–60,
    162, 166, 173

Wagner, Richard 69
Wales 3, 4, 32, 97, 99
Wallace, Edgar 1
wandering Jew, the 16
'War Poets', the 71
Wars of the Roses, the 76, 82
Weil, Simone 23, 23n, 25
Weimar Germany 21
    see also Germany; Nazi Germany
Welfare State, the 144
Welsh 96–7
Welsh, Irving 4
Wesker, Arnold 36
    Chips with Everything 36
Wesley, John 77
Wessex 66
    see also Hardy, Thomas

West, the 16, 25, 152, 160, 173
Westminster 37, 63, 75
    Abbey 32
Whitehall 57
whiteness 24
Wilde, Oscar 101
Williams, Raymond 46–7
Wilson, A. N. 11, 58–9
    Late Call 59
    Old Men at the Zoo, The 58
Wilson, Colin 24, 37
    Hemlock and After 37
    Outsider, The 24
Wilson, Harold 101
Wimbledon 63, 104
    tennis tournament 58
Wolfenden Commission, the 33
Wolverhampton 30, 36
Wood, James 171–3
Woodward, Louise 123, 126–8, 130
Woolf, Virginia 33, 36, 55, 57–9, 62–3,
    104–5, 172
    Mrs Dalloway 57–8, 62–3, 105, 172
    Orlando 33
    To the Lighthouse 59
    see also Hours, The
Wordsworth, William 35, 65, 69, 75, 77
    'Immortality Ode' 61
    'Upon Westminster Bridge' 100
World War I see First World War
World War II see Second World War
Wright, Kim 171, 171n
Wright, Patrick 109n, 113n, 138n

xenophobia 148

Yeoman of the Guard 8
Yoknapawtawpha County 175, 178
    see also Faulkner, William
Yorkshire 73, 81–2, 84, 89
    see also East Yorkshire
Young, Robert 139, 139n
    Colonial Desire 139, 139n
Yugoslavia 95, 97
Yuval-Davis, Nira 123
    'Gender and Nation' 123